George and Sam

CHARLOTTE MOORE

With an introduction by NICK HORNBY

PENGUIN BOOKS

PENGUIN BOOKS

Published by the Penguin Group
Penguin Books Ltd, 80 Strand, London WC2R ORL, England
Penguin Group (USA) Inc., 375 Hudson Street, New York, New York 10014, USA
Penguin Group (Canada), 90 Eglinton Avenue East, Suite 700, Toronto, Ontario, Canada M4P 2Y3
(a division of Pearson Penguin Canada Inc.)
Penguin Ireland, 25 St Stephen's Green, Dublin 2, Ireland (a division of Penguin Books Ltd)
Penguin Group (Australia), 250 Camberwell Road, Camberwell, Victoria 3124, Australia
(a division of Pearson Australia Group Pty Ltd)
Penguin Books India Pvt Ltd, 11 Community Centre, Panchsheel Park, New Delhi – 110 017, India
Penguin Group (NZ), 67 Apollo Drive, Rosedale, Auckland 0632, New Zealand
(a division of Pearson New Zealand Ltd)
Penguin Books (South Africa) (Pty) Ltd, 24 Sturdee Avenue, Rosebank,
Johannesburg 2196, South Africa

Penguin Books Ltd, Registered Offices: 80 Strand, London WC2R ORL, England

www.penguin.com

First published by Viking 2004
Published in Penguin Books 2005
Reissued with a new Postscript and Appendix in Penguin Books 2012
001

Copyright © Charlotte Moore, 2004, 2012
Introduction copyright © Nick Hornby, 2004
All rights reserved

The moral right of the author and of the introducer has been asserted

Typeset by Palimpset Book Production Limited, Polmont, Stirlingshire
Printed in England by Clays Ltd, St Ives plc

ISBN: 978-0-241-95660-1

www.greenpenguin.co.uk

ALWAYS LEARNING   **PEARSON**

For Jake
and
in memory of
Ruby Cruse
and
Mary Oliver
who both loved the boys

Contents

Introduction

I'm guessing – I can't know for sure, of course, but this seems a reasonable supposition – that you have picked this book up, if not with a heavy heart, then with an oppressive sense of duty. Perhaps you have an autistic grandson, or nephew – most autistic kids are boys – and you feel that the least you can do is to find out more about his condition, especially since you don't know him as well as you'd like to. (How can you, when he won't speak to you, or play with you, or possibly even be in the same room as you?) So maybe reading a book will help, somehow – will show that, even though you feel excluded from his world, you do care.

Or perhaps you are more directly affected; perhaps your own child is autistic, as mine is, in which case your need to read a book on the subject might feel more urgent. If the diagnosis has been recent, then you will almost certainly be desperate to know more. Maybe something in these pages will help to alleviate the panic you feel when you're told that your child has a condition for which there is no cure; indeed, maybe you're hoping that *George and Sam* will tell you that there *is* a cure, contrary to all the information you've been given by health professionals. Books tend to need narratives, after all, and the most popular kind of narrative for books about disability is the kind that takes us from the darkness into the light, from despair to hope, from disaster to triumph.

It would be nice to think that there might be a third category of reader, too: some of you might want to read *George and Sam* in the same way that we all read *Wild Swans*, even though many of us had no burning interest in the history of China; or Claire Tomalin's book about Pepys, despite a long-held suspicion that Pepys's diaries might be on the dull side. Perhaps you read

Charlotte Moore's brilliant columns about her autistic sons in the *Guardian* (included in this edition as an Appendix); if you did, then you'll already know that in the right hands, this subject, like all subjects, can be made to entertain, as well as educate and move. The non-fiction bestseller lists frequently prove that we all want to know more about everything, even if we didn't know that we wanted to know – we're just waiting for the right person to come along and tell us about it.

I have an autistic son, but even so, I would place myself in this last category of readers. Like a lot of people, I sense within me a reluctance to read books about disability. I think I'll end up feeling guilty, or hopeless, or manipulated, or just *bad*. (And there are so many disabilities – where does one start? Where, more to the point, does one *stop*?) And I particularly don't want to be made to feel bad precisely because I have an autistic son. As any parent in my situation will tell you, energy and optimism are precious commodities, not to be squandered, and certainly not on a book that describes a condition with which you are wearyingly familiar. So I hope you, and the author, will understand when I say that this is not the sort of book I would normally have chosen to read.

If you belong in the second category, I should tell you right now that Charlotte Moore offers no cure for autism, nor does she attempt to make you feel better about the huge chunk of bad luck that has fallen from a clear blue sky, like a chunk of frozen 747 urine, and landed right on your head. This is a clear-eyed observation of her sons and their behaviour; she makes no attempt to sentimentalize them, and she certainly doesn't attempt to tell us that they are now, as she speaks, embarked on a programme or a diet that will eventually take them to Cambridge or RADA or 10 Downing Street. She knows that her sons are autistic, and will stay autistic, for the rest of their lives, unless there is some currently unimaginable scientific breakthrough. And as a consequence, I would say that this might be the only book you need to read about your child's condition. It tells you the things you will need to know – about education, and diet, and behaviour modification, and sleep – but the advice is sensible and practical, rather than evangelical, and in any case it is not the point of the book. The point of *George and Sam* is to inform, yes, but also to entertain us and engross us and, like all the best books, to resonate.

I'm not sure I would have found it quite so entertaining a few years ago, when my son was first diagnosed. Nowadays, I'm used to glancing out of the kitchen window on a freezing November night and seeing a naked boy bouncing on a trampoline in the dark. It makes me laugh. (I don't *just* laugh, by the way, before anyone contacts social services. I go outside and get him in, too.) Back then, when I didn't understand Danny so well, and didn't really want to think about how his disability might affect me beyond the next few days, the naked trampolining would have alarmed and depressed me; it would have been yet another indication that my life as a parent was not the one I had anticipated.

This process of letting go is long and difficult, and I feel as though I'm right at the beginning of it. Charlotte Moore is, I suspect, right at the end, and there are very, very few parents who ever get there. And this is what makes *George and Sam* a great book: Moore's willingness (perhaps 'ability' is the more appropriate word, because none of us is *willing* to give up the life we had planned for ourselves) to see her boys for what they are provides her with a unique perspective. Writing is as much about character as it is about talent, and Moore's character – her wryness and flexibility, her intelligence and her lack of judgementalism, her lack both of self-pity and of self-aggrandizement – means that she is ideally qualified to tell us this story in a way that hasn't been told before.

She also has the advantage of having two autistic sons, rather than one. The word 'advantage' can only really be applied to this particular project, the one you are holding in your hands; those of us who have one autistic child, and just about manage to keep our heads above the water (and even then not every day of the week), cannot really imagine life with two, even after Charlotte Moore has explained it to us. But what it does mean is that she resists extrapolation, because experience has taught her that you cannot really extrapolate with autistic children. No two autists are alike, and this is as true of their response to therapies and medication as it is of their behaviour and abilities. Moore writes here of the improvement in George's behaviour and language after receiving Auditory Integration Therapy; when Sam was given the same treatment, however, there was no discernible improvement. Lucky for us, in a way. Moore is much too sharp to write a whole book about AIT, but she might have been tempted had there been spectacular results in Sam's case, too. Plenty of other people have written whole books about diets and such like, and though they might help a minority of children, they will not help all, and they will be of absolutely no interest to a general reader. If no two autists are alike, then in George and Sam, Moore has access to a microcosmic world of autism.

George and Sam is painfully funny, in a way that is only possible because Moore has learned to appreciate and recognize what she's got in her three boys. (This book is about George and Sam, mostly, but Jake, her youngest, who is not autistic, provides her with all sorts of usefully contrasting material.) I once heard her describe George and Sam as 'autistic through and through', meaning that, contrary to some fondly nurtured parental beliefs, there is no normal child trapped inside, waiting for release. That recognition enables her to look at her children with love and joy, rather than love and regret, to observe their behaviour with a winning delight in its eccentricity. Where else will you read about a child so obsessed with white goods that visits to the launderette constitute a treat? Or a child who, for reasons best known to himself, wants everyone to pretend that he doesn't eat, even though he does? The weirdness, the sheer otherworldliness, of autistic thinking is a never-ending source of wonder and fascination – what does it say about them, and what does it say about us? – and Moore's laconic, unshowy narration provides the perfect setting.

I began by saying that the most popular books about disability take us from darkness into the light, and that this book didn't really follow that pattern. On reflection, this isn't strictly true, because *George and Sam* is luminous. True, it doesn't provide us with the kind of redemption that allows us to weep sentimental tears and then forget all about it (which, after all, is the unwitting function of many against-all-odds books). But it does ask — and, more impressively, answer — important questions, questions that apply to all of us: to what extent are we really prepared to accommodate our children? Are we properly equipped to love them the way they are? If our lives do not turn out the way we had hoped, what is the best way of living them? Do six After Eights constitute a decent breakfast? Charlotte Moore knows, but I'm not telling. You'll have to read this wonderful book to find out.

Nick Hornby, 2003

Acknowledgements

As I hope this book makes clear, the quality of our family life depends on the goodwill of a large number of people, and I'm deeply grateful to them all.

This book came into being as a result of the *Mind the Gap* columns I wrote for the *Guardian* (reprinted for this edition as an Appendix). Thanks to Alan Rusbridger for taking me on, and to Ian Katz and Matt Seaton for their help and encouragement. Thank you also to the many *Guardian* readers who wrote to me; their messages were invariably supportive and interesting.

The idea for the book was shaped by my agent, David Godwin, and my editor, Tony Lacey. Many thanks to them and to everyone else at Viking who was involved. Thank you, too, to fellow parent Nick Hornby for his generous introduction, and to Thérèse Jolliffe for allowing me to quote from 'Autism: A Personal Account' (Thérèse Jolliffe, Richard Lansdown and Clive Robinson, *Communication*, vol. 26, National Autistic Society, December 1992).

Thank you to Saskia Baron for her patience and care when working with us on *The Autism Puzzle*. Making the documentary was integral to the book's progress. Thanks, also, to Kate Lithgow for her kindness in letting me use Crear, her beautiful Scottish retreat, to get some of the writing done.

The ASD staff at Torfield and Saxon Mount schools are too numerous to thank individually, but I'm grateful to them all. Thank you to Pat and the rest of the boys' taxi team. The generosity of The Paragon Trust has enabled me to run the boys' therapy programmes; many thanks to them and to all the tutors past and present – at time of writing, they are Sue Lynch, Vikki Kindell, Mark Lovegrove, Andie Lawler, Jan Relf, Ian Bailey and Delia Langham. Special thanks to Ian for keeping us all happy, and to Delia for years of incredible commitment and understanding.

Eva Littna did an enormous amount of work on the MS as well as putting in lots of time with the boys. Many thanks to her, and to Hilary Smith for babysitting above and beyond the call of duty. The boys and I have received a great deal of support from both sides of the family; warm thanks to all their grandparents, uncles, aunts and cousins. Our friends, too, have been wonderfully tolerant and helpful. Thank you, all of you, and most especially Em, Chris, Sophie and Iggy Clarke, and to Simon White for raising morale.

I'm grateful to all those who have shared their experiences of autism with me and in some cases allowed me to quote them. So many people have contributed to the boys' lives over the years – a big thank-you to all the neighbours, shopkeepers, doctors and dentists and their assistants, teaching staff, policemen and members of the public who have had dealings with us. I hope you know who you are. Finally, thank you to Deirdre Hazell and Freda Catt for cleaning up after us!

For the 2012 reissue, I'd like to add my thanks to the staff at St Mary's Wrestwood Road, Grove Park Sixth Form, The Mount Camphill Community, Autism Sussex, Greenwood Respite Centre and Project Art Works; also to Sam's personal assistant, Simon Bashford.

Prologue

Monday morning. We're in a hurry – of course we are. Every working mother with three school-age sons is in a hurry on a Monday morning.

George is nearly thirteen. The physical process of puberty is beginning, but he seems unaware of this, just as he's always been unaware of the effect his exceptional good looks have on people. He wanders into the kitchen, naked. He climbs on to the Aga, and sits there twiddling a piece of cardboard. I send him to get dressed; his skin is red and mottled from the heat. He returns with all his clothes on the wrong way round.

I fill a lunchbox for eleven-year-old Sam. Plain crisps, gluten-free biscuits, marzipan, an apple that I know he won't eat, but I suppose I live in hope. George doesn't have a lunchbox, because George maintains the fiction that he doesn't eat anything at all, and a lunchbox is too blatant a reminder that this cannot be the case. I smuggle his food supplies – mainly Twiglets and chocolate – into his school taxi, underneath his swimming things.

I make George's breakfast – but I have to pretend it's not his breakfast. 'I'm making this for Sam,' I announce, pointedly. I toast two slices of rice bread; Sam's diet excludes wheat, oats, barley, rye and all dairy products. I place them on two plates which George has selected by sniffing. I spread Marmite in an even layer right up to the edge of the crusts, cut them into quarters, then busy myself elsewhere. George slips down from the Aga; as long as my back's turned, he'll risk the toast. 'These are for Sam,' he states as he starts to eat. 'Yes, they're for Sam,' I confirm, without looking round.

Sam's always the last up. He's awake, but he's under his duvet, murmuring; his vocalization is somewhere between a hum and a chant, and is almost completely incomprehensible. He fingers

George and Sam

the toy owl he's had since babyhood. The owl has no name, no character; Sam has never played with him, but then he's rarely played with any toy. The owl is a tactile comforter, not a friend.

Sam won't get up and dress until the taxi driver rings the doorbell. I did try ringing it myself, to get him moving, but Sam's not daft. He only fell for that once. And the dressing process can be infuriatingly slow. Pants on – pants off again. Shirt inside out – outside in – inside out once more. Six pairs of identical tracksuit trousers rejected – the seventh finally, mysteriously, acceptable. Socks stuffed down into the toes of his trainers, pulled out, stuffed in again. One step forward, two steps back – and endless little rituals about touching things and moving things in his bedroom. If I try to intervene, the whole process starts all over again.

At last he's dressed – no time for niceties like washing or brushing teeth. Now Sam has to get down the stairs all in one go. If anything blocks his way, or if he has a crisis of confidence halfway down, he'll freeze. He takes the stairs at a gallop, gets as far as the front door. I open the door for him. Mistake! Sam has to do everything for himself. He opens and shuts the door six times before he can bring himself to leave the house.

George's taxi arrives. I note with pleasure that the toast has been eaten – but where is George? In the lavatory of course, where he spends about a quarter of his waking hours. He emerges, and makes for the front door – but wait, there's something odd about his gait. He's pulled up his trousers, but forgotten about his pants. I ignore his protests, hoick up his pants, waft a brush over his uncut hair, and propel him towards the taxi. 'Don't wave! Don't say goodbye!' he commands, and hands me a fragment of sweet paper to add to the collection that already covers the kitchen table. Two empty Fanta bottles, eight yellow lollipop sticks, silver foil, Softmint wrappers . . . hoarding litter is George's latest obsession.

A call from the playroom reminds me of the existence of my youngest child. *Blue Peter* has finished; Jake, four, wants his Ready Brek. He chats as he eats; he'd like to meet Gareth

Gates, he'd like to be Young Sportsman of the Year. Have I found his reading book? Can he have three kinds of sugar on his cereal?

I take Jake to the local primary school, where he is in Reception. He greets his friends on the way in, dismisses me with a hug and a kiss. Neither George nor Sam ever embrace me in greeting or salute.

As I leave, I peep through the window. Jake is cross-legged in the middle of the group; he is listening to what the teacher has to say. His hand shoots up. He's right in there, a proper schoolboy, a social animal. He couldn't be more different from his older brothers – but then, Jake's not autistic.

Eight o'clock. The day ought to be drawing to a close, but the boys have several hours to go. I take Jake up to bed, leaving George and Sam rampaging downstairs. I wonder what I'll find when I return. Once, Sam emptied a gallon can of olive oil all over the kitchen floor. I have locks on all the cupboards now, but Sam is cunning, and good at finding keys. Will he eat a hundred vitamin pills, or put packets of butter into the oven, or post plates into the bin, or fill the doll's house bath with honey? All these have been done.

Jake takes a good half-hour to settle. His brothers make him nervous; he has to fall asleep with the light on and an adult beside him. Once he's truly asleep, I lock his door. That way, I know Sam can't leap on him if my vigilance slips for a moment.

As I leave Jake's room, I hear a familiar squeaking. It's Sam, barefoot, trampolining by moonlight. He throws his whole being into it; his intricate hand movements make it look as though he's casting spells; his habitual vocalization has become a throaty chuckle. This free, uninhibited, physical response is an aspect of autism I really like.

The boys still share a bath without a shred of self-consciousness. They have a close physical relationship. There's a deep bruise on George's arm, surrounded by a ring of toothmarks. I ask George about it. 'It was Sam,' he confirms without rancour. I notice some reciprocal pinches and scratches on Sam's thigh. Like most brothers, they fight, apparently to their mutual satisfaction.

The long evening progresses. George watches videos – *Bob the Builder*, *Bananas in Pyjamas*, things aimed at children a quarter of his age. Sam flits in and out, uttering incantations. I eat my supper and flick through the paper, thinking wistfully of the television I inevitably miss.

Bedtime at last. I read stories to George while Sam hums and whirrs. George wants the same stories he's liked since toddler-hood – Dr Seuss, Beatrix Potter, 'The Gingerbread Man'. There's an unshakeable innocence about George which is attractive, but he'll soon be a teenager. Should I really still be reading him *Rumples and Tumbles Go to the Country*?

I switch off the light, and lie down on the sofa between their two beds. I doze off with them – this is the best way of convincing them that the day really is over. I wake with a start at midnight, take a last look at their perfect sleeping faces, and go to unlock Jake. Then to my own bed, where I'll have about three hours before one or the other joins me there.

1. Does It Run in the Family?

I suppose every child regards its family life as normal. It's only in adulthood that we reassess the things we took for granted. Certainly, nothing in my stable, effortless childhood prefigured the position I would find myself in as an adult – a single mother of three sons, two of them autistic.

I live in the house where I grew up. It's an overgrown Sussex farmhouse with a large untidy garden. When my grandfather died, my parents moved in, on 1 April 1960 – my first birthday. Thirty years later, I moved back there with my husband, Min, and George, then six months old.

The house hasn't changed much since the 1960s; the externals of George and Sam's childhood experiences are similar to mine. They sleep in the room I once shared with my brothers, and the dragons, sealions and goldfish painted on the walls by my aunts look down on them as they once looked down on us. The kitchen is still dominated by an inefficient Aga, the crumbling garden walls are still there for them to risk their necks, as my brothers and I used to. We walk through the same fields, splash in the same streams. As the boys lie in bed they hear the sounds I always heard, the creaks and rustlings of an old and draughty house, the train rumbling through the valley, the crooning of woodpigeons in the big yew tree outside.

Yet internally, their childhoods could hardly be more different from mine. George and Sam's experiences are disparate, unconnected, a series of sensory impressions that don't add up to make a pattern. When I lay in bed and listened to the train, I imagined dragons. I knew that dragons didn't exist, but I chose to tell myself stories about dragons, I involved the painted dragons on the wall in these stories. I knew that the noise was the London train, the one my father took to work each day. There was no confusion in my mind between the real and the pretend worlds, and to me, both made sense. I'll never know, because they can't tell me, but I believe that, for George and Sam, neither makes sense. When you're autistic, *everything* is experienced differently. The assumptions and explanations of the people around you are of very little help.

There were three of us children. Charles is two years older than me and Rowan two years younger. We were bookish and unsporty; Charles was quite tough and adventurous, Rowan and I were rather weedy. We went to the village primary school and brought friends home to play. We kept a great many animals. We made dens in the woods behind our house. We quarrelled fiercely over Racing Demon, Pit and Monopoly. When we weren't fighting, we played elaborate imaginative games based on invented worlds. Rowan and I ruled jointly over the whimsically named Land of Nursery. Rowan's responsibility was primarily for organizing building programmes, controlling civil wars, and colonizing outlying regions with his Hornby train set, while I concerned myself with social and domestic dramas. Charles's country, the United Moore Republic, was more austere. It was a military dictatorship with no female inhabitants.

These invented worlds were not retreats for us. They were shared. They were not a substitute for real life, but an extension of life, a rehearsal for what would concern us as adults. We moved freely in and out of each other's games, though we bickered as we did so. None of us, in other words, exhibited the autistic 'triad of impairments' – of imagination, communication and social interaction.

Play of this kind hardly exists for George and Sam. They have many toys, but few of them are put to their intended use. Their play is limited, end-stopped, and – above all – unshared. George, aged thirteen, went off to school this morning clutching three toy tank engines. He likes these engines, will move them about a bit and give them a few snatches of dialogue – lifted from his *Thomas the Tank Engine* videos – but he has no intention of inviting other children to join him in playing with them. If another child initiated a game, George wouldn't know how to reciprocate. If anyone suggested that he was too old to be playing with tank engines, he wouldn't know what they meant. Sam's play, such as it is, is even more private, because it's largely non-verbal. It's hard to tell, even, whether he is actually playing in an imaginative sense at all, or whether he's just making movements and noises for their own sake.

For me, the life of the playground was by far the most important and interesting part of school; for George and Sam, outside 'play' is just existing in fresh air. I was deeply involved in an ever-shifting network of friendships and alliances; my sons have no independent social life, nor do they appear to want one. Each day, they go to an autistic unit attached to a special-needs school in Hastings. George is interested in the other children, probably regards them as his friends, and has occasionally asked me to invite them home, but it would never occur to him to ring them up or invite them himself. Sam seems barely aware that the other children exist. As far as I can tell, neither of them imagines that they will not be at school for ever. They have no ambition, no thoughts about their adult selves, no perspective on anything except the here and now. The contrast between my experience of being a child and theirs could hardly be greater.

When, after George and Sam had been diagnosed, Min and I needed to decide whether to risk having another baby, we went to the Maudsley Hospital for 'genetic counselling'. It's now generally accepted that autism has genetic causes, that it does 'run in families'. The picture is somewhat obscured by the fact that, due to the antisocial nature of the condition, full-blown autists are much less likely than almost any other group to become parents themselves. In preparation for the consultation we were asked to note down any family members who were eccentric, depressive, obsessive-compulsive, schizophrenic, even dyslexic – and of course, any who were actually autistic.

My family has lived in the same place for a long time. They have always been great letter-writers and recorders of information, they have been socially stable, their lives have not been hugely disrupted by war or disaster, and none of them ever throw anything away. All this means that I can tell you a very great deal about my family for several generations. Don't worry, I won't – not much. But my report for the Maudsley was pretty comprehensive. I came up with some cases of mild depression, one obsessive-compulsive, no dyslexia. Lots and lots of left-handers – I'm not sure if that's relevant. No schizophrenics, and no confirmed autists – and absolutely no one who wasn't able to lead a normal life, if by that one means marrying, holding down a job, maintaining friendships, bringing up children.

There are eccentricities, as there probably are in most families. In my case, they cluster most markedly round my paternal grandfather, the one who died when I was a baby. Grandfather had extreme food fads. He abhorred fat of any kind, and couldn't bear people to eat butter or cheese anywhere near him. Although he was a kind man, he imposed his fussiness on his forbearing wife – family meals were utterly plain and monotonous. He made up his mind about something, and never changed it. 'In 1898,' he remarked, 'I ate an apple that I *almost* liked.'

Grandfather took comfort in familiar objects. When he went to boarding school, in 1894, he had a dressing-gown – 'The New Dressing-Gown'. In 1959, during his final illness, the hired nurse threw The New Dressing-Gown away. My mother is convinced this hastened his end.

Grandfather kept a diary for every day of his adult life. It is a startlingly un-intimate record. If you want to know about Welsh miners' strikes in 1919, or the times of trains from London to Chatham, then Grandfather's your man. He recorded the weather every single day. This is not so odd, given that his great love was the sea and sailing ships, but less easy to explain is his habit of recording the lifespan of each of his razor blades. It is hard to come up with a better example of 'autistic' information: '12 February 1932. This morning I discarded my razor blade, after 86 days of use.' The fact is recorded purely for its own sake. It has no resonance, no wider context.

Grandfather was a literal-minded man. He argued against the existence of angels, because in order to support their wings they would have to have a breastbone twelve feet deep. Going to the cinema with him was agony, says my aunt, because inaccuracies enraged him. 'That's not a man-of-war. Where are the puttock shrouds?' he would demand of the luckless usherette, 'How can you show such nonsense in your cinema?' He talked to everyone in the same way, making no allowances for education, age, class or show of interest. The local policeman once called in, to inquire about a shotgun licence, and was found in the drawing room, imprisoned by politeness, while my grandfather read him extracts from Swift's *Journal to Stella*.

This last characteristic was admired. He was a polite man, except when exasperated by inaccuracies of rigging, and most people felt flattered by the way he discoursed with them. My grandfather's eccentricities were generally seen as harmless and endearing, though for his children irritation and embarrassment also played a part. His Pavlovian response to the sound of the hornpipe caused my poor aunt acute distress – when he heard it played by Battle Town Band, he danced the length of the High Street. At the theatre, once, he was in a box, and wanted to make contact with his companions who were seated below, so he turned his programme into a paper aeroplane and threw it down to them mid-performance. He had no fear of heights (a common autistic trait) and loved walking round the tops of factory chimneys or the battlements of Bodiam Castle. He delighted in disregarding the sign at the railway station which said 'Passengers must not cross the line.' 'I'm not a passenger,' he would proclaim with autistic pedantry as he skipped across the tracks.

All this makes him sound like a classic case of undiagnosed Asperger's syndrome. And yet there is plenty of evidence in the opposite direction. His marriage was happy and stable, though perhaps this says more about my grandmother, who was by all accounts a particularly loving, humorous and tolerant woman, than it says about him. He was an affectionate and interested father; he wrote 'baby books' about each of his four children, recording funny remarks and charming habits as well as statistics about teeth and weight. He maintained several lifelong friendships, and seems to have enjoyed socializing. Following his father's wishes, he became a doctor. For himself, he would have preferred a maritime career. He became the Medical Officer of Health to Battle Rural District Council, and wrote detailed and sympathetic notes about the diseases – rickets, TB, scarlet fever, diphtheria – that he encountered in the cottages of the poor. But at times his sense of medical priorities was not all it might have been. During the Second World War, he was asked to give lectures on First Aid to volunteer nurses. My aunt popped in on the fourth of eight lectures to see how things were progressing. The young trainees were earnestly taking notes on the causes and spread of the Black Death.

Though Grandfather seems to have been closer to autism than other members of my family, he was far from being a diagnosable case. What of my sons' father's family? Are there any genetic clues to be found?

The Smiths – Min's father's family – came from Birmingham, and hadn't moved about very much, so we know a fair amount about the last three generations. But Min's mother, Eva, didn't know her father. He was a Czech architect who died of cancer, and we don't know much more than that. Eva's mother, Elvira, came from a highly educated Hungarian family – Jewish, but they'd given up practising. There were mental health problems – Elvira's older sister committed suicide – but, with most of the family in concentration camps, there were mitigating circumstances.

It's hard to disentangle Elvira's innate psychological make-up from the historical circumstances in which she found herself. She was a great survivor. She escaped to England before the beginning of the war, and because she was pregnant with Eva she was able to remain here. She had a second child, Marina, and she left the girls in a series of boarding schools and orphanages while she struggled to make a living. She was a single mother; she married three times, but the marriages were all short-lived. It would be interesting to know whether she felt guilt about leaving the children, because guilt is a very non-autistic emotion. I wonder, too, whether she experienced the less rational guilt at being one of the family members to avoid the camps.

By the time I knew Nana, as we always called Elvira, she was an active old woman, furiously resisting old age, and very, very preoccupied with herself. As with my grandfather, it would be stretching a point to place Nana on the autistic spectrum, but there were certain characteristics . . . like my grandfather, she talked in exactly the same way about exactly the same things to whomever she met. She had a fund of interesting stories – she had friends who were well-known artists and writers – but because she never paid attention to anyone else, she rarely added new ones, and she didn't attempt to remember whether she'd told them to you before. She was always pleased to see me, but I never got the impression that she knew me at all.

Nana was academically able. She had trained as a lawyer, spoke seven languages, and became the successful headmistress of an approved school. But when she read, or talked, she seemed only interested in finding evidence to confirm what she already thought about things. She never modified anything – her opinions, her manner, her appearance – to suit her circumstances. Her liveliness and force of character gave the impression that she was a sociable person, a 'party animal', but the impression was a false one. She was, I think, very much alone.

George couldn't bear Nana. She died just a month or so before his autism was diagnosed, and I regret that I was never able to explain away his tearful, clinging behaviour when she came to visit. Nana had a deep, resonant, heavily accented voice. She had been a very good-looking woman; in her seventies, she still wore plunging necklines, high heels and masses of clanky jewellery. She would pick her way across our muddy garden in sling-back stilettos and mink coat, utterly failing, as an autist would, to adapt to circumstances. We told her, as politely as we could, that her dramatic gestures, over-insistent hugs and elaborately presented gifts were all frightening for George, but she could not take this in.

Could Nana possibly have been autistic? She had many eccentricities. She would remove food from the table and take it home in her handbag, and she was incapable of buying anything new – for Christmas I once received a box of bath salts with a predecimal price tag. She rarely – as far as I could see – ate a proper meal, but created strange concoctions; I remember broken-up Ryvita mixed with quantities of neat tomato purée, and bags and bags of raw carrots. It would be feasible, however, to attribute this behaviour to the trauma of her experiences as a refugee. Other peculiarities, like the fact that she was unsure which part of the ear to attach clip-on earrings to, are more obviously reminiscent of the syndrome. There was something false about Nana, but not false as in scheming. It was as if she had constructed a whole persona to carry her through life, because despite her apparent sophistication, she didn't really seem to understand the way the world worked.

I'm sure other members of the family, reading this, will protest vigorously. 'Nana autistic? What nonsense!' And certainly I would never have come up with such a theory if George and Sam's condition hadn't encouraged me to subject their forebears to intense scrutiny. On the Smith side, their father's father's family, there seems at first sight to be nothing. The Smiths were a straightforward bunch who worked hard, moved up in the world, married and had children, enjoyed participating in sport, and were reasonably socially active. Several of them were successful salesmen, which suggests a non-autistic ability to observe and predict human behaviour. But then there was Cousin Artie. Cousin Artie was a pretty remote connection – Grandfather Clive's second cousin. He died a long time ago. But it is significant that, despite his remoteness, stories are still remembered about him. Artie was very intelligent, with an amazing memory for facts, but he never made the success of himself that people expected. He never married; he lived alone, sweeping up dust and storing it in jars, doing without crockery – he used an old sardine can as a dish – and burying his money in the garden. Cousin Artie had an even less accessible brother, Cousin Victor, who committed suicide. Depression and suicide are common among high-functioning autists and people with Asperger's syndrome, particularly when their condition is undiagnosed.

Our trawl through family history threw up poor long-dead Artie as the closest thing to a full-blown autist. Arguably the examination of any family could reveal such a character. Why did Min and I produce George and Sam? Did the eccentricities in both our gene pools combine to produce exactly the right ingredients for autism? People have often asked me, why have you got two? And the only accurate reply is, I don't know. In a way, it doesn't really matter. I've never raged against fate, or cast about much for explanations. Nothing in my own childhood experience led me to expect that anything would be 'wrong' with my children, but then there they were, and – well, you just get on with it.

The Maudsley estimated our chances of having a third autistic child as one in twenty. There was a much higher chance – one in six – of the child having a minor learning problem – being a slow reader was the kind of example they cited. If the child was male, the 'danger' was much greater, so of course we hoped Jake would be a girl.

I found out that he wasn't halfway through the pregnancy. There was a little scare – the midwife couldn't find the heartbeat – and I was rushed off to hospital for an extra scan. The heartbeat was swiftly located, and so were the genitals. 'Do you want to know?' asked the nurse. I hadn't thought I did, but suddenly it made sense to get the disappointment of the new baby's gender out of the way before the birth itself. So the anxiously waiting extended family had several months to get used to the idea that I would have a third boy.

Five years later, the worry seems extraordinary. Jake is not only not autistic, he's the least disappointing child it's possible to imagine.

2. The Wonderbaby

George wasn't my first baby. There was another, who would now be fourteen. Min and I married in 1987, and in the autumn of 1988 we were living in a rented flat in Maida Vale. Min worked at home, writing children's books. I was an English teacher. We both very much wanted a baby, but I don't think we imagined that having one would make an enormous difference to our lives. I certainly intended to carry on working full time. Min would look after it, supplemented by some kind of au pair, or perhaps a day nursery. That was the idea. It seems that we didn't think about it very hard.

I was twenty-nine, healthy and energetic. I became pregnant the minute I wanted to, and felt fine – the odd surge of nausea, nothing more. I sailed through the first three months, eating well, cutting alcohol down to the occasional glass of wine. I was entirely confident about this pregnancy. The first ultrasound scan was booked for the eighteenth week of pregnancy in the middle of January. We went to the old Westminster Hospital, dingy and old-fashioned, with people shuffling along the corridors and smoking and coughing their guts out. Min and I waited with other parents-to-be for the first exciting glimpse of our baby. I drank cup after polystyrene cup of water; a full bladder makes the scan easier to read.

Neither of us had seen an ultrasound image before. I lay on my back, staring at the screen, unable to interpret the swirls and loops that met and parted like oil on water. The nurse doing the scanning passed the monitor back and forth, back and forth over my stomach, not looking at me, intent on the image. 'I'm afraid I can't see all of it. Could you wait outside, to give Baby a chance to turn round?' I had no misgivings. We sat on the bench outside, cracking jokes. Perhaps I hadn't drunk enough water? I refilled my polystyrene cup.

We were called back in. Now, there were several more white-coated people in the room. A more senior-looking woman took over the scanning. Nobody said much, and it seemed to me that they were avoiding my eyes. I began to feel alarmed, but still I couldn't make much sense of what I saw on the screen.

The doctor sighed, and turned to me. My baby had no legs, and only half an arm. The head and torso looked normal, but the scanner wasn't sufficiently accurate to rule out further damage. She pointed out the relevant detail on the screen. Suddenly I saw it all. There was the baby, round-headed, jaunty, its half-arm raised like a little flag.

The hospital staff were kind, and helpful. They introduced the idea of termination as an option. But they put no pressure on us. They wouldn't let us make any decision right away. It was a Thursday – we were to come back on Monday for a consultation.

Min was sure that termination was best. I wasn't. I had lots of experience with disabled people; I had friends in wheelchairs due to spina bifida or cerebral palsy. They were all opposed to abortion – well you would be, wouldn't you? Who would wish themselves undone?

Disability had no horror for me. Before the scan, I would have said, 'Oh, I'll keep any child, whatever it's like.' But when I saw that baby twirling around in the only environment in which it would ever be wholly comfortable, I thought, if you keep this child you're asking it to be a hero, and is that fair?

Min's certainty helped me to decide. Ironically, in view of our eventual separation, I worried that keeping the baby would put our marriage under pressure. We settled for termination. In my childhood I had kept a great many cats. If a kitten was born with any kind of deformity, the mother cat would quickly destroy it. I do know that humans are not the same as cats, but I found the memory helpful.

The pregnancy had passed the stage where a simple evacuation could be carried out, so labour had to be induced. It was expected to take twelve hours. After forty-eight hours of fruitless labour I was given a general anaesthetic and the baby was removed while I was unconscious.

Throughout the labour I was given shots of pethidine, which made me feel most unlike myself; I always refused it during my subsequent labours. Every now and then I would be lifted up and told to push, but nothing happened. I dreaded seeing the baby, but at the same time I wanted to; it is a great regret to me that I never did. When I came round from the anaesthetic I asked to see him (the baby was almost certainly a boy) but the kind nurse said, 'Baby's not looking his best, dear.' Later I discovered what she meant; the baby had got stuck, and had to be cut up to be removed.

The hospital was fairly grotty, but the nurses were excellent. The sister cancelled her day off so she could see me through to the end. Another, very young nurse sat with me talking in the early hours, after the baby had gone. 'Everyone deserves to have a baby,' she said. That struck me as profoundly true. I think it still does.

One reason I had wanted to see the baby was to convince myself of the reality of what had happened. I've been appalled, since, to read about the widespread use of general anaesthetic during childbirth in North America in the 1950s and 1960s. If you're unconscious when you give birth, how much harder it must be to accept the child as really, truly yours. I was given a scan photo to keep, which was helpful. In irrational moments, when I began to worry that I had ended the life of a perfectly healthy child, I could look at the photo which showed clearly that there were absolutely no legs.

I was young and fit, and I recovered quickly. By April, I was ready to conceive again. George was soon on his way, due exactly a year after the date of the termination.

The limbless baby hadn't shaken my confidence. It felt like a random piece of bad luck. No one came up with a reason for it. 'We don't keep data on this kind of thing,' said the consultant, 'because it's so extremely rare. Actually, we had a lady in here a few weeks ago with something similar . . .' If anything, that disaster made me feel all the more certain that my next baby would be absolutely fine.

Again, the pregnancy was straightforward, almost symptomless. I had more ultrasound scans than usual – five or six in all, the first at only eight weeks. They reassured me that this baby was physically complete, but in later years I worried – could ultrasound possibly trigger autism? The incidence of autism was rising; ultrasound was a newish procedure to which the entire neonatal population was subjected. Could there be a link? I've never come across any scientific support for this idea, though ultrasound has been blamed for other problems. I still don't feel happy about bombarding tiny foetuses with rays, and tried, unsuccessfully, to prevent Jake from being scanned more than once. But this was a long way in the future. At the time, I just enjoyed watching the prawn-like George shifting the four white dots that were his limbs in miniature boxing movements.

We didn't want to know George's gender, and were not clever enough at reading scans to detect it. I felt sure that I was going to have a girl – a girl with hair. I felt confident that I would have an easy, natural birth. I was remarkably unworried about the whole business, though I do remember being given a little romper suit early on in the pregnancy, and really not wanting it. It seemed to be tempting fate, to possess clothes for a baby who was so very far off being born.

On 25 January 1990 – ten days after my due date – I was seized by a great restlessness, a manifestation of that same impulse that drives pregnant cats to turn circles inside laundry baskets and unfeasibly small cardboard boxes. Cold winds were twisting dry leaves into whirlpools on the pavements of Maida Vale; I'd invited a friend – just one – to supper, so I waddled to the shops and saw fit to buy five pounds of stewing steak, five pounds of potatoes and a quantity of suet. On the return journey, the wind blew into a gale; the carrier bags cut into my hands; my bump was vast. Every few steps I had to stop and realign my various burdens. Back at home, I unpacked the meat, and felt sick. I lowered myself into a hot bath, and felt even sicker.

I paced the flat, leaning on the backs of chairs, and punctuating the day with mugs of tea. I've yet to see a convincing portrayal of a woman in labour on television or at the cinema. In my experience there's no sudden stab of pain, no rolling of eyes and clutching of bed rails. For me, it's a slow build-up of pressure, like being squeezed by a giant elastic band.

By late afternoon I was throwing up. That's a feature of labour that Hollywood doesn't dwell on – I vomited constantly throughout all mine. I rang my friend Richard and said perhaps he shouldn't come to supper after all. I never did find out what happened to all that meat.

At about seven in the evening we set off for St Mary's, Paddington. It was a short drive, but the stormy weather meant that the traffic crawled along. I was of course convinced that my baby would be born in the car. I needn't have worried; I still had fifteen hours to go.

St Mary's is a famous hospital, but I was unimpressed. There was no attempt at continuity of care. I was examined by several different people (and, during labour, internal examinations are THE most painful thing). None of them seemed to pass on any information to each other, and all of them failed to realize that George was in the posterior position – lying spine to spine with me, and 'presenting' with his face rather than the crown of his head, which usually means a longer and more difficult labour. The delivery room was cramped and lightless, and the soundproofing poor. I could hear a woman screaming and wailing, heartbroken. I longed to ask what had happened to her baby, but I didn't dare.

I'd written a long 'birth plan'; I didn't want an epidural, pethidine, or my waters broken – I didn't want any intervention at all. I was extraordinarily confident that I wouldn't need any. And when, at first examination, they told me I was already five centimetres dilated, I was jubilant. 'You'll have your baby by midnight,' I was told.

But midnight came and went, and George was well and truly stuck. Yes, I was fully dilated, but nothing was happening. They attached me to a drip, to speed things up. They broke my waters with one of those horrible crochet hooks. They clipped a monitor to George's unborn scalp to measure his distress. A midwife with sweaty armpits and a heavy cold flumped clumsily down on my bed; the jolt was agony. Because of the drip and monitor, I wasn't allowed to get off the bed. This was the worst thing; never in my life have I so much wanted to move about.

The night wore on – high winds and screaming women. My 'birth plan' was looking increasingly like an elaborate fantasy. Still, no one had realized that George was in the wrong position. Dawn broke. A registrar appeared, and ordered an epidural. He wanted to do a Caesarean, but George was too far down. If he'd suggested cutting me open with a rusty saw I'd have welcomed it. I didn't care about anything, certainly not the baby. I just wanted the whole process to come to an end.

The epidural was set up. The pain vanished; I was laughing and joking. They tried to suck George out with the ventouse but it kept popping off his head, sending the registrar reeling backwards across the floor. They made a huge cut and inserted the forceps – the giant salad servers. I was flat on my back, with my legs in stirrups; I couldn't see what was going on, but I could see that Min was looking a bit green.

The storm was over. The small window was full of bright sunlight. At ten in the morning of 26 January, George was hauled out. He was small and thin – only six pounds five ounces, despite being ten days late. He was streaked with meconium, the blackish-green tarry stuff which new babies have in their bowels, and which they void all over the place if they are distressed. George was very distressed. He was held up to me, cord still attached – bloody, muddy, with a furious bald head and the most enormous ears. This was not the dainty pre-washed girl with hair I'd been envisaging for nine months. They laid him on my stomach; he was writhing and slippery, and I squealed, not with delight.

His Apgar scores – a series of checks on the newborn's pulse, heartbeat, breathing, skin tone, and so on – weren't great, so they put him on a machine to clear out his tubes. I mistook the whine of the machine for his newborn voice. They wiped him a bit, wrapped him up, and gave him to me to be put to the breast. 'He's beautiful,' said the nurse. I looked at her in astonishment. 'Well,' she said, 'you should see the one next door.'

The top of poor little George's head was a tender purple cap, from the suction of the ventouse. Red looping marks from the forceps were clearly visible on his cheeks. He had scaly skin, a large nose covered in tiny white spots, white-and-purple fists, and large, bright, widely spaced eyes. Those eyes, as I was soon to discover, rarely closed. Right from the start George was vigilant, alert.

He suckled eagerly. I lay there nursing him while the registrar tidied me up. Then we were wheeled off to the ward. Both George and Sam were born in subterranean delivery rooms; with both of them, the journey upwards to the ward felt like another kind of deliverance. With Sam, I remember my mother walking beside the trolley, telling me that Terry Waite had just been released, and the news seemed appropriate.

I was lifted into bed, because the epidural hadn't worn off and I couldn't stand. George was put in a cot by my side, maddeningly out of reach. I could hardly move. I'd had dozens of stitches, and felt extremely weak. One of the other mothers, a tall Jamaican woman with a tiny dry-skinned baby for whom she'd provided a giant tub of Vaseline, astonished me by lifting her large suitcase on to her bed herself. She saw how feeble I was, and walked the crying George up and down for me. Then she tucked him into bed with me. I was very grateful. I didn't want George in the cot. A baby – a little girl called, I think, Alexandra – had been snatched from a hospital by a woman posing as a social worker or similar. We new mothers followed the story with anxious attention. Alexandra was found, alive and well, after a few days. There have been several similar stories since; I always like to keep my newborns in bed with me.

I have often heard autistic people described, sometimes by

themselves, as aliens, visitors from another planet. That's certainly how George felt to me for the first few days of his life. Was that because I sensed his otherness, or was it just a pretty normal reaction to the shock of a new baby and a difficult birth? I looked at George with wonder and deep, deep interest, but it wasn't, immediately, love.

Research suggests that babies who later turn out to be autistic have often had a difficult birth. The first assumption would be that the child has been damaged by the process; perhaps the supply of oxygen to the brain was interrupted. But then, what of the countless normal children who have also endured difficult births, and who seem unaffected? And though my labours with George and Sam weren't straightforward, neither were they emergencies. I've heard of far, far worse.

There's another theory about 'autistic' births, which sounds quite plausible to me. This theory suggests that the autism is already active, as it were, prenatally. The difficult delivery is the result of the baby's failure to co-operate with the birthing process. Already, the baby's instincts are somehow awry. This idea made much more sense to me after I'd had Jake. With George and Sam, nothing that happened during labour made much sense. They were both in the wrong position with the cord wrapped round their neck, and neither of them was going to get born on his own. With non-autistic Jake, it was all quite, quite different. His labour took four hours, and was utterly straightforward. I had no pain relief at all, not even a whiff of gas and air. I had no stitches, and very little bleeding. Of course it hurt, but it was the kind of pain that made sense. Giving birth to Jake was an active process, not a passive one; it really did feel as if both he and I knew what we were doing. I actually enjoyed it.

George stayed awake all of that first day. A crowd of visitors arrived. He was passed round, and he stared at them all with his big thunder-coloured eyes. When night fell and the visitors left, I thought perhaps he'd sleep, but I was wrong. He cried all night. I suckled him and cuddled him, but he went on crying. I rang the bell for the night nurse. She was grumpy. 'Change his nappy,' she ordered. She didn't offer to do it herself. I couldn't possibly change his nappy – I could hardly sit up. And besides, I felt that George's woe was for something far more profound than the need for a new nappy.

Things improved, as they always do. I stayed in hospital for five days – quite a long time, but I had been fairly knocked about – and by the end of it George and I were both a lot more cheerful. We were surrounded by a wall of flowers and cards, and George had plenty of admirers. The need to have people admire your baby is strong, especially your first. The girl in the bed opposite was only about sixteen. She had no flowers, just one pink balloon, saying, 'It's a girl', tied to the foot of her bed. Her shaven-headed boyfriend came to visit her; they had nothing to say to each other. The baby was called Stephanie. When they left hospital, they were going to live in a B and B.

I knew I was lucky, and soon I began to feel lucky. George was healthy, and gained weight fast. The scars and bruises faded. He was obviously very bright – everyone said so. He fixed his attention on faces and objects for long periods; he focused very well. He was excited by anything red – and, thirteen years later, he still is. He would vibrate with pleasure at the sight of a teddy with a red bow. I don't know why the experts insist that new babies can't see colour, when they so clearly can.

George was breastfed. It never crossed my mind that he wouldn't be. Nor had it occurred to me that breastfeeding would be anything other than a completely easy process, like turning on a tap. It was quite a blow to discover that I found it difficult, uncomfortable, boring, and not hugely rewarding. There are pleasures – the tiny face guzzling away is a very sweet sight, and the steady weight gain, all your own work, is satisfying. But though I remained a committed breastfeeder – I fed Jake until he was twenty months, by which time he was saying things on crowded commuter trains like 'Other side now please, Mummy' – I can't say it was ever my favourite aspect of motherhood.

The midwives and health visitors encouraged demand feed-ing. The idea is that the baby takes what he needs, and the mother's supply adjusts accordingly. You are meant to achieve a perfect balance. It's a far cry from the only-every-four-hours-and-don't-you-dare-touch-him-in-between-times rule imposed on my mother's generation.

Demand feeding makes sense to me – in fact it's the only option for me, since I find it impossible to ignore a crying baby. But in those early weeks a 'perfect balance' did not seem to be what George and I were achieving. George wanted to feed *all* the time. He would feed for ages, fixing me the while with his gimlet eye. If I did anything other than return his gaze, he would stop sucking and cry. Other mothers have told me how breastfeeding allowed them to read the whole of Proust, or George Eliot, or at least watch lots of telly, but I could do none of these things. George was, and is, a very controlling child.

Poor eye contact is one of the distinguishing features of autism, yet in those days George couldn't get enough of it. Not just with me, either – his father, friends and relations, people in shops . . . George has large, bright eyes, beautifully shaped; grey-blue, with long curling black lashes. They have a Slavic slant in the corners; it is hard to deny the impression they give of sensitiv-ity and intelligence. Nowadays he finds prolonged eye contact difficult – 'Don't look at me! Look at Sam! Look at that cupboard!' But as a baby he went to the other extreme. His desire for eye contact seemed to go with his need to be held upright – he hated lying flat. He wanted to know what was going on; he sought stimuli of all kinds, particularly visual stim-uli. A psychologist later described him as 'over-vigilant', and I think that's about right.

For the first three weeks of his life he never slept for more than an hour and a half at a stretch. That meant that I didn't, either – George seemed to thrive on this regime, or non-regime, but I did not. The health visitor called. 'Get him a dummy,' she ordered, 'otherwise, you will die.' Health visitors can be very useful people. With that pronouncement she cut away all my middle-class disdain. 'He's a sucky baby,' she said. 'Some of them just are. He's using you as a dummy, so you may as well get him one.' Min raced to the chemists round the corner and came back with a fistful of dummies. He inserted one. Silence, and rest. I fell asleep at once. George didn't wake for three hours. When I woke, I felt as if I had been on a Caribbean cruise.

Why do people persist in believing Locke's idea that a baby is a blank slate? Surely only a man could have come up with that. As every mother knows, a baby is a slate with a great many things already written on it. In George's case, most of them were inde-cipherable, but 'I like putting things in my mouth' was up there in large, clear letters. It has never been rubbed off. All babies explore objects with their mouths; the lips and tongue are even more useful than the fingers for examining the peculiar proper-ties of something new. With most babies, mouthing peaks at about ten months and fades out during toddlerhood, as the child finds a variety of other ways to find out about his environment. With both George and Sam the habit began early, and has never truly ended. They would both put absolutely anything into their mouths, except, of course, food of any significant nutritional value. They moved on from rattles and rubber ducks to earth, paint, stone, cardboard, ringpulls, drinking straws, slugs, spiders . . . Sam, at eleven, still loves chewing Plasticine and biting the tips off felt-pens. When his class planted daffodil bulbs he pulled them up and bit chunks out of them.

George gave up his dummy on the day the newborn Sam came back from hospital, which was also – alas – the day he gave up his afternoon nap. It was as if he was saying, 'Don't think you can fob me off with this any more, and don't think I'm ever going to let you out of my sight again.' Sam kept his dummies for years and years. I'm ashamed to say that when, finally, I furtively binned them, like the monster mother in Jill Murphy's excellent *The Last Noo-Noo*, Sam may have been as old as eight. I do remember asking the dentist whether the dummy would make Sam's adult teeth stick out, and the dentist looking at Sam trashing his surgery, and saying, 'Well, possibly, but it's a question of priorities, isn't it? I mean, if it helps . . .'

So, at three weeks old, George was plugged, and the dummy gave a little more order and sanity to our lives. He slept more, though not much. In any twenty-four hours, George was awake for fourteen, which is an awful lot for a newborn. I now know that sleep problems are extremely common among autists. During George's insomniac babyhood I took comfort from the reassurances of everyone who met him – 'Oh, he doesn't sleep because he's so bright!'

George did everything early. I noted it all in his baby book with pride. He smiled at three weeks, laughed at one month. He soon reached out for toys, and at two months could handle things quite competently. He sat at five months, crawled at six, stood alone at seven, and took his first unaided steps on the day he was nine months old. He was an ambitious baby; I remember him dragging a huge pack of nappies, three times his size, across the living-room floor. He had one of those wheeled babywalkers that are now thought to be so dangerous; he loved it, and at six months would scoot round the kitchen in it, grabbing things. I remember him seizing a cauliflower from the vegetable rack and careering away with it, chuckling with glee.

His fascination with colour, which I had first noticed in hospital, continued, as it does to this day. He had a musical mobile of four rotating plastic bears; he would lie on his mat watching this intently, reserving his energy for the reappearance of the red bear. When this tinkled into sight he would throw himself into a frenzy, waving his arms and legs and gurgling. He was about a month old.

He found certain visual details hugely exciting – the honeycomb grid on the front of a radio, for example. I remembered this when, a couple of years later, he pored endlessly over the picture of a honeycomb in a nature book. He loved music, and the sound of running water – if he was crying, I used to turn on a tap to soothe him. All his senses seemed to be on red alert – he hated being dressed or undressed, but his bath was a great joy. He didn't reject physical contact, which is often the first sign of autism in babies, but he was never relaxed. When my mother held him she said he felt stiff, though I, who hadn't handled many babies, didn't notice. It wasn't until I had Jake, eight years later, that I realized what a 'normal' baby felt like. Jake, a neat little parcel, nestled into the crook of my arm as if he'd grown there. George wanted to be held, but he wasn't truly cuddly. He accepted hugs but didn't return them; he did stretch out his arms to reach things, and that 'thing' might be a person. George wanted to be held *up*, so that he could see things – people were useful pieces of furniture rather than comfort-givers. And he *never* kept still. From the moment he could wriggle, wriggling was what he did. I remember holding my cousin Helena's twin girls, who are exactly the same age as George, when they were about ten months. They sat in my lap, snug and plump. I thought, George never sits like this. He squirmed in my lap like a puppy. But the difference didn't worry me. I just assumed it was the difference between boys and girls.

It wasn't possible to think of the infant George as anything other than highly intelligent. Baby books rightly warn us against interpreting the early reaching of milestones as significant, but we can't help it. If a child is showing enthusiasm for picture books at three months, or sitting confidently astride ride-on toys at six months, as George was, adults just do say 'Isn't he bright?' I am not sure, now, how to interpret George's precocity, which continued until the age of precisely two and a quarter. Was it just that, being awake for more hours than other babies, he had more time to learn new skills? Or does it mean that he really does have great intelligence, which with time has become shrouded in the mists of autism? As I write, thirteen years later, George's academic skills are scant. He has basic numeracy and literacy, no more. There is no area in which he overtakes or even matches his peer group, except that he still learns songs quickly, has a good memory for both the words and the melody, and can sing well when he tries.

There's a popular belief that inside every autistic child is a genius struggling to get out. I don't subscribe to this. It's probably true that most autists have more ability than they can or will display. It's also true that they have 'islets' of ability, a few areas in which they are disproportionately skilful. Sam, who is academically much less able than George, is relatively good at jigsaw puzzles. He's not *very* good at them – all normal eleven-year-olds would be better. But he's much better at jigsaws than he is at, say, reading. IQ profiles are not a satisfactory way of assessing autists, but they do usually illustrate this intellectual profile of peaks and troughs.

My own feeling is that George, as a baby, could not rest. He sought stimulus all the time, and at that stage new knowledge and new skills provided stimulus. It doesn't now. George crammed himself with knowledge for two and a quarter years, he overloaded, and he shut down.

Min and I became boastful about our prodigious baby. I forgive us – new parents simply cannot get into perspective the importance of their offspring in the greater scheme of things. We would make him perform his party pieces, doubtless to the dismay of our friends – grandparents can take any amount of this kind of thing, but friends shouldn't have to. Did our boasting mask a faint anxiety that all was not quite well with our little star? It's possible. I couldn't help noticing that compared to other babies George was exhausting, demanding and disobedient, though I chose not to see this as a problem.

The baby book I followed most closely was Penelope Leach's *Baby and Child*. I found most of her advice sympathetic, but every now and then I would simply fail to recognize what she was talking about. She describes the time when the baby changes from being 'a totally unpredictable and therefore rather alarming novelty' and becomes 'settled into life . . . whether he's settled at two weeks or at two months, that moment will come'. Having experienced Jake, I know exactly what she means. But I remember reading this when George was tiny, and thinking, no, she's looking through rose-tinted spectacles. George didn't 'settle into life'. He didn't know night from day; he was up, laughing and larking about, at any time. The gaps between his feeds were of wildly varying length. There was no guarantee, even, of what would comfort or amuse him. What worked one day would often fail the next.

No one suggested anything was wrong. The doctor who gave him his six-week check thought he was wonderful. 'There's a baby who's in love with his mother,' she remarked, as George's gaze followed me round the room, and his little limbs waved with excitement whenever I came near. Like normal babies, George was fascinated by the human face. He became hugely enthusiastic about a photograph of Paloma Picasso on the back cover of a magazine, all black eyebrows and big red lips, when he was only a few days old. My mother and I look quite alike, and when George was a baby our haircuts were similar. George would turn from one of us to the other, puzzled, trying to work it out.

Recent research, using gaze-tracking devices, has established that autistic people focus on the lower half of the face, particularly the mouth. The 'neurotypical' gaze roves from background to foreground, from eyes to mouth to hands, taking in a whole range of clues about the intentions and state of mind of the watched person. The autist, by concentrating almost exclusively on the lower face, misses nearly all of these clues. Ironically, given that many use little speech themselves, the autist is heavily dependent on the spoken word for his understanding of a social situation, and, as most of us know, what is said and what is meant are often quite different. It would be interesting to know whether, when baby George was scrutinizing faces so intently, he was autistically only truly looking at the lower half, or whether scanning the whole face was a skill he once had but has now lost.

Three features of early infant development were absent in both George and Sam, although I only realized this when I had Jake. Babies of three to four months are supposed to play, first with their fingers, then with their toes. They spread their hands in front of their faces and wiggle their fingers; they lie on their backs, catch their feet, and bring them up to their mouths. Jake did this at the right time, just as he did everything else. George and Sam didn't. I do vaguely remember noticing that George's feet weren't going into his mouth, and thinking, oh well, perhaps he's not very flexible. It seems possible to me now that this was an early sign of autism. Adult autists report a peculiar, disjointed sense of their own bodies. Donna Williams, for instance, writes that she thinks somebody has touched her arm, looks down, and realizes that it is her own hand. Perhaps the baby who fails to establish the boundaries of his own body through playing with hands and feet is likely to experience this disconnectedness in later life.

The second possibly significant omission is about faces again. Babies usually look doubtful or even cry when they see their mother in a hat, sunglasses, with a new hairstyle, and so on. Neither George nor Sam ever had this reaction. Jake couldn't bear to see me even with wet hair, for months. Some mothers of deeply autistic children believe that their child doesn't even recognize them. I think this unlikely; I'm sure George and Sam have both always recognized me, but they may not feel the need or the inclination to display that recognition. My guess is that George and Sam didn't react to seeing me with a towel round my head, or whatever, because though they know me and, after a fashion, love me, they don't have normal expectations of what a mother should be or do. Most babies' emotional instincts conform to a pattern; those of autistic babies do not.

Their reaction, or lack of reaction, on switching from breast to bottle may fit in here. It's something that every nursing mother dreads, particularly if – as in my case – the switch is necessary because she's going back to work. One feels guilt for exchanging the baby's birthright for cold, unloving, rubber-insulated feeding, to coin a phrase. Some babies can't bear it – my cousin's baby daughter was so cross about it that Caroline found herself rushing back from the City to Wandsworth (a forty-minute trip on a good day) every four hours to give Mary another suckle.

Well, neither George nor Sam turned a hair. They guzzled down their first bottles of formula with indifferent greed. They really didn't seem to notice. I'd planned to keep the breastfeeds going night and morning for some time, but in the face of their nonchalance there didn't seem to be much point. Jake, by contrast, never had a bottle at all. His desire to be fed by me and me alone was ferocious. When he was twenty months old, my friend Clare took matters out of his and my hands. 'Go away for a weekend,' she ordered. 'You need to get your life back. I'll look after him. It doesn't matter if he hates me.' I spent a weekend in Barcelona. Jake was angry, but it worked.

Though George was a 'difficult' baby, he was also great fun. He loved peek-a-boo and tickling games; he loved to be rocked, bounced, sung to. This meant that it was easy to leave him to be looked after by other people – they found him very engaging. And, strong though his interest in me was, he didn't seem to mind my absence much. Penelope Leach tells us about 'eight-month anxiety', and I recall friends' babies crawling desperately after them, weeping, if they had the temerity to go to the lavatory on their own. Neither George nor Sam did this, and this is the third of my significant developmental differences. At the time I concluded, smugly, that my babies were so emotionally secure that they didn't need to cry. I was wrong about that. Their lack of reaction was a sign of autism, not of security. As in so many other ways, they didn't fit the pattern. Jake, who had the least 'reason' to be anxious, as I didn't go back to work after his birth and was rarely out of his sight, exhibited classic eight-month anxiety. Now, aged five, he has strong relationships with several adults and confidently spends time away from me. His emotional development keeps pace with his growing maturity and understanding; he spread his wings once he was ready to do so. For his brothers, despite appearances, babyhood was full of gaps. We're trying hard to fill them now.

3. Please Replace the Handset and Try Again

All autists have abnormal language. Some have no spoken language at all, but can be taught to use signs. A very few never achieve any means of communication at all, spoken or signed. This complete absence is rare – most will tug an adult by the sleeve or guide a hand towards a desired object, and this, although basic, is communication of a sort.

Others speak with extreme, almost preposterous, fluency. 'Talking like a dictionary' can be a symptom of high-functioning autism. This may not sound like too much of a problem, but on closer examination the speech patterns will be found to lack flexibility. Slang and idiom will be poorly understood, metaphor and simile may be taken literally. And the super-fluent speech will take no account of the listener's level of understanding; the autist will probably be unable to modify his elaborate vocabulary for the benefit of a child or a foreigner. It's highly likely, also, that the autist will talk almost entirely about things that interest or concern himself. He may have been trained to ask polite questions, but will rarely take in the answers. Even the highest-functioning autist will have difficulties with the give and take of normal conversation.

Echolalia is a very common feature of autistic speech. The autist mimics words or phrases, or even whole chunks of dialogue. He may perfectly capture the voice and intonation of the person he's imitating, but unlike a true mimic he won't be able to improvise for satiric or comic effect. He won't be able to think 'This is the sort of thing Mum might say' – he'll simply imitate what Mum actually has said. Echolalia is particularly common in young autistic children just learning to speak. It's usually a relatively good sign – any speech is better than no speech, in terms of future development. Some echolalic children – George included – build on their 'echoes' and learn to produce speech of their own. Nor should the echoes be regarded as empty of meaning. They may be – but not necessarily. Many children don't echo any old phrase. They choose phrases that are in some way interesting or useful to them, though their value may be obscure to their neurotypical listeners.

All echolalic behaviour in young children should be investigated, unless you're very sure that a joke is intended. Parrot-talk is not a normal part of language development. Of course, all children imitate – that's how they acquire speech. But very quickly, the normal child will put words together in her own way. She may pick up adult expressions and put them into her sentences, often with precocious effect, but she won't simply bounce your phrases back at you, unadorned, unless she is autistic.

Some autists invent words and phrases. These may be 'stims' (sounds that give them some kind of sensory stimulus or satisfaction) or they may be genuine coinages. Sam's invented words include 'stonkers', 'splockiator', 'splainiator', 'mushroom hands' and 'Chenta and Gleed'. I don't know what these mean, but I think stonkers and mushroom hands are something to do with clocks, and splockiators and splainiators are machines. When we visited the Science Museum Sam seemed to think there were splockiators and splainiators in it. Chenta and Gleed would be a good name for a Disney film, and indeed I think that Sam has a pair of characters in mind, possibly based on himself and George. But I'm really not sure.

It's unusual to find an autist with normal use of grammar. The ability to follow grammatical rules seems to be something innate – even deaf communities, using only signing, develop their own grammatical systems with ease and speed. But this doesn't seem to be true of autists. Perhaps their problems with grammar are something to do with their lack of 'central coherence' – they can focus on details but cannot see an overall pattern.

Nearly all of them have difficulties with personal pronouns. George couldn't use 'I', 'me', 'my' until he was six and a half;

Sam still hardly uses them. George used the second or third person. 'Do you want a drink?' meant that he wanted a drink. I remember him saying, nervously, at a party, 'Everybody here likes George.' He was really asking me a question – 'Does everybody like me?'

A psychologist might interpret this pronoun problem as the manifestation of a defective sense of self, and this could be true. I think, though, that it's more likely to be a mechanical thing, connected to the way the autistic child acquires language, through echolalia. The parent says, 'Do you want a drink?' The autistic child, who wants the drink, but has difficulty with an 'abstract' word like 'Yes', repeats the phrase. The child's lack of grammatical connectedness makes it difficult to swap 'you' for 'I'. Grammar can be learned, but for the autist it's not instinctive. High-functioning autists may use 'perfect' grammar, but like their elaborate vocabularies it will have the quality of being learned by rote. Past and future tenses seem to cause particular problems, perhaps because sequencing is a typical autistic difficulty.

It seems to me that most autistic children (I don't know many adults, yet) use language in two distinct ways. The first is to get what they want. They have learned that saying 'Biscuit' to an adult is a more effective way of getting a biscuit than screaming, arm-tugging or rolling on the floor, though it takes many of them years to reach this realization. So they use our language to us, to fulfil their most pressing needs. But they don't use our language to find out more about us as people – they don't want to hear stories about what Mummy did when she was a little girl, they're not interested in what Daddy saw when he went away on that business trip. Autists live in the moment, and the functional, concrete nature of much of their language reflects this.

Then they have a second kind of language. This kind they use for their own private satisfaction. They murmur phrases to themselves, they repeat snatches of video dialogue, they reduce words to odd, elided syllables to be yelled out or whispered. It's hard to tell whether language used in this way has any meaning in the conventional sense, or whether it is being relished purely for its sound effects. I'm inclined to think there is some meaning. George weaves phrases from different videos together to produce some kind of story of his own, or that's what it feels like. Sam's far less coherent vocalizations are often based on things that once interested him – 'The TUMble the DRYer eeeeoooaaah!' he'll chant at ever-increasing volume. This kind of language is private, and has nothing to do with communication. George now distinguishes clearly between his two modes of speech – 'I'm not talking to you, Mummy. I'm talking to myself.'

George acquired language early. By his first birthday he had several words, of the usual 'duck', 'ball' and 'brm-brm' variety, and he could show that he understood many more by directing his gaze or pointing. Yes, pointing. Lack of pointing in a baby (from about ten months) is, at time of writing, held to be the earliest indication of autism, but this needs to be assessed very carefully. Both George and Sam did point, and at the right age, too. I'm relying on memory here, because for obvious reasons I didn't take detailed data at the time, but I think the difference is that they mainly pointed on request. 'Where's the moon?' Point – 'Well done, darling!' They also pointed to get their needs met. Biscuit tin – point – result. But what they didn't use, or used only to a limited extent, was the shared-attention point. They didn't call my attention to things in order to make me see, enthuse, inform or share. I have a clear memory of George at about eighteen months, squatting, studying a ladybird. He was fascinated, and I remember thinking, fleetingly, shouldn't he want to show me that? But he didn't. He observed it for a long time, and then he stomped off.

As with so many developmental details, I didn't fully appreciate the difference until I had Jake. By ten months, Jake's arm was permanently extended in a point. If he spotted something interesting, he had to make sure that everyone else in the room had spotted it too. At the same age, Jake constantly brought things to show me, which the other two never did. I remember remarking on that to a friend. 'George never offers me his toys,' I said. 'Maybe he's selfish.' And I laughed, and thought no more about it.

For Jake, pointing and sharing toys was all about communication. Jake is a great communicator. Like George, he learned to talk early; unlike George, communication was his motivation. It's only now that I realize that George didn't acquire language primarily to communicate. He acquired language because he enjoyed language; words were a major stimulus. They still are. Like many autists, George has extremely acute hearing. His imitations of accent or tone of voice are exact. When he was attending the village school, aged about five, I wanted to know whether gym was called gym, PE, PT, or whatever. 'George,' I asked, 'when you put on your shorts and plimsolls and go into the hall, do you call it gym?' 'No,' said George, 'you call it George.' I began again, elaborating on my question. 'Do you call it gym or PE?' 'No,' said George, in immaculate estuary English, 'you call it pay-ay.'

There seemed to be nothing unusual about the early stages of the baby George's language development except that it was pretty fast. If I'd been very alert, I'd have noticed the absence of babble and gobbledegook. George had made the usual coos and gurgles, but he'd never gone in for the long nonsense sentences, the strings of syllables that imitate the pattern, though not the meaning, of adult speech. Right from the start, George spoke clearly and precisely, in a melodious voice. He still has this – when he's not shrill and agitated, his voice is musical and attractive. I'd like to make a bit of a point about this lack of infant babble, but my point is undermined by that fact that Sam babbled and burbled away with the best of them. Directing a flow of nonsensical speech-pattern babble towards a listening adult was one of Sam's specialities.

George's baby book records that at fifteen months he knew forty-three words, and that there were many more he had repeated two or three times and then seemed to forget. This is a lot for his age, but it is not astonishing. I also note that he will follow instructions to jump, dance, wave bye-bye, clap hands, and so on. It is perhaps significant that gestures are supplied on request, rather than produced spontaneously. However, George at that age didn't lack spontaneity. There was nothing passive or robotic about him. In the same entry I mention that 'he has become very tyrannical with his stories, fishing them out and bashing people with them to imply they should read them to him'. I also remember him following me round the kitchen, holding out a book and pleading 'In-a-minute,' because that was a phrase he'd associated with adults and story-reading.

His appetite for stories was the most unusual aspect of his early language acquisition. When he was sixteen months old I discovered that if I paused when reading a familiar story, he could supply the missing word. He could do this with any word (including 'and', 'the', etc.) at any point in at least fifty stories. The same applied to songs and nursery rhymes. By eighteen months, George could sing really well. By Christmas, a month before his second birthday, he could sing several carols, including long ones like 'Good King Wenceslas', note- and word-perfect, though I do remember him getting stuck on the 'Glorias' in 'Ding Dong Merrily' – a bit like not knowing when to step out of a revolving door.

This prodigious memory is fairly common in autists. Of course at the time we interpreted it as yet another manifestation of his amazing intelligence. George still has a retentive memory, though he's less interested in using it. He still learns new songs quickly, and knows the dialogue of his videos by heart. It's the closest either of my sons gets to the 'savant' skills possessed by a small minority of autists. Savant skills feature disproportionately in the public consciousness. This isn't surprising, because it is fascinating to come across someone who can do calendar calculation in the blink of an eye, or someone who has only to glance at a complicated architectural structure in order to reproduce it on paper with accuracy and panache. But it should be reiterated that most autists have no such skills.

And even if they do, their talents may be of limited value. With autism, one skill doesn't lead on to another in the way one might assume. The boy who can tell you the day of the week for any date you care to fire at him doesn't necessarily have ability in any other mathematical area. I knew a child who at five could reproduce sections of road maps; this hasn't led to any wider interest in cartography or town planning. It was just a knack. George's early love of language didn't encourage him to learn to read or write. The basic literacy skills he now has are the result of the efforts of determined teachers who have gone on and on at him and plied him with Refreshers. It's still very, very unusual for George to use reading or writing for his own pleasure or information. A phrase comes back to me from one of the boys' school reports – 'All new skills must be built on the back of existing ones.' Excellent educational theory, but extremely difficult to apply to autistic children, whose skills resemble an archipelago of islands scattered across a sea of confusion. Most of the islands aren't even within hailing distance of each other.

Just sometimes, autistic skills come together and cohere to excellent effect. Temple Grandin's ability to think in three dimensions has combined with her instinctive understanding of the link between physical pressure and the control of anxiety to make her one of the world's leading designers of cattle-handling equipment. This is excellent for all concerned, not least for the destressed cattle. But Temple Grandin is an unusually productive autistic adult. More often, the talent just sits there, a source – arguably – of some pleasure to the autist, and of pride giving way to frustration to the parent, who slowly comes to realize that their child's perfect pitch or gift for calculus or ability to memorize the number stamped on every manhole cover they pass on their daily walk to school is a discrete, isolated skill, not the key to unlocking a 'normal' intelligence.

There was nothing mechanical about George's early language, despite his amazing capacity to learn by rote. He relished language. He loved poetry – R. L. Stevenson's *A Child's Garden of Verses* was one of the books he frequently bashed me with, and this was before Sam was born, so George was considerably less than two. He would stand on a chair to recite: 'Dark brown is the river, Golden is the sand, It flows along for ever, With trees on either hand . . .' This was cute, and unselfconscious. His poetic tastes were catholic. He memorized the greeting inside all the cards he got for his second birthday and carried them round, intoning, 'Hello there lickle two-year-old, Your happy day is here, And that's the time for wishing you, Fun throughout the year, Lots of love from Aunty Gill.'

He used the phrases he'd learned from stories and deployed them in conversation. This was George's version of echolalia, and he used his echoes so cleverly that we were slow to perceive it as a problem. His twin cousins, William and Katharine, are just a little younger than him; they were scuttling about the kitchen, getting into everything. George, regarding them from his high chair, looked doubtful. 'These Things will not bite you,' he said. 'They want to have fun.' This is a line from *The Cat in the Hat*, and indeed the twins were very like Dr Seuss's anarchic Thing One and Thing Two.

George's echolalic fluency masked a serious deficit. He could point to the sky and say, 'There were fluffy white clouds in the pale blue sky' (*Ant and Bee and the Rainbow*), but he couldn't say, 'Look, Mummy – clouds!' He could look at our cleaning lady and say, 'There in the doorway was a huge green alligator,' but he couldn't say 'Jane's got a green dress.' When he picked up a toy telephone, he didn't say, 'Hello, Daddy,' or improvise any kind of imaginary conversation. Instead he said, in a perfect computerized voice, 'Please replace the handset and try again.'

In short, he had real difficulty constructing sentences of his own. He was like a foreigner with a phrase book; he stored memorized sentences, and pulled out whichever seemed best fitt d to the occasion. He did sometimes put his own words together. I remember him seeing a photograph of the recently deceased Robert Maxwell with his mouth open, and saying, 'Man done a yawn.' But his ability to create his own sentences and inflexion was limited, especially when compared to his huge vocabulary. And his tremendous enjoyment of fairly 'advanced' stories and poems led us to overlook the inadequacies of his comprehension. He had a book about Labrador puppies, a factual book with quite a difficult text, aimed at eight- or nine-year-olds. George loved this book as much as any, and listened to it again and again.

One day I paused during the reading, and pointed to a picture of the puppies. 'What are these, George?' I asked. 'Two pigs,' he replied. He'd heard *The Puppy Book* read a hundred times, but he hadn't realized it was about puppies.

By his second birthday, George could recognize all the letters of the alphabet, and could form a few short words with magnetic letters on the fridge. Sam, though much less precocious, could also identify letters early on. In the only home movie we have from their early days, Sam, aged twenty months, is poring over *Dr Seuss's ABC*, and, interestingly, calling my attention to his favourite letters. He finds W particularly amusing. I had good reason to assume I had a pair of early readers on my hands. How wrong I was. At thirteen, George has a reading age of maybe six or seven. Sam, now eleven, after long hours of labour and many Dolly Mixtures, can identify a handful of words – 'Sam', 'pig', 'sun', 'hot', 'cat'.

Watching Jake learn to read was completely different. Jake is an effortless reader. He could read a bit by three and a half; now, at just five, he's quite fluent. Words like 'laughed', 'excited' and 'through' cause him no problems. For Jake, everything is connected. His intellectual world is all joined up. He uses reading without noticing he's doing so – for computer games, in shops, for filling in the puzzles in children's magazines. He reads recipes aloud to me while I cook. He can see that reading tells us what we need to know.

George learned letters quickly because he has sharp eyes and a good memory. He learned to recognize words as discrete shapes; he still finds it difficult to break words down phonetically. But it never occurred to George to put his 'reading' to any use. Even at the height of his passion for stories, George never showed curiosity about a new book.

During his third and fourth years, as his autism closed him in, he became resistant to any new books at all. He would sit on the floor, surrounded by his old favourites, each one open at a particular page; he would turn from one to another, mixing extracts like a DJ mixing tracks. For George the language of the books was moving further and further away from its meaning.

Our scrap of video footage shows George at three and a half. Like most children of that age, he is talking all the time. He's talking to me, as well, or at least with reference to me – he frequently looks in my direction, requiring a response. But if I give the 'wrong' response, he overrules me. He's looking at *The Mixed-Up Chameleon* by Eric Carle. He is 'reading' – reciting – it, with considerable expression. But he doesn't think that the illustration of a seal is a seal. He thinks it's a pigeon. 'It's a purple pigeon,' he repeats. He looks to me for confirmation. I point out that textual evidence suggests it is, in fact, a seal. George denies this. 'It's a purple pigeon,' he reiterates several times, firmly and without rancour.

George's voice is clear, rather singsong. By this stage, there are quite a lot of his own constructions as well as some echolalia. An untrained observer would probably not suspect a problem. What is most autistic about George's speech is its omissions. I'm his mother; I'm holding a camcorder for the first time. He doesn't ask a single question. If it had been Jake, there'd have been a stream of them – 'What's that?' 'What's it for?' 'Why are you doing that?' 'Can I have a go?' George doesn't even seem to notice.

Three-year-olds are often described as being 'like sponges', soaking up enormous amounts of information about the world around them. They ask endless questions (and don't always seem to listen to the answers) because they are powerfully driven to find out as much as they can. Knowledge is power. George – bright, vocal, bookish George – asked no questions, beyond the most basic – 'Where's Sam?' Sam didn't even reach that level. Now, George does ask questions, on the lines of 'Where's X?' 'What's that?' 'What day is it today?' Sam only uses questions that he has learned by rote – 'Can I have a sweet?' (He's only learned

'I' by rote, as well.) Neither of my autistic boys has ever used the word 'Why?'* Curiosity is unsettling; it feels as if, beyond the boundaries of the here and now, they sense an immense bewilderment. They don't want to venture into that territory. Instead, they annex only small pieces of information, fence themselves in with concrete certainties. 'That's a purple pigeon!'

On 23 March 1993, I recorded everything George said during a fifteen-minute period. George was three years and two months – still ten months before his diagnosis. We were alone in the kitchen; Sam was asleep upstairs. I said nothing to George during the fifteen minutes, so all his remarks were self-generated. I reproduce this monologue in full, because it illustrates several of the key characteristics of autistic language, though of course I didn't realize that at the time. My commentary is in square brackets:

Yellow and blue mixed together make green. [Playing with Play-Doh.]
(Sings own 'song' – incomprehensible.)
What shall we do now? [Not directly addressed to me.]
(noises)
Look – they're doing painting. [Pointing into space.]
Look!
They're doing painting.
Are they in Sam's room?
No they're not in Sam's room.
Are they in George's room?
No they're not in George's room. [I didn't know who or what 'they' were.]
What shall we do now? [Imitation of adult voice.]
Mummy, I can't see you. [Repeated five times, in singsong. He could see me. This was a line from one of his books, about a little hippo.]

---

* Stop press: April 2003. George asked me, 'Why is Tom [the cat] sneezing?' and since then has asked several more 'Why?' questions. Progress does happen!

Mmm mmm mmm mmm.

There – that's enough. [Referring to Play-Doh.]

Beetles! [Looking at scrapbook with insects on the cover.]

(laughter)

That says Mummy!

That says George!

Granny! [The words 'Mummy', 'George', 'Granny' are written in the scrapbook.]

A comb for Granny. [Quote from *Lucy and Tom's Christmas* by Shirley Hughes.]

A handkerchief for Grandpa. [Quote from same source.]

Oh no!

(squeal)

Oooh.

There – go and play.

(laughter)

A calendar for Granny.

A packet of seeds for Grandpa to grow flowers from when springtime comes. [More *Lucy and Tom*.]

[Goes to Aga, points behind it. Addresses me directly for the first time.]

We go that way? [There's not much space behind the Aga!]

That way?

This way! This way! This way!

George – I'm going to get your nose. [Reference to a chasing game played by Delia, his nanny.]

George!

Sam – I'm going to get your nose. [Repeated five times, running up and down the kitchen. Sam is still upstairs in bed.]

Sam!

Boo!

I got Sam's nose!

Aaaah . . .

Got George's nose!

Got your nose.

George – I'm going to get your nose. [Repeated twice.]
(noises)
Here I come . . . aaah . . . got it!
George – I'm going to get your nose. [Repeated twice.]
Yes I mam – no – yes I *am*. [All this section imitating Delia's
   intonation.]
Go up! [To me, meaning, upstairs. I don't respond.]
We go up?
Put Mummy's slipper back on. [My slipper wasn't off.]
Each Peach Pear Plum.
I spy Tom Thumb.
I spy the three bears. [Quoted from *Each Peach Pear Plum*
   by Janet and Allan Ahlberg.]
(something incomprehensible)
I think . . . oh no, Teddy, we take you back. [No teddy in
   sight.]
Another . . . yes . . . there. [Arranging Play-Doh pots on the
   edge of the playpen.]
[Long silence.]
Some orange perhaps.
Right. Right. Blue time. [Picks up blue lid.]
No, put them away.
Now put them away. [Stacking pots.]
There. There.
Put them away. [To me.]
We go to toilet? [Fills nappy.]

There's a marked difference between the relative sophistication
of the quoted material ('A packet of seeds for Grandpa . . .') and
the rather awkward, unpractised quality of George's own phrases
('We go that way?'). There's a certain inconsequentiality – seeing
'Granny' within the scrapbook is enough to send George off into
Lucy-and-Tom land. There's little symbolic play; the most
extended piece of play is the nose-catching game, and here George
is simply rehearsing the way Delia played with him and Sam,
without any improvisation. The speech is very clear, and he

corrects his one mistake ('mam' for 'am'), but it lacks the organic connectedness of 'normal' language.

And, perhaps above all, George seems to have so little need of an audience. Most small children will talk to themselves as they play, but they'll frequently call an adult's attention to their activities if one's available. And I was very available, just standing there, writing things in my notebook, but George, though fully aware of my presence, hardly draws on this human resource at all. Just as neither George nor Sam has ever asked 'Why?', so neither of them has ever said, 'Look at me' – that defining request of neurotypical childhood.

4. Two in the Family

George's autism was diagnosed just before his fourth birthday. At that time, as the doctor's notes record, we had 'no worries' about two-year-old Sam – indeed, we used some of Sam's abilities, such as pedalling a trike, to highlight George's deficits. It may seem odd, having one autistic child, that we failed to spot the symptoms in our second, but right from the start Sam was very, very different from his brother. We got used to the idea that one set of characteristics – George's – amounted to autism, but there seemed to be little overlap between these characteristics and Sam's behaviour, eccentric though that often was. And besides, I'd never heard of more than one autistic child in a family. It didn't occur to me that it could happen. I've since discovered that it isn't even particularly rare.

Sam's apparently cheerful nature also delayed the need to worry about him. George was such a bundle of nervous energy – volatile, ethereal, powerfully attractive. Sam, from birth, was the opposite – placid, quiet, a creature of habit, the kind of baby you have to remember to notice. He wasn't a model baby. He did wake at night, though not as often as George, but at least he seemed to know night from day. Unlike George, he would lie quietly in his cradle, not asking for anything. Like George, he smiled early, but he didn't have the same passionate attachment to me. Sam quite liked people, but it was a long time before he seemed to distinguish between them.

I expect I attributed Sam's early placidity to a combination of my greater experience and his easier birth. The labour was longish – thirteen hours, and unpleasant for me, but not, I think, especially stressful for Sam. Like George, he was in the posterior position, which prolonged the early stages, but the midwives massaged me hard to avoid another forceps delivery; Sam turned just in time, and was actually born quickly, without intervention. I could sit up and watch. I have a clear memory of his head coming out, like a tortoise poking out of its shell.

Sam's Apgar score was good, and he fed easily and immediately. He weighed six pounds fifteen ounces, and put on weight very fast. George had looked like his father at birth; Sam resembled no one, except, my mother claimed, Lester Piggott. He was born at lunchtime on 18 November 1991 – Monday's child, but no one at that stage could claim that he was fair of face.

Later that day, he turned deep purple and choked on his mucus. The nurses kept him with them for much of the night, to keep an eye on him. There didn't appear to be any lasting damage, but he was inclined to snuffle for much of his babyhood, and beyond.

Sam passed a number of milestones early, but with nothing like George's accelerated development. He was strong and muscular, and could sit up early, but there was nothing remarkable about his progress. If anything, there seemed to be a subtle lack of – what was it? Spark? Engagement? Curiosity? Sam smiled, handled toys, looked at pictures, but he didn't truly explore the world. At this early stage he showed no distinct tastes or preferences, for people or for things, unless it was for his soft owl, who shares his bed to this day.

And he was very quiet. Rereading his baby book, I find I have written that Sam at seven months is 'still very quiet and makes no consonant sounds at all – he just says "Ah ah ah," and that not very often. However he is not deaf as he always turns his head to his name, and enjoys certain tunes very much.' Later this was to change, and Sam, as mentioned in the previous chapter, became a great babbler, producing long inflected nonsense sentences accompanied by earnest hand gestures.

It is common for an autistic child to be suspected of deafness before the correct diagnosis has been made. Mothers are often puzzled by the child who ignores all their remarks but comes running from the bottom of the garden at the sound of a bag of crisps being opened. Sam didn't ignore us; he could follow instructions, and was soon responding to 'Wave bye-bye', 'Clap hands', and so on. But he didn't seem alert to adult speech in the way that, later, Jake was, and I now realize that he never turned his head from one speaker to another to follow conversation.

Sam acquired language slowly but surely, until his second birthday. He had a couple of words by his first birthday; at eighteen months I list twenty, the usual mixture of animal noises and useful commands – 'up', 'no', "gain'. I comment, 'He has many fewer words than George had, but he uses them more effectively.' In a funny way, this remained true. Even though Sam has never achieved verbal fluency, and at one point almost gave up talking altogether, the few words he did retain were those that would get his needs met.

Sam didn't echo, except in the way that babies always repeat new words. His voice was, and is, unusually deep and husky, not musical like George's. He often speaks much too loudly. He didn't pronounce words clearly; when he was three, this revived the idea that he might have some hearing loss, and he was checked for glue ear. I now realize that his lack of interest in and co-operation with his hearing tests were the most significant part of the exercise. In the test room were a number of toys that would entice most three-year-olds – wooden men in a boat, trains, that kind of thing. There were also three black boxes which magically lit up to reveal three toys – a pig, a penguin and a helicopter. The pig and the penguin danced, the helicopter's propellers rotated. The idea was to see if the child turned his head in the right direction in response to sound. Sam didn't, not because he couldn't hear, but because he wasn't interested, except, mildly, in the helicopter. His response to these lovely toys was, to say the least, muted. And he didn't want to fit the wooden men into their boat when the doctor asked him to, either. At the time I didn't attach much significance to his lack of interest, but having had Jake I now know that a normal three-year-old, unless he's ill or very tired, *will* be attracted by toys, *should* co-operate, *should* want to show the doctor what he can do. It's a bit like those notices people put up at college, which said SEX in big red letters, and then underneath gave you some information about something like the Debating Society. If you're normal, you just can't help paying attention to certain things.

The question of Sam's glue ear dragged on throughout his fourth and fifth years. Perhaps he did have it – he certainly produced excessive amounts of mucus. It was obvious, though, that he had no serious hearing loss. Though not echolalic, he was very good at imitating certain sounds. At sixteen months, I write that 'he does an accurate imitation of the sound of the water draining out of the bath', and he soon extended his repertoire to include imitations of washing machines, drills, microwaves (even though we didn't have one), food processors, and the like. The idea of hearing loss was finally laid to rest when, aged five, some time after his autism diagnosis, he was given a general anaesthetic and had his hearing tested by a computer. His hearing was perfect.

Would it have been possible to detect Sam's autism during infancy? I wrote a full account of him at twenty months:

Sam is very solid, with thick muscular arms and legs and a large tummy. He has thick fairish hair with more than a hint of red in it, and light brown eyes. He is extremely sturdy, walks for miles, runs, jumps, kicks and throws balls, climbs all over the place. He jumped out of the bath yesterday, and has escaped from his cot. It is no longer possible to write a list of the words he knows as he now copies such a lot . . . He joins in several nursery rhymes, supplying the end words. He does not pronounce words clearly, for instance his word for mummy is 'nen' and baby is 'de-dun' or something like.

He likes books, though again not as much as George did – he favours those with photographs and is not interested in stories so much as naming objects. He tries to eat the picture of a biscuit in one of them. He plays very independently and never minds being on his own. His favourite activities include grubbing in muddy puddles, etc. He shows no especial preference for any type of toy – except soft toys which he loves, especially Owl – but will play with whatever comes to hand. He loves music, and dances with vigour.

He eats very heartily; mainly jars of baby food. He is not interested in what adults eat. He feeds himself entirely and is good with a spoon. His especial love is salty snacks like Pringles. If given a chance he will push up a chair and climb up and raid the biscuit tin ('kikkit').

He is better with his hands than George was and enjoys filling containers, sorting shapes, etc. He has been known to take his T-shirt off. [George was extremely slow to make the slightest attempt at dressing or undressing.] He is quietly sociable and enjoys meeting other children. Most of the time he is easy and sunny but if thwarted (e.g., not allowed to open the fridge) he will roar for several minutes at incredible volume.

He wakes at about 8.30 and always has to carry everything that was in his cot – Owl, Teddy, dummy, empty milk bottle, etc. He has one long nap 2.30–5.00 but will forgo this if we are out. We put him to bed about 7.30 but he is often awake until about 9 – he will lie burbling to himself. He usually wakes once during the night and has a bottle of milk. Not brilliant, but better than George at that age – or indeed than George now . . .

Does this make Sam sound like a child with a profound life-long disability? I think not. Even bearing in mind that the writer is me, his mother, biased, and doubtless casting a rosy glow, it is hard on a first reading to see this as anything other than the description of a robust, happy, normal toddler. Our little bit of video coincides with this time. With George, yes, you can see . . . he's a gorgeous golden-haired three-year-old, but his movements are unusual. There's lots of flapping and jumping, and he's going on and on about that purple pigeon . . .

But Sam – Sam just looks like a healthy toddler enjoying himself. He's very, very bouncy – he's jumping and tumbling on an old mattress that I've put out for the purpose. He cuddles his soft toys. He points to things – the clock, for instance – names them, and *draws my attention to them*. He turns over the pages of *Dr Seuss's ABC*, showing delight in naming a few letters – and, again, looks at me for confirmation. He climbs up to the window and looks out, interested in the world outside. It's nap time; I tuck him into his cot. He smiles, snuggles down with Owly and a bottle of milk. I leave; he doesn't object. What a contented, well-adjusted child!

Does this mean that at twenty months Sam was not autistic? Did he become autistic later, as a result of MMR or some other insult or trauma? There's been a tenfold increase in the number of children diagnosed with autism over the last two decades. Opinion is divided as to whether this is a 'real' increase, or whether it's simply due to a more accurate diagnostic process, a greater understanding of the condition among doctors and psychologists. In the past, autism was often called 'infantile schizophrenia' or 'infant psychosis'. This was at the severe end of the spectrum. At the more able end, children who would now be recognized as having Asperger's syndrome might have been called lazy, disturbed, eccentric or just plain awkward. So, yes, a large part of this apparent increase in incidence must be attributed to a broadening of the diagnostic criteria.

Most experts subscribe to this view. But like many parents, I can't shake off the feeling that there's been a 'real' increase as well. If the number of autists has remained constant, where were they when I was growing up? Some were inappropriately locked up in mental hospitals and children's homes, and some were floundering undetected in mainstream schools, as is probably still the case; I suspect the condition is still under-diagnosed. But in all my childhood, even my early adulthood, I never came across a child who I can identify retrospectively as an undiagnosed autist. When I visited my friends' houses, there was never a little brother twirling and flapping in the corner. On buses, in shops, in parks, I don't remember normal-looking children shrieking or hooting or picking up the used bus tickets. I often see such children now. When I was young, I never heard any talk of children who had been 'put away'. I don't even remember any markedly eccentric children. We often saw visibly handicapped children, with Down's syndrome ('Mongols', as they used to be called), or 'spastics' in wheelchairs, their heads lolling to one side. But if the incidence of autism was really one in a hundred, as it's now said to be, it seems strange to me that I never came across even one. I'm no scientist, and I have no convincing hypothesis to put forward to account for the increase, but my instinct tells me that better diagnosis doesn't account for all of it.

Many theories for the 'epidemic' (a term I dislike, as it suggests a catchable illness) have been put forward. The MMR vaccine is the most notorious, but heavy metals and other pollutants, or food intolerances triggered by changing diet patterns and modern methods of food production, have all come under scrutiny. I simply don't feel that I know enough to nail all my colours to a single mast. But, thinking about cheery twenty-month-old Sam, it's easy to see why so many parents believe that they have 'lost' a normal child to autism, and why they devote so much time and effort in trying to find that sunny baby again. I don't wish to contradict such parents. I can't rule out the possibility that, in some cases, autism was triggered by some external disaster. But I feel certain that this is not what happened to either George or Sam.

George and Sam were born autistic. It's just that nobody noticed. And nobody can be blamed for not noticing, because the signs were so subtle. I have an idea that the regression often observed in autistic children of two or three years is something to do with what's expected of them; their brains are struggling and failing to cope. The parent, who nearly always believes they have a normal child, pushes the child in directions which would be wholly appropriate for a neurotypical, but which the autist simply cannot follow. Take language development. Many autists can manage nouns with ease. 'Car', 'cup', 'shoe'; these come in different shapes, colours and sizes, but they are recognizably themselves, in or out of context. Concepts, or abstract words, are much less reliable, and therefore threatening. Verbs like 'eating' or 'walking' aren't so bad, but adjectives and adverbs are dangerously unstable and emotive. It took George years to use words like 'angry' or even 'thirsty' (though he could easily ask for a drink). Sam still hardly ever does. When Sam was small, adults often asked him what his favourite colour/food/game was. Sam couldn't cope with 'favourite'. He turned it into a noun. He just couldn't get the hang of its real meaning even though he said it often, and over time, by some association of ideas, it became more or less synonymous with 'rainbow'.

In babyhood one is only expected to use nouns – 'teddy', 'ball', 'cot' – or a few unambiguous prepositions like 'up'. Adjectives are limited to the most visual or tactile, the least abstract – you'd say 'blue' or 'hot' to a baby, but you wouldn't say 'emotional' or 'confusing'. My theory – based, I admit, on the observation of my own sons – is that autistic babies are quite happy with 'concrete' words, but when language needs to reach beyond the here and now, when language casts out nets to capture thoughts and feelings, past and future, possibilities, plans, it slips out of the autist's grasp, and so may be discarded altogether. George tried to cope by using his quotations, which fulfilled the pattern of conversational exchange, and sometimes trawled in information that was useful to him. When George, at two and a quarter, asked visitors, 'Do only insects have antennae?' he wasn't looking for an answer, and he certainly wasn't showing off. He was demonstrating that he knew that talking was appropriate human behaviour, though he didn't really understand why. And he wasn't interested in any response the visitor might make. Whatever they said, George would supply the right answer: 'No, woodlice have antennae.' George wasn't interested in antennae (though he did like putting woodlice in his mouth). It was just something he'd learned by rote at Drusilla's Zoo.

George circumvented with his sophisticated form of echolalia; Sam used simple, concrete words, singly or in pairs, for as long as he could, and then he stalled. He tried babbled 'sentences', into which he eventually inserted one relatively distinct word – 'Aba dala loola laaa *icekeem*.' He did learn to put words together, slowly. At Easter, when he was two and a half, he said, 'Choc-choc egg – g'een one – Ham want it' (he called himself 'Ham' for a long time). I recorded this as his longest-ever sentence. This utterance was motivated by intense desire; nothing could have motivated Sam more than a chocolate egg. But the usual motivation for a child learning to talk, which is the desire to understand the world through communication with older beings of his species, wasn't really there.

Language development, then, after the early stages, makes too many demands on the autistic brain, which can result in 'overload' and 'shutdown'. Social interaction, similarly, can seem normal in the first year or so, before it degenerates. Perhaps this is because babies are not aware of themselves as separate entities. The world comes to them; they have not sufficient reserves of memory and experience to consider themselves objectively, as beings with relationships and social responsibilities. Autists seem to have a weak or confused sense of identity. Both my sons show indifference or aversion to photographs or films of themselves. Most children like stickers or mugs with their own name on, are interested in what other people say about them, want to read their own school reports. Autists seem to find all this baffling, boring, or frightening. If George finds any mention of himself in, say, a letter from school, he will furiously ink it out.

Some autistic babies are aloof from birth, stiffening or crying when touched, avoiding eye contact, happiest when left alone. These are the children likely to receive the earliest diagnoses. Others, like mine, are smiley and responsive. Both George and Sam nearly always responded favourably to social advances from both children and adults during their first two years. With hindsight I can see an unusual quality in their social reactions, but the reactions were certainly there. In the second and third year of life, hugely much more is expected of a child than that they should smile back at a smiling face. The child separates itself from the mother, learns to play and share with other children, finds its instinctual behaviour directed and channelled by moral and social judgements – in short, learns to become a social being. Most children achieve this transition successfully. They are hardwired to do so. Autistic children are not. The fact that autistic behaviour becomes apparent during the second and third years, that the child regresses, loses or abandons skills, cuts himself off, becomes uncontrollable, may be the result of him coming up against a set of expectations which he is not equipped to fulfil.

To use a crude analogy: a dog is a pack animal, a cat is not. It is very, very difficult to train a cat to behave like a dog. It is very, very difficult to train an autistic child to behave like a social being.

To return to my rather partial account of Sam at twenty months: if you know what you're looking for, the warning signs are there. Even in the physical description, there are hints. Sam's extremely impressive musculature, for instance, was partly the result of autistic restlessness. To this day, Sam's body is like a drawing by William Blake. He no longer has an ounce of fat on him, but the muscles on his legs are the result of eleven years' incessant bouncing. His big tummy has gone now. For years he had a stomach like a beach ball. When I removed gluten and casein from his diet, it went flat, as it has remained. I discuss the autistic reaction to gluten and casein in Chapters 7 and 12, but for now it suffices to suggest that Sam's round twenty-month tummy was partly due to an intolerant reaction to wheat and milk.

His escapology, here limited to jumping from bath and cot, became a huge problem later, when Sam took himself for long, unaccompanied walks, which often resulted in a 999 call. I had extra locks put on all our doors; we couldn't leave a door or window open on a warm day. Once, Sam watched yet another lock being put on the front door, thought about it, and climbed Tom Kitten-like up the chimney. I heard the fall of soot, and came into the room to see a pair of sandalled feet dangling above an (unlit) fire.

With the cot-jumping goes my comment that he 'climbs all over the place'. Autists, so full of social fears, often have little sense of physical danger. They can have exceptionally good balance (although, confusingly, the opposite can also be true) and an amazing head for heights. Both boys have had phases of being extremely physically adventurous, including, in Sam's case, a tiresome summer spent mainly on the roof of our house, pulling out tiles. I'm tempting fate to write this, but neither of them has ever had a serious accident. Once, Sam fell off our garden wall and scraped his face, and George fell downstairs at eleven months, but that's it. Most families I know have spent more time in A and E than we have. Could it be that autists are protected from danger by their lack of awareness of it? Sam, scrambling sure-footed across a slippery roof, doesn't pause to take stock of his situation, whereas another child might stop, panic, and slip. They are protected, too, by their aloneness. Most cracked heads and greenstick fractures are caused by playground skirmishes, but an autistic child won't come near anyone else at playtime if he can avoid it.

Sam continues to prefer books of photographs over stories. Most babies start with images of familiar objects, of the dog/apple/socks variety, and move on to stories later. Sam did learn to enjoy some stories, but usually because they referred to his special interests. He liked *The Tiger Who Came to Tea* because cakes featured prominently, *Jemima Puddleduck* because he had a thing about eggs. *Peace at Last* by Jill Murphy, about a family of bears going to bed, was a favourite for ages because it had an alarm clock, a cuckoo clock *and* a grandfather clock. Sam used to point out a space on one page where he felt another clock should have been. But his taste for stories like these was only an extension of his early interest in books that featured photographs of biscuits. I think it's true to say that Sam has no fictive imagination. He has never identified with a fictional character, never shared their hopes and fears. He has never listened to a story and wondered 'What happens next?' He doesn't care whether Jeremy Fisher gets swallowed by the trout or not; he just likes the bit about digging for worms because there's something about worms that intrigues him.

'He plays very independently and never minds being on his own.' Isn't this every mother's dream? After George's wakeful, watchful babyhood, Sam's 'independence' was a relief. But I now feel that a twenty-month-old *should* mind being on his own. The ability to amuse oneself is valuable, but a very young child should also be in constant interaction with his mother or mother-substitute, showing, asking, sharing. The adult enables the infant to access the world, scale it down, bring it within his grasp. Sam, contentedly alone, was strengthening the barriers to knowledge and understanding that autism was erecting around him.

I note Sam's taste for 'grubbing in muddy puddles, etc.' Sam was, of course, not the only toddler to enjoy puddles, but he was – and still is – more deeply enthralled than most children by the physical properties of things. So is George, though Sam's approach is more hands-on. Paint, mud, water, soap, butter, wind, ice, Play-Doh, shit; Sam kneads and mashes and splashes and throws himself about in these things. Both he and George have an intimate relationship with the four elements, and on the whole this is an aspect of their condition I really like. It's lovely when they run and run, with the wind in their hair. It's lovely, though nerveracking, to see them entranced by the shifts and crackles and falls of fires. It's less lovely when they rub excrement into their hair, the curtains, the cracks in the floorboards. This isn't a sign of emotional disturbance, or even deliberate naughtiness. It's just another manifestation of the desire to poke about in puddles. Lacking normal social instincts, neither of them has a sense of revulsion, or shame. It's been hard work training them to accept the difference between poo and Play-Doh, but we do seem to be winning. It's been several years since smearing was a major problem, though it's still not safe to leave Sam alone in the bath . . .

Sam's twenty-month lack of preference for any particular toy could also be symptomatic. A characteristic of autism, one of the clearest signs in a toddler, is that toys are rarely put to their intended use. Babies simply explore the physical properties of toys – soft, rattly, bouncy, chewy – but by twenty months they should have moved beyond this stage. Cars should be pushed along the carpet, dolls should be fed, put to bed, and – I'm afraid – scolded. As time goes on, soldiers should fight, trains should stop for passengers, balls should be aimed towards goals. Of course, 'normal' play is hugely flexible. A toy soldier can inhabit a doll's house, a soft rabbit can become a football, cars can have characters and conversations. But at a remarkably young age the normal child will pick up the toy manufacturers' intentions, even if they then decide to put the toy to rather different use.

Autistic children show a diminished interest in toys. When they do pick them up, they explore them physically, rather as a baby would. The child will often hold a toy car close to his face and spin the wheels repeatedly. Both George and Sam would run little trains quickly past their eyes. Bricks or trains will be laid out in rows, and woe betide anyone who moves them. Soft toys, like Sam's Owly, may be obsessively fingered and sniffed, but it's unlikely they'll be given a personality. Autistic play is essentially static.

It's striking how very young neurotypical children will home in on toys that correspond to their own nascent interests or aptitudes. Most children will try out a range of playthings, but a particular bent for animals, vehicles, buildings, or whatever, soon manifests itself; early interests are nearly always observable in later life, even if their outward form has changed. Sam's lack of preference for any particular toy resembles his lack of discrimination between people, his failure to engage with most human activities. There is a kind of blankness.

I mentioned Sam's early love of music. That has never altered. George is 'the musical one', with a good singing voice and an excellent musical memory; Sam has a voice like a bullfrog, but he too, in a lesser way, has a large repertoire of songs, and he shows pleasure and animation when music is played. He likes a strong beat – reggae and ska always get him moving.

It's extraordinary, now, to read that Sam once ate 'very heartily'. Eating problems are almost universal among autists. I'm so used to it, so out of touch with normal eating in children, that I still hold my breath when Jake happily eats fruit and vegetables – it looks miraculous to me. At twenty months, Sam's diet and eating habits seem normal and healthy enough, but a note of warning is struck by that phrase 'He is not interested in what adults eat.' Penelope Leach suggests parents include the child in their meals, offer tastes of whatever's going. Sound advice, except that it depends on the natural curiosity of the neurotypical child. Most toddlers do want to know what their parents are eating, even if they then reject it. I remember Jake, the Christmas before he was two, asking for chestnut stuffing simply because he'd never had it before. This would have been unthinkable with either of his brothers. This isn't simply about fussy eating; some toddlers are fussy eaters, some are not. It's about eating as a social, shared activity, and for Sam it simply wasn't. When, years later, I decided to take gluten and casein out of his diet, people said, 'Oh, but won't that be sad because he won't be able to share your meals any more?' But he never did share our meals, so it wasn't sad.

My description of Sam as 'quietly sociable' is a little rose-tinted. I don't think Sam ever sought the company of a child other than George, to whom he is genuinely close. But, unlike George, he showed no anxiety about the proximity of other children. If older children kissed him or picked him up he would smile. If another child wanted his toy he would hand it over without hesitation or complaint. He never, I think, offered toys to children or made overtures of any kind other than smiles. Sometimes the antics of others amused him, but apart from the most basic chasing, bouncing and splashing games, Sam has never sought to join any group activity.

His roaring when thwarted sounds like classic toddler behaviour, which indeed it was. Unlike other toddlers, he didn't grow out of it. Just last night, he and I had a fight over Chipsticks – a difference of opinion about opening a new packet before the old one was finished – that lasted on and off all evening. The roaring has been replaced by jumping up and down and biting his hand, but the single-mindedness is still there.

His sleeping habits were not exceptional at twenty months – they were to become so later on. It's unusual, though not unheard of, for so young a child to lie awake for an hour and a half without calling for attention. Taken on its own, it sounds like an entirely good thing, like the independent play, but it can also be seen as a symptom of unnatural emotional detachment, a short circuit in Sam's social wiring. I well remember Sam's need to take everything out of his cot every morning. He would waddle into the kitchen, bowed under the weight, blankets trailing behind him in bridal fashion. Was this an early manifestation of obsessive tendencies, of the need to create rituals? Later, aged about five, he went to the opposite extreme, and stowed objects under his duvet. I once uncovered a cache of sixty-three different items – the usual soft toys and picture books, but also things as disparate as a cheese grater, my party shoes and a cereal-packet plastic statuette of Alan Shearer.

So, yes, with hindsight and vastly increased knowledge of the subject I can identify my account of Sam at twenty months as the unwitting profile of a child with autism. But I'm not at all surprised that I didn't spot it at the time. Nobody did. Sam and George were seen, in the usual way, by midwives, health visitors and doctors. Until George was three and a half, none of them noticed anything wrong at all.

5. Diagnosis

How does one arrive at a diagnosis of autism? There have been three important stages in reaching the current definition. In 1943, Leo Kanner was the first to describe 'classic' autism, which is sometimes called 'Kanner's syndrome'. The two characteristics he emphasized above all others were 'an extreme aloneness, from the earliest days' and an intense desire for 'the preservation of sameness'.

Hans Asperger, only a year later in 1944, published his own findings. Asperger's case studies tended towards the high-functioning end of what is now generally accepted as the autistic spectrum. While Kanner's children were withdrawn, aloof, locked in a limited world of their own, Asperger's had stronger social instincts, but a poor and eccentric understanding of how to operate on a social level. Asperger emphasized that, despite 'considerable and very typical difficulties of social integration', 'his' children had 'particular originality of thought and experience, which may well lead to exceptional achievements in later life'.

Kanner and Asperger were working independently of each other. Kanner was in Baltimore; his account was published in English, and quickly became well known. Asperger was in Vienna; his paper, written in German and published during the Second World War, received little attention. It was not until the 1990s that Asperger's work became well known in Britain and America. Now, 'Asperger's syndrome' has become widely used as a description – crudely speaking – of 'able' autistic people. But there is still catching up to do; for many years, due to a quirk of history, it was Kanner's definition that reigned supreme.

In the early 1970s, as a result of a London study by Lorna Wing and Judith Gould, a 'triad of impairments' was established. This triad is still the main diagnostic criterion. To be counted as autistic, the child (or adult) must have impaired communication, impaired imagination, and impaired social interaction. The degree of impairment varies enormously. Wing is insistent on autism as a 'spectrum disorder', ranging from extreme intellectual and behavioural disability to mild social handicap.

Then, in 1985, Simon Baron-Cohen, Alan Leslie and Uta Frith augmented the diagnostic picture by adding the 'theory of mind'. The autist has no theory of mind; he is mind-blind. He does not fully understand that your experience of the world is different from his own. This applies whether his IQ level is low or high. This was demonstrated by the 'Sally-Anne experiment'. Autistic, normal and Down's syndrome children were all shown a scenario enacted by dolls. Sally has a basket, Anne has a box. Sally has a marble. She puts it in her basket, and leaves. While Sally is away, Anne removes Sally's marble and places it in her own box. Sally returns. The child is asked, 'Where will Sally look for her marble?'

Anyone reading this book will (I assume!) know that Sally will look in her basket, because that's where she believes the marble to be. The non-autistic children gave the correct answer, so did most of the Down's children. All but a few of the autistic children gave the wrong answer. They said Sally would look in the box, because that's where the marble actually was. They could not understand that Sally didn't know this.

These three stages towards diagnosis – the 1940s papers, the 'triad of impairments', and the 'theory of mind' discovery – do not quarrel with one another. Wing does not contradict Kanner, Frith does not supersede Wing. They augment each other and, put together, indicate the immense complexity of this condition which defies any simple diagnostic test.

Taking Kanner's criteria in isolation, neither George nor Sam would be classed as autistic. Neither of them is, or has ever been, 'extremely alone'. When George's behaviour first gave me cause for anxiety, the idea of autism did enter my head, but I dismissed it, thinking, 'He can't be autistic – he's too affectionate.' George has always sought people out, and discriminated strongly between them. His relationships are lopsided and peculiar, but they are full of feeling. Aged thirteen, he still climbs into my bed most nights and cuddles me, and he's not just using me as a human hot water bottle. Sam, though more aloof than George, also has favourite people. He, too, enjoys physical contact on his own terms, and seeks it out. At times he has established an 'in-joke' with a particular person, which is reserved for that person alone. For instance, he goes, laughing, to Ian, our nanny, and says, 'One-two-three!' meaning, please pick me up and throw me in the air. On the telephone to Grandfather Clive – always a favourite person – he used to say, 'Grandfather Clock – Grandfather Clive!' plainly with humorous and sociable intent.

So, my boys are not 'alone' in Kanner's sense, though their human relationships are all profoundly odd. Neither do they conform to Kanner's second criterion; they are not strongly motivated by a desire for 'the preservation of sameness', though this is observable in a dilute form. Kanner was thinking of the kind of autists who insist on wearing exactly the same Buzz Lightyear pyjamas, day and night, or who won't tolerate the slightest rearrangement of the furniture, or who need to eat nine Smarties at eleven o'clock each morning, and woe betide anyone who disturbs the colour order in which those nine Smarties are assembled. The lives of many families are dominated by such insistences. I'm lucky in that both my boys are – relatively – flexible. We've had phases when George would only wear black or red (currently, it's pink and tartan, but with some leeway), and both boys find some kinds of change quite difficult – Sam was recently incensed when I removed a fireguard, so I put it back, because it didn't matter much. But I've been able to move things round in their bedroom, get a new car, take them on certain kinds of holiday, and move them from one school to another, without extraordinary fuss.

So they would have slipped through Kanner's net; what about Asperger's? Asperger avoided concise formulations, and was perhaps more cautious than Kanner in his conclusions. His emphasis is on social integration, and the uneven pattern of intellectual achievements. My sons would have fitted on these counts, though

Sam's intellectual achievements are far, far lower than those of any of the children Asperger studied. And neither of them has the 'excellent ability of logical abstract thinking' that he describes – neither George nor Sam remotely conform to the 'nutty professor' stereotype. Asperger notes the 'characteristic peculiarity of gaze' and 'poverty of facial expression', but in George and Sam these characteristics are subtle, easy to miss. Both can maintain eye contact, and both have a considerable range of facial expressions, though some are missing – pride and embarrassment, for example. But I've seen such non-autistic expressions as guilt and mischievousness clearly shown on both their faces.

Neither George nor Sam fits neatly with Asperger's case studies, though George comes closer. What of Wing's 'triad of impairments'? It's interesting that despite being so different from each other this umbrella does cover both boys. It's important to emphasize that word 'impairment'. Impaired communication doesn't mean no communication. Very few autists have no communication at all, though many have no speech. The children in whom communication is most profoundly impaired are those who appear to have no desires – the state of 'Nirvana' admirably described by Clara Claiborne Park in *The Siege*, her account of her successful battle to create desire, to introduce motivation, into the closed world of her daughter, Jessy.

Some autists, as mentioned in Chapter 3, have clear, fluent speech, and use immense vocabularies with more than usual ease. Where, then, is the communication impairment? Look closely, and it will always be found. The autist may be literal-minded, baffled by irony and metaphor – though some use striking metaphors of their own construction. Phrases like 'You'll be the death of me' or 'I cried my eyes out' can cause distress and puzzlement to autists. George, sitting quietly in the kitchen with a glass of water, overheard us adults talking about George Best and his drinking problems. Best had been treated with a drug that turned alcohol into an instant, deadly poison. Someone remarked, 'If George Best has one more drink he'll die.' Our George began to weep, silently. It took me a long time to discover the reason.

'If I have that drink I won't die!' he exclaimed at last, dolefully regarding his tumbler of blameless water.

However apparently fluent the speaker, if he is autistic he is unlikely to use slang or colloquialisms with any ease. And, most significant of all, communication will be one-sided. The autist may want to tell you about computers or tornadoes or the Highway Code, but is unlikely to listen carefully to what you say in return, unless you provide information which happens to dovetail with their particular interest. Female readers who have sat through dinner parties smiling politely while their male companions hold forth may protest that this is not an exclusively autistic characteristic – and indeed, researchers from Asperger to Baron-Cohen have suggested that autism may be a form of extreme maleness. Some autists may be excellent at one-way communication, speaking fluently and intelligently on a chosen subject, but when communication is considered as a two-way business, the impairment soon shows.

It's quite often said that autistic people have no imagination. This is wrong, and here I'd even take issue, just a little bit, with the admirable Lorna Wing; I'm not sure that 'impaired imagination' is quite right. It's absolutely true that autistic children don't have the same imaginative play as neurotypical children. This is one of the earliest warning signs. The two-year-old who will never feed, scold or say goodnight to her doll, or who will only do so when prompted, needs to be investigated. The neurotypical imagination is amazingly inventive but also, at root, extremely predictable. In the same way that there are said to be only six plots for stories, though any number of variant details, so the foundations of human imaginative play are 'samey' the world over. This is because they are built on the child's own experience. The child will make toys eat, fight, hurt themselves, compete, sleep, embrace, converse, receive instruction, get lost and found again, the emphasis depending on the child's gender, life experience and natural inclinations. Jake's teddies run races a lot; his cousin Stella's are more likely to be sent to school. Play reflects and enlarges upon what the child already knows.

Play also reinforces the child's sense of connectedness with other people. When a mother and child conspire to pretend that a teddy is alive, they are using imagination to strengthen their emotional bond through a pleasurable activity. Less obviously, the child is learning that her mother has an independent, imaginative 'inner' self. Even the youngest child understands that Teddy will not really drink her juice; neither does she seriously think she's fooling her mother into believing that he does. The game is strengthening the child's understanding that other people have minds that are separate from her own, that she and her mother can collude to enjoy a 'false belief'. Shared imaginative play, in short, teaches the child to have a 'theory of mind'.

This aspect of imaginative play is almost entirely denied the autistic child. When George was little he would play with dolls; he had two baby dolls called 'Sam' and 'Max', and he would accept suggestions from me – 'Sam' needs to sleep, 'Max' wants a biscuit, and so on. But there was no two-way play, no turn-taking. 'Sam' and 'Max' had no characters; their activities never developed beyond a crude imitation of the kind of physical care needed by the real Sam, then a baby. 'I know, Mummy, you pretend that Max is ill, and I'll be the doctor . . .' That sort of play never happened for George. Sam's imaginative play was even less social. It was usually concerned with machines, and only rarely involved humans or human-substitutes.

It's very hard to write about autistic imaginings because, like their dreams, autists so rarely describe them to us. But it seems to me that they don't fully enact social situations through play because social situations have little meaning for them. A normal child uses toys to explore the ever-increasing complexities of her interconnectedness with other people. She has more control over her toys than she does over the animate world, so she is able to go over the most interesting or difficult bits to her heart's content. The toys help her to think flexibly and creatively about the social structure of which she dimly perceives herself to be a part. When she is ready, she can incorporate another child into her fantasy, and accept the contributions the other child will make. It's noticeable that though two-year-olds are interested in one another, they're not good at sharing pretend play without adult help, but by five they are able to listen, take turns, and build on one another's suggestions in a mutually satisfying creative dialogue.

Toys are useful and important to the normal child, but if there aren't any she'll provide her own. Safety pins, wood chips, bits of fluff off the carpet – once she realizes she is truly left to her own devices, she'll anthropomorphize absolutely anything. She'd rather have a doll, but a clothes peg can become a person for her – can even become a person for whom she feels affection. I remember feeling very fond of a cupboard-full of rolled-up socks, because I chose to call them kittens. At the same time, the child is able to keep a sense of perspective. However powerful her imaginings, she knows they are different from reality. If the socks had been thrown away, I would have been upset, but not as upset as I would have been at the disposal of a litter of living kittens.

Presented with a group of mixed toys, the normal baby will handle them, mouth them, explore the sounds they make. So will most autistic babies. For the first year of life it could be extremely hard to tell the difference. There are some autistic babies who are oddly passive, and don't respond to anything much, but George and Sam certainly did not fall into this category. The normal toddler will attempt to put the toys to their intended use – pretend to drink from a doll's cup, push a car across the floor, put a teddy into a pushchair, maybe circle a toy aeroplane in the air. Gender differences will show even before the age of two, with most (though not all) boys selecting the car and plane, and most (though not all) girls going for the cup and teddy. The autistic toddler *may* also use the toys 'appropriately', especially if prompted by an adult. He is, however, more likely to seek out those aspects of the toys that stimulate his senses rather than his emotional intellect – he'll spin the car's wheels near his ear, or run the plane past his eyes, repeatedly, very close. The autistic toddler is also much more likely than the normal one to ignore the toys altogether.

Still, at this stage it would be quite easy to mistake autistic play for normal play. A couple of years on the difference would be far more obvious. Presented with disparate toys, the normal child would attempt to make connections between them. She'd weave them into some kind of story – the teddy would travel by plane to a holiday destination where he would drink something unusual from a cup – the cup alone would stand in for a whole café. A little boy might make the car and the plane race, crash or fight – with Teddy as adjudicator. If the provided toys didn't conform to the child's imaginative desire, they'd be recast; the car would become Teddy's mother, the cup could be a football for two competing vehicles.

The autistic child would not do this *at all*. Autistic children do not use toys as flexible props in the telling of their own stories. Some, like Sam, are struck by physical resemblances – a stalk of cow parsley was sufficiently similar to a vacuum cleaner to allow Sam to hoover most of our orchard. But there was no story here. Sam was not 'being a mummy cleaning the house'. He enjoyed the physical behaviour of the vacuum cleaner and wished to recreate this effect, but the 'game' was devoid of emotional meaning.

Others, like George, become interested in the characters in stories or videos. If, in my hypothetical group of toys, the four-year-old George had found something that resembled, say, Pingu or Thomas the Tank Engine, he could have played with it. To the casual observer he would have been acting out a story in an imaginative way. But, looked at closely, the story would have been a close copy of the one he already knew. Thomas would have got stuck in imaginary snow, for instance – and after being dug out he would have got stuck again. And again. Thomas would not have been provided with any previously unscripted lines. Pingu would not have stepped, or waddled, out of role to create a new plot line. And the 'story' would not have had a beginning, middle and end. It would have been a snatch of story, a single event, isolated, out of context. And George's interpretations could be tiresomely literal. I found him, once, sitting in a pool of his own urine, quoting from *The Tale of Mrs Tittlemouse*

– the part where Mr Jackson the toad drips water all over her nice clean floor.

George rarely 'took on' a character. Sam never did. George seemed worried by the idea, as if he feared losing his own identity. Sam just didn't understand the concept. Some autistic children, however, do assume a character. When they do, it takes over. The child becomes Buzz Lightyear, 24/7. All right, says the eager mother, delighted by the emergence of some apparently 'normal' play, you be Buzz, I'll be Woody. But Buzz doesn't want his mother to be Woody, unless, perhaps, she has as accurate a memory for dialogue as he has, and can re-enact favourite scenes from *Toy Story* to the same obsessively high standard. Buzz doesn't need a Woody because he doesn't need to give himself a social life. Something about Buzz's appearance or tone of voice has entranced the child, and all he wants to do is relive it over and over again. Is this imaginative play, or just another 'stim'?

When George was at mainstream primary school, aged about six, he developed an intense interest in Disney's *Snow White*. He was given photocopied sheets of characters from the film and would colour these in, from memory, with complete accuracy. Dopey's hat, Doc's belt, Sneezy's boots – George knew the colours by heart, and never made a mistake. And he 'became' Bashful. He decided he *was* Bashful. At school, he would only answer the register to 'Bashful Smith'. This lasted for about a term. But he didn't act out the part of Bashful. He didn't alter his behaviour in any way. He just announced that Bashful was who he was.

A little later, *Pinocchio* took over. This time George didn't call himself Pinocchio, but he repeatedly acted out moments from the film ('scenes' suggests a completeness that was distinctly lacking from George's performances). He put a half-lemon on top of his head, like Pinocchio's yellow cap, held a strand of raw spaghetti to his nose, and carefully threw himself down our stairs, singing a snatch of 'I've got no strings to hold me down – whoops!' When Pinocchio is made to perform by Stromboli, the cruel puppet master, on his début appearance he falls down some steps, pierces a floorboard with his nose, and pulls up said floorboard, to laughter from the crowd. George would try to burrow his nose into our dining-room parquet, but failed to achieve the desired result.

George thought about Pinocchio a lot, and drew pictures of him, including one of him coming down the stairs in a Duchamp-like blur of legs. It's tempting to think that he was exploring the Pinocchio story to draw imaginative parallels with his own situation; did George feel himself to be not quite human, a puppet who might one day turn into a real boy? It's possible – just as it's possible that he chose Bashful as the dwarf most emotionally linked to his autistic state (though some days, Grumpy would have fitted the bill, too). But equally, it could have been something about the smile, movements, or tone of voice that attracted him; in other words, the characters might have provided sensory rather than imaginative excitement. It's very hard to know.

Very able autists sometimes create elaborate fantasy worlds, with rules and outlandishly named countries and warring tribes. What is there to distinguish these fantasies from the sub-Tolkien imaginings of many a normal nine-year-old? One difference is likely to be accessibility. The autistic or Asperger's fantasist may decide to tell you all about the world he has created but he's unlikely to welcome any suggestions you make. The normal nine-year-old can't wait for his friend to come round on Saturday so that they can both charge about the garden bashing Orcs with sticks. The Asperger child can't accommodate a friend, unless the friend is prepared to obey his every command. Other people are all right, says John Peters, a grandfather with Asperger's speaking on the BBC documentary *The Autism Puzzle*, as long as they do exactly what you want.

There'll be another difference, too. Normal little boys are notoriously bloodthirsty, but there will be some emotional content in their play. Goodies and baddies will be clearly distinguished, and betrayal, courage, honour and friendship will feature in some form, however vestigial. The Asperger imagination is far more taken with rules and structures than with feelings. The imaginary world of the autist is likely to be immensely detailed, ordered and emotionally static.

I'm only guessing. Only a handful of autistic adults have been able to tell us about what they imagine. I know almost nothing, for instance, about autistic dreams. I suspect that it is harder for an autist to know when the dream ends and reality begins. I recall only two occasions when George or Sam seemed to be telling me about a dream, and in both cases the dream seemed to have some kind of physical reality for them. Once George stood up in bed, screaming with terror, pointing to a corner of the room where, he said, he could see 'Oliver the Western engine'. There was no toy engine there, but George was running a temperature. Perhaps this was more a hallucination than a dream. Sam once complained about 'snakies and snailies in the night'. I took this to be a dream, but I did discover some lumps of sucked bread in his bed – perhaps these were the snakies and snailies. Jake, by contrast, gives me regular bulletins about his dream life. He was only two when he dreamed about 'a wife in my cot cutting down trees wiv a axe'. Good old Freud.

To return to the diagnostic criteria – is it fair to call the autistic imagination 'impaired'? It certainly operates in a very different way, and is not put to the same uses. The neurotypical child uses her imagination in learning how to think and how to feel. Through symbolic play, she works out that different people have different perspectives. An idea is not a fact, but something open to interpretation. By hiding Teddy and having Rabbit look for him, the child is moving away from the simple, concrete world of milk, biscuit, ball.

The autistic child cannot access the common stock of symbols. He may develop his own set of symbols, but he does not instinctively accept the transference of meanings that allow normal children to play imaginatively with one another. The autist can go some way down our symbolic path, but he will soon meet a dead end. The hardest thing for an autist to grasp is that other people have different thoughts, different feelings, from his own. Playing with toys doesn't help him to understand social complexities because, it seems, the neural pathways that should guide him to this kind of understanding are blocked.

Simon Baron-Cohen and his collaborators have devised a test intended as an early-warning system to pick up autistic symptoms. The CHAT test (Checklist for Autism in Toddlers) is now used by some health authorities as part of the eighteen-month developmental check; it's carried out by a health visitor, who will have had some training in its use. It's a good idea, but it's by no means infallible. If I'd been asked whether, at eighteen months, George and Sam used pretend play, the answer would have been 'yes' in both cases. A close look at the frequency and quality of their play would have revealed deficits, but it would have taken an exceptionally alert health visitor to pick them up. Did they push cars along the carpet, making 'brm-brm' noises? Did they hold cups and spoons to the mouths of stuffed animals? Yes they did – occasionally and half-heartedly.

Lorna Wing's third impairment, that of social interaction, is the one most easily observable in very young children. Does a baby greet a parent with enthusiasm? Does he raise his arms to be picked up? Does he offer toys to adults as a way of initiating social contact (as opposed to needing help with the toy, for instance to mend it, or switch it on)? Failure to do these things should be investigated.

It is unlikely that any baby, unless severely brain-damaged, will make no social contact at all. Once again, it's the quality and the frequency of the overtures that count. I've said that both George and Sam were affectionate, smiley babies, and so they were, but I now believe they lacked the automatic, instinctive social skills possessed in spades by Jake. Sometimes they greeted me effusively; sometimes they seemed to be in a kind of trance, and there was no greeting. My cousin Caroline described how, when she went away, her son Toby would 'punish' her for her absence by turning his face away and rejecting a cuddle on her return. I waited for George and Sam to behave like this, but they never did. They had no awareness of the effect they could have on my state of mind. Toby's behaviour was socially sophisticated. He knew that he had a fair chance of altering his mother's behaviour if he played mind games. George and Sam could express pleasure and woe, but they could not scheme, or feign, or cajole. An autistic baby is never coy.

Abnormal social interaction is likely to be the first of the three impairments to show, but it's still quite easy to overlook in babyhood. Babies spend an awful lot of time being over-tired, windy, cutting teeth, hatching colds, and so on – or at least, their mothers think they do. And interpreting pre-verbal behaviour is difficult. I asked a friend, Elspeth, whether she'd noticed anything odd about my boys before they were diagnosed. Well, yes, she said, when Sam was about nine months old and we'd been on holiday together, she'd tried quite hard to engage him in play, and had been completely ignored. Not actively rebuffed, not rejected as in go-away-you're-not-my-mother. Sam just acted as if she wasn't there. Oh, well, thought Elspeth, maybe it's just because I'm too boring. But of course, that wasn't it.

As time goes on, the impairment becomes more marked. Lack of co-operative play with other children, lack of interest in adult activity, and – in my opinion, most crucially – failure to imitate adult behaviour, all indicate a fundamental problem. Poor play skills can be attributed to shyness, emotional disturbance, or lack of practice – 'He'll be all right once he's at school.' But social obliviousness is harder to explain. The child who sits at the bottom of the slide, deaf to the pleas of others that he move over; the child who passively allows toys to be snatched from him and exhibits no animosity towards the snatcher; the child who shows no interest in or understanding of simple social games like ring-a-roses or hide-and-seek – this child is displaying the kind of social impairment Wing meant.

Toddlers love to imitate their parents. They want to stir saucepans, sweep floors, waft imaginary razors over their cheeks. They're nosey – they want to know what's on their father's dinner plate, what's in their mother's handbag. They delight in child-sized versions of adult equipment, whether it's a tool set or a doctor's kit. The reason for this kind of imitation is obvious; it's part of the long process of learning to be an adult.

George and Sam didn't imitate – or rather, they imitated a few, selected activities, but they never built up a repertoire of copied, learned skills. Sam imitated mixing a cake because the beaters excited him, but he didn't copy me when I was gardening or writing a letter. George could accurately repeat a phrase I would use, in my exact tone of voice, but he couldn't build on this to imitate my conversational pattern with friends of his own age. When George or Sam imitated an action it was in a subscribed, end-stopped way. The action was performed for its own sake, not as part of a greater, more meaningful whole. Thus George saw the Aristocats splash paint over a piano, and so he painted our own piano keyboard. Jake, though, aged three, would bash away at my word processor – 'I'm writing for the newspaper to get some money for us, Mum.'

Communication, imagination, social interaction – the three are, of course, closely linked. You could, however, have one impaired, with the other two pretty much fully functioning – in which case you would not be autistic. A deaf child, for instance, would by definition have impaired communication, but his imagination and his social instincts – though affected by his deafness – would remain intact. He would need help to achieve full social inter-action, but his desire for that interaction would be as strong as in a hearing child, and his innate inclination to communicate would eventually enable him to find alternative ways of doing so. In an autistic child, the links between the 'triad' have never been forged, perhaps cannot be forged. The autist is differently wired.

What does Simon Baron-Cohen's 'theory of mind' add to the diagnostic picture? The 'Sally-Anne experiment', with the dolls and the marble, illustrates what Wing's impairments actually mean in terms of living a life. The autist may be highly intelligent, or mentally retarded, but what he cannot do is use his imagination to understand that other people experience things differently. He cannot communicate properly because he doesn't know what needs to be communicated. He cannot interact socially because he has no perspective on himself as a social being.

On a practical level, the lack of a 'theory of mind' has many frustrations for both autists and carers. 'Want it, want it,' chants the child. He doesn't know that he has to tell his mother what 'it' is. A child cuts his hand, badly, in the school playground. He says nothing to the teacher on duty. He can't guess that she won't know the cut has happened until he tells her. I know a little boy who developed peritonitis – he'd had appendicitis for a while, but it hadn't occurred to him to tell anyone about the pain.

I knew, for certain, that Jake wasn't autistic when he was about fifteen months old. He had just learned to walk. He had a biscuit in his hand, and he toddled off into the garden, round the corner, out of my sight. He came back, empty-handed, weeping. 'Want bikkit,' he wailed. He guided me, pointing round the corner, to where the biscuit was, wedged in the spout of a watering-can. He knew he had to tell me where the biscuit was. He knew I didn't know.

The other two would not have done this. They might have wept; they might have used the word 'bikkit', but more to imply that they should have another one than to tell me what had happened. At fifteen months, George appeared to be a gifted child, Sam seemed like Mister Cheerful Average, but neither of them understood that, if they didn't tell me what had happened, I couldn't know.

Theory of mind is a uniquely human attribute. One animal can guess from scents or movements how another animal is likely to behave, but they can't, as far as we know, step into the shoes (or paws) of another animal. They can't make a supposition about what the other animal might have experienced, and how it might have reacted to that experience. A normal child, even one of low intelligence, can not only predict where Sally will look for her marble, but also guess how Sally will feel when she finds it's missing. An autistic child, whatever the IQ level, is unlikely to be able to do this.

Does this mean that the autist is more like an animal than is the neurotypical human? Actually, the reverse seems to be the case. George and Sam are animal-like in that they use all five senses to explore their environment more actively than do most children. Their response to illness or injury is also animal-like; instead of seeking help, they lie still and wait until the pain has abated. They don't waste energy moaning and worrying, they just curl up and sweat it out. But in terms of the way they spend their time, they are further removed from animal behaviour than most of us. Animals spend their time either using or practising their survival skills. The kitten pounces on cotton reels; the cat pounces on mice. Squirrels run along walls and leap from branch to branch to exercise the muscles and balancing skills required for treetop life. Jake, in a far more sophisticated way, is unconsciously practising his own survival skills. When he plays football, he's learning to outrun and outwit his competitors. When he plays on his Gameboy, he's honing his mental reactions. The world is too big to experience everything at first hand; when Jake reads stories he's enlarging his knowledge of the world, partly through metaphor. He's also improving his verbal skills, which are of supreme importance in twenty-first-century human society.

Very little of Jake's time is put to no kind of use. The reverse is true of his brothers. Left alone, George and Sam do little apart from 'stim'. They flap, twiddle, bounce, hum. George tears sweet wrappers into tiny pieces and piles them on the windowsill. Sam bangs balloons up and down between his hands to make a loud, intensely invasive sound. Apart from keeping their muscles from atrophying, it's hard to construe their repetitive self-stimulation as in any way useful or linked to any other activity. The squirrel doesn't run back and forth aimlessly along the same branch. The kitten moves on from cotton reels to mice; cotton reels are not the be-all and end-all.

This leads me to the aspects of autism that I think have been overlooked by the currently accepted diagnostic criteria. Autism is a condition with physical as well as mental or behavioural symptoms. All autobiographical accounts by autists have described their heightened sensory experiences. These can be 'good' or 'bad'; colours may be amazingly rich and vibrant, but the noise of ordinary household appliances may cause acute discomfort.

The fact that autists sense the world differently is manifested in unusual physical behaviour. Even the most able can be distinguished by peculiar gait or quirky mannerisms. Bill Gates, the putatively Aspergerish head of Microsoft, is said to rock back and forth continually, as well as having an overloud, harsh, monotonous voice. Walking on tiptoe, hand-flapping, head-banging, are all common. One of the first oddities I noticed about Sam was that he loved to run up and down beside a straight line – a hedge, a wall, a washing line – with his head twisted to one side. At the extreme end of the scale, this abnormal response to sensation tips into self-mutilation. George has never gone in for this, thank goodness, but Sam began biting his hands during his big regression at age nearly six, and at one time they were always raw and bleeding.

Diagnosis of autism is always based on observation of behaviour. There is no medical test that can be administered, and, at time of writing, no prenatal test. The emphasis is placed on social behaviour and verbal development. I believe that more attention needs to be paid to the physical symptoms. The constraints these place on the life of an autist can be a great barrier to social integration and learning. Imagine how you would feel about going to school or to work if strip lighting caused you violent discomfort, or the smell of a certain cleaning fluid made you want to vomit. Then add the problem that you are unlikely to be able to communicate these difficulties to anyone with the power to help you. How daunting and impenetrable the neurotypical world must seem! No wonder so many autists retreat into their own.

6. Our Path to Diagnosis

At two and a quarter – Easter 1992 – George was charming, sociable, interested in most things adults showed him, bookish, playful, humorous, and willing to perform his party tricks – singing and reciting – to any audience. Less than three months later, all this had gone.

I can be precise about the dates, because there were two trips to visit his paternal grandparents in Devon, one at Easter, one in late June. The first was a success, the second a disaster. In June, George was an unhappy child. He was clingy and fearful, he didn't want to 'perform', he didn't want to be shown anything new.

There was a crucial difference between the two visits. On the second one, I wasn't there. I was working, taking a school group on an outward-bound expedition to Snowdonia (which for me, incidentally, is atypical behaviour). Min took George and Sam to Devon during my absence.

Five days is a long time for a two-year-old to be parted from his mother. I attributed George's unhappiness to that. It had been a bad idea to send him to Devon, even to the grandparents of whom he had always been so fond. He would have felt more secure, I concluded, if he had stayed at home.

I'd left him before, for work-related reasons, and he'd coped well. But he was a 'terrible two' now; two-year-olds are famously moody and volatile. George's behaviour didn't improve during that summer. Friends urged me to send him to nursery school; mixing with other children of his own age would help, they said. He did a trial morning at nursery school, and spent the whole time hiding in the Wendy House. When I came to pick him up, I heard him sobbing 'Oh, Mummy, where are you? Oh, Mummy, where are you?' (By the way, even this heartfelt cry was a quotation; he had a book of that title.) I had the distinct impression he'd kept this up all morning.

He just wasn't ready for nursery. I deferred his entry until January, when he would be three. His behaviour problems continued. He was happy and lively at home, doing just what he wanted, but he couldn't cope with new places or new people. At birthday parties he would scream. On one memorable occasion he pulled the cloth with all the magician's tricks on it off the table. Hats, wands, false-bottomed boxes, all crashed to the floor.

His intellectual development, which had seemed so startlingly quick, plateaued. He still liked books and songs, but only the same ones, over and over again; he fiercely resisted anything new. His speech no longer seemed precocious; I was beginning to realize how much of it was echolalic. He was disobedient without being mischievous, as if he really didn't understand the concept of 'No'. He had a little train, 'Mike', that went round and round a track. He stared at it and put himself into a trance; it became difficult to attract his attention. Eating and sleeping were still chaotic. Potty-training was a non-starter.

He turned three; nursery school began. It was a pleasant nursery. The children's behaviour was orderly, the teacher sensible and intelligent. George settled in, up to a point. He still tended to take refuge in the Wendy House and sometimes had to be coaxed out with biscuits. However, he showed enthusiasm for some activities, like trampolining, and he enjoyed learning songs with actions. 'My goodness,' said the teacher to me when I collected him one day, 'I never knew "Twinkle, Twinkle, Little Star" had so many verses.'

But George's favourite thing at school was the register. Back home, alone in his room, I could hear him reciting it to himself. His imitation of his teacher's voice was uncanny. He enjoyed the names of the other children even if he seemed shy in their presence. When our peachicks hatched, George named them after three of his classmates, Millie, Chloë and Elliott. He would also repeat phrases he'd heard his teacher use often to Joyce Grenfell-esque effect. 'Andrew, I said TAP OFF! Corinne, unlock the door!'

When he was three and a half, the health visitor called for his routine development check. George was not especially co-operative, but she was satisfied with his performance. She thought he was very bright, and that his speech was advanced. I pointed out to her that much of it was parroted. She produced an inset puzzle, showing an elephant's trunk arching over a row of other jungle animals – monkey, hippo, snake. She asked George to name the animals. 'That's an elephant,' he said. 'Good. And what's that?' she asked, pointing to the monkey. 'That's a coffee cake,' said George. The health visitor laughed. George didn't react to her laughter. 'What's that?' 'That's a cherry cake,' said George, solemn-faced. He went along the row of animals – 'That's a chocolate cake. That's a almond cake. That's a cream cake.'

'Well,' said the health visitor, preparing for departure, 'at least he's got a sense of humour.' I wasn't sure that he had. It had dawned on me that the position of the elephant's trunk relative to the row of animals was similar to an illustration in one of George's books, *The Elephant and the Bad Baby*, where the elephant reaches over a row of labelled cakes to take a bun. George had been identifying the jigsaw animals purely in terms of their spatial relationship to an elephant's trunk. He had ignored all other identifying criteria.

I explained this to the health visitor. She still thought he was fine, but said that if I was worried she would refer him to a speech therapist. I agreed. The speech therapist saw George for several sessions. I suspect she guessed the truth straight away, but it's not her job to give a diagnosis. She referred him to our local hospital. These things take time to arrange, though they shouldn't. Our wait was much shorter than that of some parents, but it wasn't until December, several months later, that the hospital saw George and pronounced him physically fit and normal. They made an appointment to have him assessed by Dr Gilly Baird, from Guy's Hospital, in January 1994, just before his fourth birthday.

I knew what autism was, or thought I did. In my teens I had been very struck by a book called *For the Love of Ann*, the true story of an autistic girl who had made a rather miraculous 'recovery', largely, as far as I recall, through interaction with the family dog. I had seen an exhibition of the brilliant, energized, Picasso-like drawings of a girl called Nadia, and had been saddened to read that as her acquisition of life skills increased, so her remarkable ability ebbed away. I remembered a couple of autistic children at the special-needs school where I had helped in my teens – a handsome, unsmiling boy called David who didn't speak but drew pictures of electrical circuits, and a huge, frightening girl who rocked back and forth and gnawed at the scars on her hands. And of course I had seen *Rain Man*.

None of the people I had read about or met bore any resemblance to George. I can't remember what I expected from our meeting with Dr Baird, but it certainly wasn't a diagnosis of autism. By pure chance, apropos of a conversation we were having about someone else's child, a friend lent us a copy of (I think) the *New Yorker* which carried a long article about Temple Grandin. Neither of us had heard of Asperger's syndrome before; Asperger's work was only translated into English in 1991, by Uta Frith. We discussed the article. Yes, George was quite like Temple Grandin in some ways, but in others he was quite different. As requested, we compiled a list of his main peculiarities to submit to the hospital. I reproduce it here:

Has a good ear, very good vocal imitator, but very little imitative behaviour. He is unusually good at singing.

Mixes up pronouns. Poor grammar.

He talks through quotations and by imitating adult speech, doesn't use words as discrete semantic items very much.

Has poor social interaction. Doesn't know how to play with others.

Avoids eye contact with strangers.

He is very excitable (easily aroused, not easy to calm).

Can't keep still.

He complains about strong stimuli, such as the sun, loud noises. Sleeplessness.

He is a dreamer, living to some extent in 'his own little world'.
Abnormalities of attention, including the ability to shut people
out and be absorbed in something trivial for a long time.

Loves nature, will stand and look at the moon for as long as he
is allowed, despite freezing weather.

Good with animals. Keen on and gentle with babies.

Has a strong aversion to strangers, groups and crowds, but manages
to go to school all right.

Obsessive.

Ritualistic.

Lines up bricks in rows, or matched by colour, doesn't build.
Always destroys.

Poor fine-motor control, but balance and gross-motor control
seem OK.

Physical contact good, embracing, etc., will offer cheek for a kiss
but doesn't know how to give a kiss.

Doesn't ask for potty, seems not to know when urination is immi-
nent. Dry at school for three-hour stretch.

Occasionally plays with faeces.

'Resistant' to being taught. It is very hard to explain things to
George.

Doesn't dress or undress – just beginning to put on trousers and
coat.

Food – sticks to a very limited menu for a few weeks then
switches to something new.

Throwing and catching poor.

Doesn't draw, doesn't hold pen properly.

Knew all colours at eighteen months, all letters at twenty months.
Could recognize simple words at twenty months.

Has a strong reaction to colours.

Can't describe an event.

Never asks questions except where is Mummy, Daddy, Sam.

Doesn't argue, simply states the contrary: 'No, Mummy is NOT
going to work.'

Only just starting to correlate facial expression of others to
emotion.

Puts everything in his mouth still.

He knows several hundred books off by heart.

Doesn't mind physical discomfort. Very brave about knocks. High pain threshold?

Ribena and (probably) most berry fruits seem to have a catastrophic effect on George's mood and behaviour.

Is there a blood sugar problem?

And at the end of this account, Min, definitely a step ahead of me, has written 'Asperger's syndrome??'

People often ask whether receiving the diagnosis was a terrible shock. I can't honestly remember much about my state of mind, but I don't think 'shock' is the right word. There was even some element of relief. My all-but-four-year-old was still in nappies and still had the sleep habits of a newborn baby – now I knew this wasn't entirely my fault. Dr Baird said he had Asperger's syndrome (it was changed to 'autism' a couple of years later) and I took her opinion seriously, but I tended to accentuate the positive. 'He'll find easy things difficult, and difficult things easy,' she said. That didn't sound too bad. We were told that there was no cure, that the right education was the only appropriate treatment. I don't remember much in the way of follow-up advice as to what the 'right' education might be. When I left the room I didn't have the impression that I had a child with a lifelong, all-pervasive disability. I just had George, and now I had an explanation for some of his problems.

During the session, much of my attention had been taken up with keeping George amused and under control. This is always a difficulty when mother and child are seen together. There should be further sessions when the parents can be seen alone, so that the implications of the child's condition can be discussed in detail, without distractions. We were visited at home by a special-needs nurse a couple of times, but all I remember her saying was that learning to ride could be good for George, and that I shouldn't give him drinks at night. She was more concerned about Min, who had a very bad reaction to the news, and who was in fact about to have a full-scale nervous breakdown.

I do remember that we were both insistent that we had no worries about Sam. We used Sam as a point of comparison. Sam, nearly two years younger, could pedal a trike, whereas George couldn't. Sam wasn't clingy and nervous – you could take Sam anywhere. At that stage nobody suggested that we were wrong.

As the year wore on, Sam's problems did begin to emerge. But Min's and George's loomed much larger. Sam seemed a little slow, a little odd. His speech was certainly garbled. The possibility of glue ear cropped up. So, too, did the notion that George was a peculiar role model for him, that any eccentricities were a result of copying George. I don't know why I gave this much credence, as Sam's behaviour wasn't like George's and nor were his speech patterns. Having had Jake, I know how strong the instincts towards normality are in a non-autistic child. Children copy, certainly – that's how they learn. But they choose their role models with care. Jake has never copied his brothers in anything other than the most transient and superficial way.

I'm ashamed to say that I can't recall the exact chain of events leading to Sam's diagnosis. I paid so much less attention to Sam. That is partly because I was already so preoccupied, and partly because Sam has never sought attention. George does, and always has. You can't ignore George, because he doesn't want you to ignore him. Even now, when he repeatedly orders us, 'Don't look at me! Don't talk about me!' it feels as if he doesn't exactly mean it. If we truly screen him out, he redirects our attention to himself with ever-shriller commands – 'Mum, I *said* don't look at me!' And I wasn't.

Sam has never been like this. Sam doesn't mind whether you look at him or not. Sam is indifferent, whereas George is thin-skinned. Sam will sometimes tell me to 'Go a-WAY,' and give me a push; this is either because I'm the bearer of bad tidings, e.g., it's time to get dressed for school, or because he, Sam, has embarked on an enjoyable course of action, such as emptying shampoo down the drain, or flushing socks down the lavatory, to which he knows I'll put a stop. But most of the time Sam doesn't react strongly to the presence or absence of other people. His impassivity has always meant that he gets less attention than the other two.

So, no, I can't quite remember who first started worrying about Sam. I do remember that he was visited at home by the educational psychologist – perhaps the health visitor, or the ENT specialist, had sounded some warning notes. I do remember that he wouldn't co-operate with the activities provided by the ed. psych. – simple puzzles, handling scissors, building with blocks. 'Oh, he can do all this,' I assured her, 'he just doesn't want to.' 'The point is, he *should* want to,' she said, and it was then that I realized something was up.

I raised the suggestion that some of his stranger behaviour was the result of copying George. She shook her head. 'You can't copy something as fundamental as eye contact.' I was so used to Sam that I hadn't noticed anything unusual about his eye contact. Often, it takes an impartial observer to pick up on these things. She recommended that he go to a special-needs nursery two days a week, where he would be assessed.

The Torfield Assessment Unit, as the nursery was called, was excellent. It has since been closed, on the ridiculous grounds that because it could only serve a limited number of children, it was unfair on those without a place. Would one argue that because, say, kidney transplants could only be provided for a limited number of patients, they should be stopped altogether? I think not.

The Torfield Unit provided the kind of early-learning experience every special-needs child should have. There was one staff member to every two children, plus a speech therapist. It was housed in a sweet little child-friendly building, not unlike a doll's house, with a different activity in each room – paint, water play, a large train set. Not all the children were on the autistic spectrum. Most, including Sam, had yet to receive any firm diagnosis. But all had language delays or developmental problems. They attended the unit for a year, and at the end, depending on their assessment, they went either into a mainstream or a special-needs primary school.

Sam did so well at the unit that his assessment tests showed him performing at nearly age-appropriate levels in most areas. The verdict was that he could cope in a mainstream school. He could not – but more of that in Chapter 13.

On the days when he didn't go to the unit, Sam spent the mornings at another, mainstream nursery school. Here he did not thrive, but nor, after the first fortnight, did he show unhappiness. He was simply peripheral to most of the activities. It was a homely, unstructured place, not the right environment for someone as potentially chaotic as Sam, but it gave me a few hours to myself.

Sam still had no official diagnosis. I'd never met anyone with more than one autistic child. I'd never even heard of such a thing. I just didn't know it was possible. And the two boys were so very different from each other, that my brain went on resisting the idea for far longer than it should have done. Besides, Sam was still 'easy'. He was odd, but his oddities didn't impinge on other people much, or make him unhappy in the way that George's did. As long as Sam was doing what he wanted, such as jumping up and down in front of washing machines, he was cheerful and equable. It was almost impossible to teach him anything new, but it took me ages to understand how deep a problem that is.

The educational psychologist, who was very sensible in every other way, said that we didn't need to 'push for a label'. 'Let's just put down "language delay",' she suggested. I came to disagree. This is an issue I now feel very strongly about. Every late-diagnosed Asperger's or autistic adult I've ever come across has spoken of the relief they felt when their condition was finally identified. Luke Jackson, a teenager with Asperger's, writes eloquently in his excellent book *Freaks, Geeks and Asperger Syndrome*, 'My first reaction was relief. It was as if I had a weight lifted off my shoulders . . . If anyone is wondering when to tell their child that they have AS, then in my humble opinion, the answer is *right now*!'

The child who goes without a label is in danger of going without the right kind of help. He may fail to qualify for a statement of special educational need. This will lead to his education being managed far worse than it could be. It's easier to convince people that the child is not just spoiled or naughty if you can say, 'My son is autistic.' If you've got a label, you may qualify for Disability Living Allowance. You get a Disabled Parking Permit. What good does it do not to have these things? If there's no label to say 'Please look after this bear,' how is anyone to know that the bear needs help?

There are still doctors who withhold diagnosis. This is at best misjudged, at worst morally culpable. The only sound reason for not giving a diagnosis is if the doctor or equivalent authority figure is genuinely unsure. Autism, as I've stressed, can be difficult to detect in young children. There's no blood test, no absolutely defining physical characteristics. At present, autism can only be identified by observing behaviour. If there is doubt, then second and third opinions should be sought before the parents are given a definite label. But those opinions should be sought as quickly as possible. The younger a child is at time of diagnosis, the better. There are several therapies and intervention programmes that really help, and the earlier these are introduced, the greater the results.

Why are some professionals reluctant to label a child? There are two main reasons – one, to spare the parents' feelings. This is cowardice dressed up as compassion. Autism is a lifelong condition. It is not going to go away. The parents *need* to know; how else can they do their best for their child? Of course breaking the news is hard; of course some parents will react very badly. There's not enough support for families post-diagnosis, but whoever's in charge of the child's case should take it upon themselves to ensure that the parents have access to whatever help there is.

The best kind of help is a family support worker who visits the home, gets to know the child, puts the family in touch with local support groups, guides them through the rigmarole that establishes whether they are entitled to Disability Living Allowance, free outsize nappies, speech therapy, respite care . . .

Parents may be too stunned to take it all in at once, but repeated visits over time can help them to accept what they may have at first rejected. We were given contact numbers for other families, but Min didn't want to use them because he thought it would be too upsetting. But eventually I did start meeting other autistic children and their parents, and found it interesting and useful.

The second main reason for withholding diagnosis is the idea that a label stigmatizes a child. This is woolly thinking, particularly in the case of autism. Autists are the group on earth least likely to care about being stigmatized, because their condition usually means that they are socially indifferent or unaware. I'd make a distinction between autism and Asperger's syndrome here. Some Asperger's children do care about what other people think of them. It might be better, in some cases, to help them keep their 'label' secret if they are coping well in a mainstream environment and fear teasing if the truth is known. But this decision should be made by the person with Asperger's after a discussion of the implications. It's always wrong to withhold the diagnosis from the individuals affected if they are capable of understanding it. To quote Luke Jackson again: 'I personally think that a child *should* be told, and the sooner the better. Believe me, I know!'

There may be more sinister reasons for withholding diagnosis. Some parents suspect that a vaguer label like 'language delay' may turn their child into a cheaper package for the health and education authorities than 'autistic spectrum disorder'. I hope this is not a motivation. If a doctor or psychologist is sure that his patient has a particular condition, then it goes without saying that he should be honest about it. With Down's syndrome, the physical evidence means that no one can be in any doubt for longer than a few hours. Honesty is inevitable. With autism, in the absence of such evidence, honesty is the doctor's responsibility.

In short, I disagreed with the ed. psych. who said that we didn't need a label for Sam. I pushed for a full diagnosis, and in April 1995, when Sam was four and a half, we were seen by Dr S, a top paediatrician at our local hospital.

Dr S was a cold fish. I knew what he was going to say before he said it, so I was able to sit and listen to him and think, in a detached way, you're not making a very good job of this, Dr S. 'Yes, he's on the autistic spectrum all right,' he said. I was sitting with my chair against the door to prevent Sam escaping. Sam was behind the doctor. He had licked a fruit pastille and was tracing patterns with it, like sticky snail trails, all over the back of the doctor's chair. The pastille was inching ever closer to Dr S's tweed jacket. 'But I wouldn't worry too much,' continued Dr S. 'They can be very intelligent, you know. Some of them go to Eton.' Sam began revving up to make his washing-machine noise, which was almost as loud as an aeroplane taking off. I smiled and nodded, but I thought perhaps I wouldn't put his name down for Eton quite yet.

So there it was. Two very different boys, same diagnosis. But knowledge is power, up to a point. Once you know what you're up against you can start planning the best ways of dealing with it.

7. Is There a Cure?

There is no cure for autism. That's a controversial statement. There are plenty of parents who believe that their child has made a full recovery from autism; there are websites dedicated to accounts of such recoveries. I'm not in a position to challenge these parents. I don't even disbelieve them. I think it's perfectly possible that some children with, for instance, strong food intolerances can show autistic symptoms. Correcting the diet, and providing appropriate educational intervention to make up for lost developmental time, can all but eradicate the 'autistic' behaviour. It seems that the earlier the problem is addressed, the stronger are the chances of recovery. And because children with severe intolerances often manifest them early on, the likelihood that their problems will be quickly addressed is quite high.

However, I don't believe that, in the majority of cases, autism is caused by intolerances, or by inoculations. (I'm deliberately skirting round the subject of MMR, because I don't feel I've got anything useful to say about it. Both George and Sam had the usual inoculations, and appeared to be unaffected. But I wouldn't rule out the possibility that inoculations are a contributing factor in some cases. As far as I'm concerned, the jury is still out.) What I do believe is that the vast majority of autistic children are born autistic. There's a new theory that brain development may be affected by a testosterone surge in early pregnancy. That sounds plausible to me, but investigation of this idea is still in its early stages.

I believe that autism can develop in a huge variety of ways. I also believe that some of the symptoms can be made worse by food intolerances, some illnesses, or perhaps a reaction to inoculations. In cases of extreme early neglect – the Romanian orphanages, for example – children may develop some autistic symptoms, especially self-injurious behaviour, repetitive routines, gaze-avoidance and poor social interaction. I think it unlikely that such children would display autistic talents. My feeling is that these behaviours are a kind of pseudo-autism. I'm absolutely certain that full-blown autism is never created by parental abuse or neglect.

So, I don't believe there's any real cure, and I do believe that instances of recovery are extremely rare; to pin one's hopes on them would be foolish. But there are lots of therapies and interventions that may improve the quality of life for you and your child. Most things are worth trying, as long as they're safe, and as long as you feel strong enough to cope with possible disappointment.

Like dealing with sleep problems, choosing a treatment depends on the temperament of the individual parent. (It also, unfortunately, depends on the parents' budget.) No one can be sure about the efficacy of anything, because no one can know how the autistic person would have developed without the treatment. If someone has cancer, is treated, and subsequently is found to be free of cancer, it seems fair to say that the treatment has worked. If an autistic child embarks on a therapy and shows improvement, it is still only informed guesswork to say that the therapy is helping, because autism is an unpredictable, one-step-forward-two-steps-back condition. There are no certain outcomes, and no two autists are the same. The improvement might have happened in any event.

Assessing the value of any course of action therefore involves a meeting of belief and common sense. It seems likely that the parent is the best judge, because no one watches a child as closely as a parent. On the other hand, parents so desperately want things to work out that they can be tempted to over-accentuate the positive. So it's good to keep other, more disinterested adults informed of what you're doing, and ask them for their unbiased opinion. Recorded evidence is also useful. I wish I had more video footage of George and Sam, but, being a female-brained technophobe, I've never mastered a camcorder, so I've only got a few scraps here and there. Keeping a diary or notes is good, but of course they won't be free from bias.

Instinct tells some parents to leave their child alone. They feel that any therapy or intervention would put undue stress on the child, and on the life of the family too. Others – and I would guess this is the more common reaction – want to do whatever they can for their child, and can't bear to feel that they might have let something go due to lack of energy or lack of funds. I think it's a mistake to discourage such parents on the grounds that 'it might not work'. Powerlessness is bad for parents. If trying a diet or a behaviour-modification programme makes them feel that their frustrated love for their child is being put to good use, then that's a good thing.

I've tried a lot of treatments, and have gained something from most of them. The usual pattern is that I'll read about something in the paper or hear about it through friends, dismiss it as too expensive or too difficult to implement, have a few conversations about it, and eventually conclude that I really ought to give it a try. At the moment, I feel I've done most of the things that sound sensible, so I'm in the happy and probably temporary position of aiming for nothing other than maintaining the status quo. The only therapy left on my wish list is swimming with dolphins, and that's only because it sounds like fun.

After seven years of interventions both major and minor, the front-runner for us has been ABA therapy, which has mutated into something called Verbal Behaviour. This is an effective strategy for learning, and has become a way of life. I can't foresee a time when the boys will cease to benefit from it, because it adapts to their changing needs. If – Heaven forbid – I should find myself with an autistic two-year-old all over again, I would embark on an intensive ABA programme in place of nursery school. I do believe it to be the best way of maximizing the autistic child's capacity for learning.

ABA stands for Applied Behaviour Analysis. It's a system devised

by Ivar Lovaas in California in the 1960s, and is sometimes referred
to as Lovaas therapy. Its most devoted practitioners believe that
it can make even quite profoundly autistic children 'mainstream-
able'. Useful though ABA is, I would urge that such claims be
treated with caution.

It is a behaviour-modification programme. Learning is broken
down into tiny chunks, and the child is rewarded – 'reinforced'
– for every success. The reinforcers are whatever motivates your
child. If your child likes stickers or small toys, great. If, like Sam,
your child is motivated by little except sweets, then you may
have to sacrifice a few teeth in the interests of education. The
point is that many autistic children don't learn because they
lack motivation. Unlike mainstream children, who accept the
socially imposed value of a gold star or being clapped in
Assembly, most autists are only motivated – if at all – by something in itself, not by the significance others attach to it. George
chooses sticking plasters or a minute spent sitting on the heater
as his rewards. Not many thirteen-year-olds would be gratified
by the receipt of a Band-Aid, but then George is not most
thirteen-year-olds.

Originally Lovaas used aversive techniques, including slaps, as
well as rewards, but these days the approach avoids the punitive.
Reinforcers may be withheld until the correct answer is given,
but they will not be withdrawn for a wrong answer. 'No' is used
for information, not for admonishment. 'Errorless learning' is the
aim, so new material is embedded within what the child already
knows. To give a simple example: if the task is to teach the child
to identify farm animals, and he already knows horse, cow and
pig but not goat, then the goat picture will be slipped in with
pictures of the known animals. As the child names the animals,
the therapist will insert the word 'goat' and ask him to repeat it.
'Drills', as they are called, are kept short. Up to thirty drills may
be covered in a two-hour session.

Several different tutors work with each child. George and
Sam have three apiece. The tutors have a meeting with the
consultant every few weeks; the consultant watches them in

action, corrects their mistakes and provides new material for them to work with. The consultant is specially trained but the tutors need no previous experience – they receive their training on the job. Sam's current tutors are Delia, our neighbour, Ian, our nanny, and Andie, a friend of George's tutor Mark. George's tutors are Mark and Jan, who are both classroom assistants at the boys' old school, and Vikki, who read an article about us in the *Mail on Sunday*, wrote to me, and discovered that the house she was about to move to was two miles away from us. Sue, our consultant, is supplied through an organization called PEACH (Parents for the Early intervention of Autism in Children).

You can use family members as tutors, which saves money, but the child might find it difficult to accept a familiar adult in an unfamiliar role. Granny Eva tutored George for a while, but George objected strenuously. Parents are often not much good at it. They are too close to the child, often not strict or consistent enough, and unable to step out of role. I use the tutor time to give good attention to Jake. For me, one of the many benefits of ABA is that it gives Jake time off from his brothers.

Verbal Behaviour, which has replaced ABA for the boys, is a freer, more flexible system, but, like ABA, it aims to fill the gaps that neurotypical children fill for themselves. VB does not follow a prescribed curriculum, though it does insist that certain skills have to be mastered before certain others can be introduced. It adapts itself to what the child in question needs to learn, whether 'academic' or behavioural. The first part of the training is always to establish compliance. If the child cannot sit still on request, then he cannot learn anything else until that behaviour is in place. Even if it takes months, compliance has to be achieved before work can continue. The child, who all his life has successfully ducked out of adult commands, will go through 'extinction bursts' at first – screaming, rolling on the floor, even biting and kicking. These have to be weathered. George and Sam, to my surprise, got through this stage in less than a day, though one may find less extreme extinction bursts recurring whenever new, unwelcome tasks are introduced.

The consultant and parents discuss what the priorities are. Behavioural and self-care problems are tackled as well as academic deficits. So, in any one session, the child may have drills about putting on socks, eating with a spoon, and not spitting, as well as naming shapes, completing a jigsaw, modelling with Plasticine. Verbal Behaviour puts more emphasis on building up a good relationship between child and tutor, learning imaginative play, and taking the child out into the community – catching a bus, handling money, posting a letter. For a fuller account of both programmes contact PEACH; details are given in the back of this book.

Both boys have therapy sessions on weekday evenings for two hours, and again on Saturday morning, which I suppose makes it the equivalent of homework. I receive no funding, except for a generous donation from a private charitable trust. It is expensive, and the more hours the boys do, the more it costs; the tutors are paid by the hour. It puts a great strain on my finances, but it is an absolute priority for me. It doesn't work miracles, but it does slowly expand the boys' range of skills. It provides them with affectionate relationships with several adults, and it chips away at the great blankness and boredom that can characterize autistic life for the child who doesn't know how to occupy himself except by 'stimming' – that is, self-stimulatory behaviours such as flapping, hand-biting, twiddling string, humming, hooting, tearing up paper . . . the list is endless. It improves the quality of Jake's life, because I can spend non-autistic time with him, and because sometimes the tutors involve him in the work they're doing with George and Sam. Jake learned to read and do sums very young, because he wanted to copy what George was doing. More importantly, he can see a benefit in having brothers like his, because the tutors come to the house bringing with them fun and interest and sweets.

The way we run our programmes is unorthodox, and would shock a Lovaas purist. But, like most aspects of childcare, it makes sense to adapt the rules to what suits you and your family. For years, I put off starting ABA because I thought it had to be done for a minimum of forty hours a week, and that the child had to be taken out of school. Eventually, when George was nine and

Sam was seven, I thought, no, I'm not going to take them out of school – they're too old, school's good for them in many ways, forty hours of therapy (eighty, for two) is too expensive, and I can't stand the thought of having them at home all day. So I'll just have to fit the therapy round what they already do. So that's what happens. Maybe their progress hasn't been as rapid as it would have been on forty hours a week, but there has been real progress on their limited timetable. The therapy supports and improves our family life; we'll carry on with it for as long as I can afford to do so.

When George was first diagnosed, we were told that appropriate education was the only treatment that was any use. An education programme rooted in behaviour management, such as ABA, is the best way of coping with the child's intellectual and social problems, but autism is also a physical condition, and some treatments can alleviate some symptoms in some cases. There are a lot of 'somes' in that sentence. Caution should be urged, because it's easy to invest a lot of money and a lot of hope in a treatment that makes no appreciable difference to your child. But it does not follow that the treatment is mere quackery. George's version of autism is very different to Sam's and so it is not surprising that they have had different responses to the same treatment.

Auditory Integration Therapy (AIT) is the most striking case in point. Also called Light and Sound Therapy, this seeks to reduce the child's auditory hypersensitivities by 'retuning' his hearing. The child is given an audiogram to assess the level of his hearing distortion, then music, altered by computer, is played to him through a headset. The child sits in a darkened booth watching a light box rotate through a colour spectrum. Light and sound together seem to stimulate the brain into easing sound distortions. The child has two half-hour sessions per day for a fortnight.

George was six and a half when we set off to North London for AIT. For years he had spent a lot of time with his hands clapped over his ears. Many sounds really distressed him – crowd noises, party noises, some deep male voices, hand-driers in public lavatories. On a long car journey it was impossible for me to use a lavatory – because of the hand-driers, he wouldn't come in with me, and I couldn't leave him outside. He wouldn't use any kind of lavatory himself, at home or anywhere else. I assume this was because of the gurgling of the cistern. A physiotherapist had given us a giant potty with built-up sides, designed to give stability to children with cerebral palsy. This was what George used, when he wasn't using the garden path or the bedroom floor.

Some kinds of music were intolerable to George. He has a strong response to music, and may well have perfect pitch; he's very 'controlling' of his musical environment and hates to have music put on which takes him by surprise. Before AIT, the 'wrong' music would send him into a hysterical state. One year, his class had two Christmas carols to perform; one sent him into raptures, the other into a panic.

In short, George's hypersensitivities were affecting his life to a considerable degree. AIT offered to reduce them, and it succeeded. The Light and Sound Therapy Centre was an ordinary North London house, staffed by Hasidic Jews, all women. The married women wore stiff black wigs; this led George to address the lead therapist as Cruella, but either she didn't hear or she was too polite to object. George's preferred 'flapper' at that time was a palm cross. I felt embarrassed when he entered the therapy room holding the cross in front of his face, as if repelling vampires, but nothing bothered the calm, good-tempered staff. Their quiet confidence must have communicated itself to George. I had doubted that he would submit to the regime of wearing headphones and sitting still, but after a few minutes of resistance he relaxed and co-operated. He seemed mesmerized by the distorted music and the glowing circle of colour that moved through the spectrum. When Min joined us, after a few sessions, George, who didn't usually invite people to share his activities, grabbed his father by the tie and hauled him into the therapy room, as if to show him what he'd been doing.

After AIT, George's use of 'normal' language increased hugely and never declined again. He started using the lavatory for the first time, tolerating the cistern and the flush. He had usually referred to himself in the first or second person – 'George is here'; 'You [I] want a drink.' Suddenly, he used 'I' and 'me' with ease. He began using words to do with feelings and preferences, which he'd always avoided in the past. In true story-of-a-miracle fashion, he said, for the first time ever, 'Mummy, I love you.'

The improvement was obvious to all – family, teachers, friends. And the gains held. He stopped putting his hands over his ears – when he does that now it's a sign of guilt, as if he's anticipating the telling-off he's going to get. He doesn't much like the noise of driers, vacuum cleaners, and so on, but he'll put up with it. He never muddled his pronouns again. The sheer volume of his language continued to increase, as did his readiness to use the vocabulary of emotion – which Sam, to this day, doesn't use at all.

AIT didn't remove the autism, but it broke down some of the barriers between George's world and our world. He still has supersensitive hearing – the other day he was at the end of the garden, a long way off, so I put on 'The Ride of the Valkyries', which Sam loves and George detests. The doors and windows were closed, but still George heard it, and came storming in from the garden to turn it off, shrieking, 'I hate this music!' But though George still has pronounced auditory likes and dislikes, his hearing seems to trouble him far less.

Sam never had this problem. He never put his hands over his ears, and he positively relished sounds like gurgling drains and helicopters. But his sensory experiences are clearly very different from ours, and he hums and vocalizes a great deal, as if to create a kind of 'white noise' to keep the world at bay. When we enrolled Sam for AIT, we hoped it would reduce the humming, calm him down, and improve his concentration, which by this stage – he was also six and a half – was non-existent.

Sam was at his very worst when he did AIT. He was incapable

of sitting still for a second. Eating and sleeping were terrible, he had lost all his interests, and his self-harming (mainly hand-biting) was high. He couldn't pay attention to a story, or even a video. Only strenuous physical activity – running, 'swimming', trampolining – seemed to help him at all. So it was even more surprising than it had been with George that Sam sat and co-operated with the light-and-sound treatment.

Alas, that co-operation was the beginning and end of the treatment's success. It just didn't do anything for Sam. I thought I detected a slight improvement in concentration when he was watching TV or listening to music. He'd sit for five seconds rather than three. But it certainly wasn't twelve hundred pounds' worth of improvement. Sam's speech had all but disappeared at this time, and AIT did nothing to bring it back.

For George, AIT really was a turning point in his life. If we'd 'done' Sam first, we'd have dismissed it as tosh, and its practitioners as frauds. For George the great success has been AIT, for Sam it has been the gluten-free/casein-free diet. The diet is controversial. Most parents who've implemented it swear by it, most of the medical profession frown on it. I've outlined the 'opoid excess' theory on which the diet is based in Chapter 12, but I do urge that, if you're interested, you should use the information at the back of this book. Some of the symptoms which indicate that a child (or an adult) may benefit from the diet are a constant, restless craving for the foods containing the listed substances, a distended stomach, a pale face with dark-shadowed eyes, one or two red ears, diarrhoea, constipation or flatulence, floating stools (if you're lucky enough to get a look), excessive sweating, excessive thirst, an apparent indifference or reduced response to pain, poor sleeping habits and wild behaviour, including destructiveness or self-harm.

Sam has some of these symptoms, though not all – I never noticed any sweating, for instance. By his sixth birthday, he had taken to arching his back and screaming as if in colicky pain. This happened every day, and the screams could go on for two hours. There was a lot of incoherent, tearless crying. His appetite was extremely poor. His general health seemed good in that he wasn't prone to infections, he never vomited, and his muscle tone was, as it always has been, quite splendid. But he seemed endlessly restless, physically uncomfortable. He was either hyperactive, or slumped in a glazed, unreachable, trance-like state. His sleeping was simply appalling, and he produced loose, pale, floating stools.

Doctors don't like the gf/cf diet because it's hard to provide the child with the whole range of nutrients. A fair point – except that the child isn't providing himself with the full range of nutrients anyway. There are some autistic children who eat healthy, balanced meals three times a day. There must be. I'd guess it would be most unlikely that the parents of such children would consider tampering with their diet. There are many, many more children who, like Sam, live on a diet of crisps, fingernail clippings and fresh air. When you decide to change a diet like this you've not a lot to lose, and possibly a great deal to gain.

I sent Sam's urine off to the controversial Paul Shattock at Sunderland University. The analysis showed a typically autistic profile, though with a much stronger reaction to gluten than to casein. This may have been simply because, through his own choice, Sam ate few dairy products – the days of swigging bottles of milk were long gone. But his diet did revolve round gluten – biscuits, bread, croissants ('squeeze-buns', he called them), grissini and 'loopy Ys' (Honey Nut Loops). On Paul Shattock's advice, I removed the gluten first. The casein, in the form of milk chocolate, ice cream, and the odd smear of butter, remained in for another year. So did the aspartame and the MSG, though I now think these are what produced the worst reaction of all.

If I had to give up gluten, I wouldn't find it so very hard, because I like the whole range of fruit, vegetables, potatoes, rice, pulses, meat and fish. Sam never liked any of these, except for a few potatoey things and, occasionally, rice. My problems with such a diet would be mainly social. Sam has little social life, and doesn't feel left out if other people are eating differently, unless what they're having is a sore temptation. We never have croissants at home, and I don't eat bread in front of him. But pasta's fine, because he's not interested in it. People often ask, 'But isn't it so difficult, making separate meals for him?' The answer is no, not really, because since infancy Sam has never participated in a family meal.

Gluten is everywhere. Most pre-prepared foods are thickened or coated with something glutinous. There are gf substitutes for bread, biscuits, pasta, cake mix, and so on, but they're very expensive and, in my opinion, quite nasty. Sam nibbles the biscuits – bourbon and custard cream wannabes, pallid and brittle. Sometimes he eats rice bread dipped in egg and fried. Products come and go, irritatingly. Sainsbury's stocked some very passable gf grissini for a while, but they've gone. Casein, often in the form of whey powder, is also ubiquitous. If you're going to try this diet, you have to resign yourself to reading labels carefully, and making a few more things at home.

For the first gluten-free fortnight, Sam was irritable. I started it during the school holidays so that I could monitor him closely; it was important to be absolutely strict in order to assess the effect it was having. He couldn't be taken on his usual outings to public swimming pools and soft-play centres because he was inclined to snatch things like Kit Kats from other people. The changes happened quickly. His sleeping improved, he became less restless, his hand-biting lessened. His screaming decreased; and now, he never screams, though he does still cry and whinge. His stomach went flat, the shadows under his eyes faded. The craving for sugar, which had dominated his life, ebbed away. Now, he still likes sugary things, and sweets are still, regrettably, his main motivators, but that old junkie craving has gone.

His appetite improved. It's still not good. Sam, at eleven, is undersized and pale. I'm not happy with his eating; he rejects most protein, most fruit, and all vegetables except a little raw fennel and raw onion, but it really is better than it was. In any one day he'll eat a small amount of up to twelve different foods; pre-diet, it would have been two or three.

He simply can't be getting enough iron or calcium, but then

he couldn't have been pre-diet, either. A dietician has been consulted – the doctor will always tell you to see a dietician before embarking – but an old adage about horses and water springs to mind. Sam's dietician provided him with a beautiful powder containing all the nutrients he wasn't getting, but inserting the powder into Sam is almost impossible. You're supposed to dissolve it into drinks, but he just tips them down the sink. The only way he gets any at all is if I freeze it into home-made ice lollies, but to give him the recommended daily dose would mean making about thirty ice lollies, and even Sam would baulk at that.

Since I've ditched casein, MSG and aspartame as well as gluten, Sam's calmness and ability to concentrate have continued to improve. It would be good to take the diet still further – reduce the sugar and salt, buy nothing that isn't organic, be more stringent about the flavourings in the sweets he gets for his rewards. Perhaps, soon, I'll find the strength to tackle the next stage, but I'm not ready yet. About twice a year I think, 'Maybe he's grown out of his intolerance,' and let him have something from the proscribed list, but he still reacts badly. I always know when he's got hold of something he shouldn't have, because his eyes go red and he starts to whimper. Last Sunday he had a Cornetto – a mini-Cornetto, in fact – and he spent the afternoon howling and throwing himself about the room.

I'm not a faddy mother. Really I'm not. I've no natural inclination towards alternative remedies of any description. I'm rarely ill, and my physical condition doesn't interest me very much. I can go for a year at a time without taking any kind of medication at all. My general attitude towards food is that you should eat what you feel like or what you're offered, depending on the circumstances. I've never consciously altered my own diet in my life, except, slightly, during pregnancy, when I followed the guidelines. But desperation drove me to try the gf/cf diet for Sam, and it has had a good effect.

It's a bore, and expensive – or it is if, like me, you lazily buy special bread and biscuits instead of making them yourself. Some

GPs let you have some of the food on prescription – not mine. But I don't begrudge the cost; the years when Sam lived on fresh air were cheap, so it balances out. The best, the noblest way to do it, would be to adopt the diet oneself, and never let the forbidden items darken one's doors, but that, frankly, would be just too disagreeable.

It would also, of course, be hard and perhaps unfair to impose the diet on George and Jake. Ironically, though Sam is more severely affected by autism than George, it's often easier to impose restrictions on Sam. I suppose it's because Sam doesn't question or challenge. If Sam's thwarted in a desire, he'll try hard to find a way round it, as when I put a new lock on the door and Sam climbed up the chimney. But he doesn't argue, even in a rudimentary fashion, and he doesn't appear to bear a grudge. Because Sam doesn't compare his lot with that of other people – because Sam has a limited awareness of the existence of other people – he doesn't have much capacity to think, 'It's not fair.' At least, as far as I can tell.

Changing your autistic child's diet seems to me to be one of the more obviously benign interventions. If you do it responsibly, and make every effort to fill the nutritional gaps (huh!), then it can't do harm, and may well do good. And if it doesn't work, well, you can just abandon it. Less easy to justify is the use of any form of drug. To date, no particular drug has been found to be of much use. Temple Grandin uses anti-depressants to control anxiety, but she's an adult and can make that choice for herself. In America, I believe Ritalin is quite widely used. Ritalin is helpful in controlling hyperactivity in some children, so when Sam was at his very worst I approached his paediatrician about it.

She warned me that it didn't have a particularly good record in managing autism, but said that as it was not addictive and had no long-term side effects it might be worth a try. She added that the most common short-term side effects were insomnia and reduced appetite. Well, I thought, Sam doesn't eat or sleep anyway; it can't get much worse.

How wrong I was. In the four days that Sam was on Ritalin,

the only 'solid' food he ate was one ice lolly, and his head barely touched the pillow. I can't remember how I got the drug down him – nowadays he won't take any medication at all – but somehow I did. It had a noticeable effect, but not a useful one. He was calmer at school, but it was a torpid calm; he wasn't able to learn anything. And in the evening, when the dose wore off, he was wilder than ever.

I threw the Ritalin away. But I was still desperate for treatment of some kind. A year later, when Sam was seven, a lot of publicity was given to secretin injections. An autistic boy in America had been treated with the enzyme secretin in connection with a bowel disorder. To his mother's astonishment, his autistic characteristics all but disappeared. Other children received the injections, often with excellent results. Parents began to clamour for this miracle cure.

The medical profession were understandably sceptical. The long-term effects of the treatment were unknown. In this country, it was never possible to treat an autistic child with secretin on the NHS, but a few doctors provided it privately, at considerable expense.

The way the boys are now, I wouldn't feel justified in injecting them with anything about which so little was known. But Sam's condition at that time had deteriorated so much that I'd have tried almost anything. So, off we went to London for a secretin injection. And I'm glad we did, because if we hadn't, I would always have asked myself if I had turned down the chance of a truly miraculous treatment. And though no miracle was worked, Sam did improve after secretin.

It's hard to be very clear about its effects, because I'd removed the gluten from his diet a few weeks before, so I'm not sure which improvement to attribute to which treatment. In theory they should have worked together, since they are both intended to correct a leaky gut. The doctor who administered the secretin told us to wait for a few weeks before the next injection, and to have a subsequent injection only if Sam had begun to deteriorate again. After the third shot, Sam plateaued, and never seriously regressed again, so that was the end of secretin for him.

After secretin (and gluten-removal) Sam immediately started sleeping through the night. Before, he'd been going to bed at midnight and waking seven or eight times before rising at seven. This, combined with George's extreme early rising – often three or four in the morning – and Jake's normal-but-wakeful baby-hood, meant that I was seriously deprived of sleep.

Since secretin, Sam has nearly always slept through. He goes to bed later than I'd like, but averages half past ten rather than midnight. I have to rouse him in the mornings, but now he wakes up smiling. Before secretin, I used to dread the thump on the stairs that meant Sam was on his way, because when he woke he was always in such a gloweringly awful mood, like an infant ogre.

Before secretin and gluten-removal, Sam's hands were raw and bleeding because he bit them and banged them so much. He had deep red horseshoe-shaped weals on them, and his fingers were scabbed and swollen. Now, he still has patches of rough skin, and he'll mumble on his hands as an occasional protest against being made to do something he doesn't like, but it's nothing to what it was. He used to harm himself in other ways, too, like knock-ing himself under the chin and pinching and scratching himself all over. He doesn't do any of this any more.

In March 1999, just before my fortieth birthday, Sam's phys-ical discomfort was at its worst. He was screaming almost all the time, he would hardly keep his clothes on, and his whole body was pinched and scratched like Tom O'Bedlam. He was admitted to hospital to be checked for appendicitis, but noth-ing was found. Naked and still screaming, he ran up and down the hospital corridors for half a day. He was given something to relax his stomach, which seemed to help a little, and then they discharged us with their usual sigh of relief. He had the secretin injections later that year, and he's never been anywhere near as bad again.

Secretin also seemed to clear some of the fog that had arisen between Sam and the rest of the world. His use of language had

dwindled to almost nothing, and it had become increasingly difficult to get through to him. I was never sure whether he'd heard
me and was choosing to ignore me, or whether it just took him
a long time to process what he had heard, or whether he hadn't
realized that he was being spoken to at all. After secretin (and
gluten-removal . . .) his language very slowly crept back, and his
responses became much prompter. Now, he usually responds
immediately when he's spoken to, even if the response is negative. He makes a clear distinction between remarks addressed to
him and all other kinds of speech. He hardly ever reacts to what
is said unless his name is used.

The first time I took Sam to London for his shot of secretin,
he climbed into the train's luggage rack and remained there, spitting, for the rest of the journey. He ran barefoot through Charing
Cross; I had to bundle him into a taxi by main force. After visiting the doctor we had lunch with our friends Chris and Elspeth
– or rather, I had lunch, and Sam rampaged through the house
and ate Elspeth's contraceptive pills. The second time, he was a
whole lot calmer. He sat on the train seat, kept his shoes on, and
allowed me to entertain him with toys and books for much of
the journey. There's a big difference in Sam's behaviour pre- and
post-secretin, but what I find hard to assess is how direct a part
the injections played in the improvement.

I'm out of touch with the secretin issue. I believe it's fallen
from favour. It's certainly not a treatment to be undertaken lightly.
Quite apart from the possible side effects issue it's traumatic for
the child to travel to an unfamiliar place and be jabbed in the
arm – though the jab itself *may* be less horrible for an autist than
for a normal child, because of the high pain threshold, and because
the dread of anticipation isn't there. Sam didn't seem to mind it
as much as I'd expected. I was never tempted to submit the relatively calm, cheerful George to the procedure, but Sam's extreme
distress called for desperate measures.

I'm even less clear about the merits or demerits of anti-candida
treatment. Both boys received this – in fact it was the first medical
intervention we tried. There is a theory that autistic people are

more likely to suffer from candida (thrush) than others. I took George and Sam (again, privately) to a paediatrician who subscribed to this theory. He prescribed Nystatin, which kills thrush, and we were told to cut yeast and sugar out of their diet, because this is what thrush feeds on.

Yeast more or less went. I didn't manage to cut sugar out, though I did reduce it. Once the treatment was under way, George's body seemed to undergo withdrawal symptoms. Thrush appeared all over his bottom, like a nappy rash. He was restless and distracted for a few days, and then his behaviour and concentration started to improve. He chose a low-sugar diet for himself – for several months it was plain porridge, chicken Kiev, and very little else. He won't eat either of those things now.

Killing off the candida seemed to kick-start an intolerable sugar-craving in Sam. Day and night, he thought about nothing else. He picked pockets and emptied handbags in search of sweets, he snatched lollies out of people's hands in the street. His class made peppermint creams for Christmas. They were left out to dry, and Sam ate *all* of them. He ruined pudding for the whole school; eighty portions of lemon meringue pie were laid out on trays, and Sam raked his fingers through the lot. He would break into the school kitchen and climb up into the cupboards; he would hijack the tea trolley on its way to the staff room and snaffle the custard creams. Like a junkie in search of heroin, there wasn't enough sugar in the world to satisfy Sam's craving. And it didn't make him happy. Once he'd eaten sugar – which of course he managed to do, despite my efforts to limit it – it would make him cry.

His longing for sugar blotted out everything else. Nothing could hold his attention. The only books he'd look at were recipe books with pictures of iced cakes. All his obsessive interests, the washing machines, oast houses, cuckoo clocks, vanished almost overnight. He no longer drew, or used toys, or danced, or even smiled.

The doctor who prescribed the Nystatin also prescribed an army of supplements – evening primrose oil, magnesium, zinc, vitamin B6. At that time, both boys were still drinking out of baby's bottles. It was quite easy to spike their drinks with these supplements, so they must have received the recommended amount for at least a year. But I eventually decided to remove the bottles, for the obvious reasons that one removes baby's bottles from children of six and eight, and after that it became much, much harder to get them to take the supplements. In the end I gave up. I can't honestly say I noticed much difference.

We went through the whole business again a couple of years later, when I had their stools analysed. Collecting the samples for analysis was not plain sailing. I'd devoted a great deal of energy to persuading the boys to defecate in the lavatory rather than in nappies, trousers, beds, toy boxes, baths, on carpets, windowsills, climbing frames, trampolines and garden paths. Now I needed uncontaminated specimens; fishing them out of the loo was not allowed. I had to undo all the good work, and encourage them – reward them even – for pooing in accessible places.

The bath was the best bet for Sam. The samples might have been mildly contaminated by bathwater but it was the best I could do. Samples had to be collected on three consecutive days – not too much of a problem for Sam, who produces little and often, but George only ever 'goes' about twice a week. It is hard enough to get any child to change the habits of a lifetime, but autistic children are famously unpersuadable.

So, I waived the 'three consecutive days' rule for George. I turned him out into the garden as often as possible, and at last saw what I wanted steaming on the garden path. I rushed out with my plastic scoop, then hesitated. George was nowhere in sight. What if this was nothing to do with him, but the deposit of a fox or badger? I looked forward to the laboratory report. 'We recommend you no longer feed your child on slugs, earthworms and old crisp packets . . .'

Once collected, the samples had to be mixed with a special liquid until they resembled pea soup, labelled with the date and hour of production, and posted to the diagnostic laboratory. The report came back. The boys' guts were full of the bad bacteria and low on the good, though thankfully they were now free of thrush. I bought the various supplements and corrective medicines they suggested. But, alas, the boys no longer drank out of bottles. They wouldn't touch any of it. I mixed things into drinks, baked them into gingerbread, ground them up with icing sugar. No good. I stirred them into ketchup, strong enough to mask most flavours. The ketchup turned pale yellow. I gave up. So, for all I know the boys' digestive tracts are still full of rampaging bacteria, and I certainly can't comment on the usefulness of the recommended treatment.

Some treatments may be useful in a limited, specific way. At the suggestion of various friends I took Sam to see a cranial osteopath. He was a very nice man, he struck up a good relationship with Sam, and Sam quite enjoyed our little outings. The The benign involvement of another adult is always a good thing for an autistic child. Cranial osteopathy is very gentle and non-invasive. It made Sam a little more relaxed. It also made it much, much easier for him to tolerate having his head touched. From babyhood, he'd hated people to go anywhere near his head. Washing and cutting his hair, and brushing his teeth, had always been immensely difficult. After the osteopathy he submitted with a much better grace. When he was two, he screamed so much during a haircut that he gave himself a hernia. Now, it's still not easy, but it is possible. On a good day, we can even search his hair for nits.

It's hard to discuss the treatments we tried without sounding evangelical, either for or against. I can only reiterate that every autistic child is different, and that what suits one may do little for another. George and Sam, for instance, have had little need either for sign language (Makaton) or PECS – a picture-exchange system. However, both of these have made radical differences in the lives of autists who cannot achieve speech. Speaking entirely from my own experience, if I had my time with the boys again, I would put them on the diet, and start an ABA or Verbal

Behaviour programme as early as possible. Autistic children get set in their ways; it's best if you can point them in desirable directions. The later you leave the intervention, the harder your struggle will be.

8. Sam's Crash

'Mum, one word from you and Sam does as he likes.' George was, as usual, adapting a quotation – this time from Jill Murphy's *The Last Noo-Noo* – and, also as usual, his remark was apt. As Sam developed from toddler to child he became increasingly non-compliant. Disciplining young children relies on the removal of desired objects, or on banishment from company, or – at a more extreme level – making the child feel ashamed. Of these, only the first had any impact at all on Sam. The other two play on social sensibilities which in Sam's case were simply lacking.

So, if (when!) Sam smashed a window, grabbed another child's sweets, cut his T-shirt to ribbons, or pulled down the curtains *and rail* in his headmaster's study, what was I to do? It was no use giving him 'time out', because he didn't particularly want 'time in' – he'd just blithely wander off and do something else, something equally undesirable. Making him say 'sorry' was just eliciting a parrot-like response; he couldn't *feel* sorry, because he couldn't see anything from the other person's point of view. If I removed something he liked, it would upset him, but he wouldn't learn from the punishment, because he couldn't make the right connections. 'If you flush your socks down the loo, then I'll take away your Barbie Laundry Center' – Sam couldn't see any sense in that, and I'm not sure that I can, either.

When I was in Houston, staying with my friend Sally, we went to a parenting class where 'behavioural issues' were discussed. We were shown video clips of various misdemeanours, such as scribbling on walls and throwing sofa cushions on the floor. (My heart began to sink as I realized that in my household, throwing cushions was regarded as good-to-normal behaviour.) Then 'right' and 'wrong' approaches to chastisement were suggested. The 'right' thing to do was to kneel down so you were at the child's level, look him in the eyes, and explain in a soft, sweet voice that you worked so hard to give him a lovely home, and when he scribbled on the wall it made you feel 'kinda discouraged'. This was before the boys were diagnosed, but I remember thinking that the children these people were talking about bore very little resemblance to my own darlings.

Fear and pain are, of course, the old-fashioned, politically incorrect props of infant discipline. Sam wasn't afraid of a frown or an angry voice, though George was; indeed, Sam seemed to enjoy the unusual audio-visual effects produced by an irate adult. I disapprove of smacking, but, like many parents, that hasn't stopped me from resorting to it on occasion. The threat of a smack was an effective deterrent for George. But for Sam, it just didn't work at all. Autists often have a high pain threshold; to make any impact, I'd have had to hit him really hard. And besides, for most children the real pain of a smack is the humiliation – another emotion outside Sam's repertoire. I only ever smacked Sam a few times, and I always regretted it. I soon realized that smacks seemed to be something he actively enjoyed. My father is the least aggressive of men. He never laid a finger on any of us, and he would be, if that's possible, even less likely to smack a grandchild. But Sam would take him by the wrist and try to make him inflict punishment. 'G'anfather Richard, smack Sam, smack Sam,' he would chortle.

Autists are often disobedient without being truly naughty. They ignore your reprimand, but in ripping up a book or disembowelling a cassette they may not be showing defiance or even wilful destructiveness; it just seems to be an activity that gives them some sort of satisfaction. And much of the time, Sam's wild-boy behaviour didn't seem to matter so very much, because he was usually cheerful with it. It's hard to feel cross with a child who's getting so much pleasure from trickling molehill earth on to his head and chanting, 'It's rainin'-it's pourin'-oldmanisnorin''. 'Where did Sam come from?' I asked George, to see whether he had absorbed the very basic sex information I'd given him. 'Sam came out of a puddle,' replied George, and yes, most of the time Sam was absolutely filthy. But he was cheery, adventurous, full of life. He loved jokes – he called our friends' oast house 'the toast house', and laughed so much he fell over. We took him riding, and he was fearless and enthusiastic about 'Orange Debbie', as he called his pony – 'Get outta da way, horse, Sam's comin'!' Visiting a school, he ran into an empty classroom, sat at a table as if in a café, and said roguishly, 'Right, Sam, what would you like to drink?' He had to be escorted briskly out of the flower festival in our local church, because he sat on a flower arrangement in the shape of a hassock, claiming that he was sitting on eggs in a nest.

He took an intense interest in some aspects of the world around him, though others he blanked out. We found a slow-worm in the garden: 'Bye bye boa constrictor, see you next week for a cuppa tea,' said Sam. A scab on his leg was a source of fascination, and he gave a running commentary on its changing colours: 'Lickle bit orange . . . lickle bit green . . . bit bit purple.' He stuck foam alphabet letters all over himself in the bath, pretending they were scabs. By the stream, he would pretend to be a dog, pick up sticks in his mouth, and throw them in. Colours mattered a lot. 'It's a blue rainin' and a black windy,' was how he described a storm, aged just three. At the same age he was tearing up and down the slippery garden paths, wearing a black jumper. 'O be careful, black darling,' he instructed himself. If the rain was really, really heavy, he and George would strip naked and dance about in the garden. One January evening, they occupied themselves by dipping their long fringes into the icy water of the birdbath and then flicking the drops at each other, laughing uproariously.

Sam's habit of spotting visual correspondences was strong. 'Look at all those lubbly worms!' he exclaimed, about catkins. He intoned 'Mirror, mirror, on the wall' to a shiny circular doorknob, and pretended to blow out the hairbrush bristles as if they were candles on a cake. I offered him a plate of tagliatelle. 'I like seatbelts, mmm, 'licous.' His word coinages were equally idiosyncratic. 'Gourlagourd' and 'saunters' were nouns, 'ponk', 'glimp' and 'tuit' were verbs. I was never sure of their exact meanings, but I think Sam was.

I know he said all these things because I wrote them down. What I recorded wasn't the speech of a normal child, any more than George's utterances were normal. While Sam, aged four and five, was wittering on about gourlagourds, George, aged six and seven, was saying things like, 'Oh the television is ripped and full of toothpaste,' or (seeing Sam having a haircut) 'All Sam's feathers are coming off.' When I asked George what he'd been doing at school, he said, 'Watching the shadows dance,' and it transpired they'd had Music and Movement. He pointed at me and said, 'She was a wonderful writer, artist and countrywoman,' which I took as a tremendous compliment until I realized it was lifted straight from a video about the life of Beatrix Potter. George used to narrate the story of his own life as it was happening, always in the third person. 'He jumped into the bath with a tremendous splash'; '"Where can Daddy be?" exclaimed George anxiously.' 'He clutched his spoon tightly. The sausage bounced off the plate, but he caught it.' My all-time favourite was when he was eating a McDonald's hamburger. He pulled out the slimy, khaki slice of dill pickle and handed it to me, saying, 'Mum, this is my conscience.'

At this age, a great deal of George's speech was still adapted from memorized sources. As time went on, he worked in more and more phrases of his own, and his use of language has steadily become more normal. We can now have short conversational exchanges, even discussions, though he still finds it hard to cope with dissent, and is very controlling of the conversation, correcting one's word order and tone of voice. Certain words and phrases irritate him, usually those which don't have a precise meaning – 'Don't say "OK then", say "Yes"!' George's gnomic utterances of earlier days seem to have laid the foundations for the stronger, more 'useful' verbal structures he has managed to build more recently. Sam's language, however, has made no such progress. The garbled chatter, the humour, the ability to comment on life, which were so marked at five and a half, had all vanished within six months. All that was left was a handful of syllables. These were used only to get needs met. They weren't even whole words any more, but eroded sounds – 'ju' for 'juice', ''way' for 'leave me alone'.

Sam was five years and five months when Jake was conceived. I was feeling quite complacent. George was increasingly settled, Sam was lawless but happy; I felt, at last, that I could take on the extra labour and responsibility of a third baby. That August, four months pregnant, I took the boys on holiday to France, on my own. I joined my mother out there, but I managed the journey with them alone, and thought little of it. Six weeks later, I could barely take Sam out of the house.

So, what happened? Regression is a common, though not inevitable, feature of autism. Usually, it happens in the second year of life. The child loses language, loses interest in play; the desire for social contact dwindles. In some cases, these skills are slowly regained; in others, the withdrawal is permanent. Sam's regression was unusually late. I wasn't expecting it, and it took a long time for me to notice what was happening, as is often the case with things that lie under our very eyes. I kept finding reasons for his restlessness, his agitation, his crying, his frantic destructiveness. It was due to illness, exhaustion, or being in an unfamiliar place, I thought. It took me a long time to realize that the old happy-go-lucky Sam had gone.

Sam's 'stimming' was taking over his life. Proper talking was being replaced by a jumble of apparently meaningless noises. He was starting to harm himself, biting his hands and knocking himself under the chin. All his obsessive interests disappeared overnight, as I described in Chapter 7. Washing machines, vacuum cleaners, cuckoo clocks and the like, which had made him literally jump for joy, no longer kindled a flicker of interest. He seemed to be suffering from colicky cramps, and would arch his back and scream, sometimes for a couple of hours at a stretch. Either he couldn't keep still, and just wanted to run and run, or else he would slump on the sofa, almost comatose, feeding bottle dangling from the corner of his mouth, indifferent to everything happening around him.

He wasn't like this absolutely all the time. I have photographs from this time which show the old cheeky grin (that's a cliché, but there's no better way of describing it), and there were still a few activities he enjoyed, on good days. But for far too much of the time he was aimless, disorientated and distressed. It was terribly hard to get through to him; often he didn't even seem to hear what was said to him, let alone understand it.

In October 1997, his Uncle Warwick got married. Sam's behaviour at the reception was particularly difficult. The year before, Sam had caused chaos at my friend Cathy's wedding, but at least as far as Sam was concerned it had been happy chaos, borne with noble fortitude by the bride and groom. On that occasion, it had been George who was clingy and tearful, alarmed by the crowds and desperate to get back to the car. At Warwick and Heather's wedding, George was relatively relaxed and confident, surrounded as he was by familiar family members, but Sam behaved like a tiger escaped from his cage. He made constant dashes for freedom; when restrained, he would almost snarl. At one point he shook off his pursuers and careered through the massed ranks of a second wedding group, gathered to be photographed on the steps of Greenwich Town Hall. I put his behaviour down to too much icing.

I may have been partly right. I don't fully understand the reasons for Sam's crash, but I'm convinced that he underwent a profound internal upheaval, and that this was linked to what he was eating, and possibly to what he was not eating. In babyhood, Sam had been placidly, indiscriminately omnivorous, but since the age of one his diet had become more and more limited and nutritionally impoverished. For a long time he had consumed mainly refined carbohydrates and quantities of milk. Had an intolerance of casein and gluten been slowly building up, to reach, suddenly, an intolerable level? This seems quite likely to me.

What, if anything, did his treatment for candida contribute?

To this day, I really can't be sure. Was I right to embark on the treatment in the first place? Was I right to continue it once such a violent reaction had apparently been provoked? Was the regression an agony that had to be gone through to reach the calmer, clearer-headed Sam we have today? I find these questions impossible to answer. Any decision-making on behalf of any child involves an element of risk, however small. Have you chosen the right school, the right musical instrument to learn, the right orthodontic treatment? One can never know what might have been.

What else could have caused Sam's crash? It happened when he was unsuitably placed in the mainstream primary school, where despite everyone's best efforts he must have felt panicked and bewildered. Perhaps his language fell away because he'd got tired of being misunderstood; his idiosyncratic coinages and muffled pronunciations made it difficult for most people to know what he was saying, which must be disheartening, to say the least. But though these could have been contributing factors, instinct tells me that Sam was in the grip of a physical process way beyond his control.

These days, Sam is easier, more relaxed. He's more manageable than he's been since babyhood. He never runs away, and he's not seriously destructive any more. Thanks to his ABA/Verbal Behaviour therapy, he's infinitely more compliant both in public and private. His use of language is improving; he still has to be prompted to speak in full sentences, but he's light years away from the handful of broken syllables which was all that was left to him six years ago.

Some of his humour and sense of fun have been restored. He can be affectionate again, and just occasionally he seeks out the company of a specific person. But he is still not the bright-eyed rascal that he was before the crash. He never chats for the sake of it; most of his utterances are still to do with getting his needs met. He still has no real interests; the gap left by the white goods, oasts and bottles of Harpic, as described in Chapter 11, has never been properly filled. He spends a lot of time restlessly trying to find the thing to eat that will satisfy him – a feeling I remember from pregnancy – and he gets angry when nothing does the trick.

As a small boy, pre-crash, Sam was quite 'transparent'. He expressed things, reacted to things, much more immediately. I remember him aged five, on a beautiful autumn evening, running in to me from the garden – 'Mummy, come and see the moon! Mummy, come and see the lawnmower!' This level of spontaneity and interaction has never returned, though he does now frequently present me with things – a crisp, a Lego brick, a balloon whisk, whatever. Sam is guarded, and wary. He now keeps his inner self hidden for much of the time. People, he seems to feel, put too much pressure on him. It's interesting that the one relationship that held good throughout his crash was with George – the only person, perhaps, who exerted no pressure of any kind.

It's still hard to find things that motivate Sam, because admitting to any kind of enthusiasm would mean letting his defences slip, and he's rarely prepared to do that. Emotionally, Sam is more 'autistic' than he was pre-crash; life in the mental padded cell he has created for himself is boring, but it's more comfortable, less threatening, than the outside world.

A common belief among people not deeply familiar with autism is that there is a normal child trapped inside, struggling to get out. That's a false belief. I reiterate that Sam has no 'normal' core. He is autistic through and through. But there was a time when his autism was more penetrable, when contact with the neurotypical world was more pleasurable and easy for him. That's what I want to restore. I think we're getting there. Even on a bad day, Sam is never now anything like the lost, howling child he once became. As long as I can feel that progress is being made, I can cope with most things. For me, Sam's crash had been the worst part of the whole autism business, far worse than the initial diagnosis. The powerlessness that results from finding your child in the grip of some torment you don't understand is horrible.

9. Off the Couch

In describing Sam's great regression I omitted one possible explanation for his changed behaviour, the kind of explanation that would most readily spring to mind when discussing behaviour changes in any normal child.

A psychologist would have looked at Sam's family life, and suggested emotional causes for his increased aloofness, loss of language, his unexplained crying, his insomnia, his self-harm. Until October 1997 Sam, though clearly autistic and not easy to control or teach, was cheerful, busy, and, in an eccentric way, sociable. By the spring of 1998 he was all but unreachable.

What changes happened in family life during this period? Well, Jake was born, on 26 January 1998 – on George's eighth birthday, as it happens. So, did Sam's behaviour demonstrate his deep unease at being displaced by another baby? I might have thought that if the change had happened after Jake's birth, but it began mid-pregnancy. And, I would argue, my pregnancy hardly affected him. It was trouble-free. I never took to my bed, never stayed in hospital (before the birth itself) or gave up doing any of the things I normally did with Sam.

A psychologist might disagree. The child will have been affected by the news of the pregnancy. He will have overheard conversations, he will have brooded on the explanations you have given him, he will have sensed change on a subconscious level. And besides, there'll be other issues. What about tensions between me and Min, attempts to remove Sam's bottle, the changes, perhaps, of people in his life – babysitters, teachers, children at school? It would be easy to find explanations of this kind for Sam's disturbed and disturbing behaviour.

Easy, but, I believe, misguided. I respect psychology. I don't dismiss it as a non-science. Psychoanalysis and psychotherapy may be only as good as the people who practise them, but at best that can be very good indeed. No one system – no science, no religion, no philosophy – has all the answers, but I think that psychology has enhanced our understanding of human behaviour to a considerable degree. I believe that aberrant behaviour in children can often be attributed to emotional disturbance. And yet I don't believe that Sam's regression had anything to do with the obvious psychological upheavals. Why?

It seems to me that autism is uniquely and intriguingly resistant to psychological analysis. Autists have emotions, but they don't have the emotional instincts that are shared by the majority of the human race. As I suggested in Chapter 5, they don't cotton on to the set of symbols and archetypes that form the basis for key mythologies and folk tales the world over. If you read a collection of American Indian stories, another of Russian stories, and another of African, their similarities will be more striking than their differences. Of course, one can find many exceptions to every rule, but consider recurrent themes like the eventual success of the put-upon youngest son (usually the third son), the concealed beauty of the youngest (third) daughter, the cruelty of the stepmother, talking animals, forests you get lost in, the setting and accomplishment of seemingly impossible tasks. Consider child-eating ogres, magic seeds, enchanted sleeps, garments that make you invisible. Consider seven-league boots, swords that cut through anything, wishing-wells, flying carpets. These devices, or their equivalents, crop up with astonishing regularity in all cultures from the Innuit to the Australian Aborigine.

Folk tales are about wish fulfilment, and about the raising and assuaging of fears. They deal with all the big events and emotions of human life – love, treachery, desire, jealousy, death – and fit them into a manageable framework. They achieve this by using archetypes – the wicked stepmother, the handsome prince; and symbols – the briar rose, the red riding hood. You can take the symbols a long, long way, but while many readers will be sceptical about accepting, say, the glass slipper as a vagina, most will respond to the basics – Red Riding Hood straying from the path, the deceptive allure of the gingerbread house. There is a deep, wide commonwealth of imagination which links us all in our response to these stories. If you tell a tale to a group of five-year-olds, you'll get the same 'oohs' and 'aahs' and 'no, nos!' at the same moments. Normal children don't have to be taught such responses. They appear to be innate.

Normal children respond in a similar way to the pattern and shape of folk tales – and most of them are highly patterned, with events falling into groups of three, or a phrase repeatedly chanted with slight variations. 'Fee, fi, fo, fum! I smell the blood of an Englishman. Be he alive or be he dead, I'll grind his bones to make my bread.' 'Run, run, as fast as you can, you can't catch me, I'm the gingerbread man!' Presumably these repetitions were useful aide-mémoires in the days when stories were passed down orally, but there's something about them that children find deeply satisfying. Children don't like a story to be interrupted or disrupted. Even if they've heard it before, and know what happens, they want to hear it out, to savour the cosiness of resolution. Indeed, when I was doing my primary school teacher-training course, in 1981, we were told that we should never leave a fairy tale half-finished, to be resumed the next day, in case the lack of resolution gave the children nightmares. This is sound advice.

As we all know, fairy tales are full of grotesquery and horror. Bluebeard's murdered wives, Hansel fattened in a cage, the wolf gobbling up Grandmother – when the real-life equivalents of these events are reported in the newspapers, we don't want our children to know about them. Shocking events such as the disappearance of the Soham schoolgirls lead to discussions about the best way to filter the information for our children, who are bound to pick up on it in this media-saturated society. Why, then, do we think it appropriate to tell stories full of horror to young children? Because if such tales are related in the right circumstances, they help the child to cope with fear. The adult teller, whether parent or teacher, should have a bond with the child, a bond of affection and respect. The telling of the story strengthens that bond. The tale addresses the child's fears, and the affection of the teller reassures the child that fears are normal, and shared. Human life does contain violence and sorrow. It also contains beauty and joy. Fairy tales shape these extremes into something the child can manage, and the telling of them lets the child know that he is not alone in the frightening, enthralling adventure of life. The adult is beside him, guiding him, consoling him, implicitly letting him know that, yes, I've felt the things you're feeling now. Fairy tales properly told are resonant and thrilling; danger and beauty are closely linked. Fairy tales should never be bland.

Fairy tales are also a receptacle for cultural memory. They pass on experience from one generation to the next. They present good advice, both practical and moral, in a palatable form; don't wander off the path; be brave and truthful. The normal child has no difficulty in generalizing the advice. She can see that *Hansel and Gretel* is not warning you against nibbling houses made of gingerbread, it's letting you know that things – and people – are not always what they seem. Similarly, the normal child has little problem in distinguishing goodies from baddies. Archetypes survive and flourish because they do have universal meaning. Even a three-year-old can detect the wiles of the smiling fox, feel anxious on behalf of the foolish goose.

And the normal child will swiftly find someone with whom to identify. She'll place herself in the story; she's not just a passive listener. A girl will usually identify with a female character, a boy with a male, though of course there'll be many exceptions. And the huge range of stories provides plenty of role-model choice. I had little time, myself, for the passive Sleeping Beauty, trapped in suspended animation until the right man came along. I identified with the brave, resourceful little girl who goes to call on Baba Yaga, the bony-legged Russian witch, and wins the support of the dog, the cat, the servant girl, the creaking gate and the birch tree. With their aid, she outwits the witch and lives to tell the tale.

For autistic children, very little of this applies. I read the simpler folk tales aloud to George and Sam from an early age, and they found favourites among them. George, far more book-orientated than Sam, had a stronger response. His favourites were – are – 'The Three Bears', 'The Three Little Pigs', 'The Gingerbread Man', 'The Little Red Hen' and 'Jack and the Beanstalk'. He quite likes 'Red Riding Hood', and 'Snow White' and 'Beauty and the Beast' reached him via Disney. George's story choice has always tended to dominate, so, mainly due to exposure, these are also the stories Sam has shown most interest in, especially 'The Three Little Pigs'. The stories they like are strong on repeated phrases. '"Who's been eating MY porridge?"' '"I'll do it myself," said the Little Red Hen'; '"I'll huff and I'll puff, and I'll BLOW your house down"'; both boys find such phrases satisfying and amusing, and for George there's also a pleasant frisson of alarm. The props are solid, and come within the boundaries of their experience – the porridge bowls, the house of bricks, the giant's egg-laying hen. The stories are linear, uncluttered, and do not rely heavily on deception and magic, both of which confuse the boys. The more complicated, fantastical tales, like 'The Twelve Dancing Princesses' or even 'Cinderella', fail to hold their attention, because they call on powers of imagination which George and Sam just haven't got.

So, the boys aren't indifferent to folk tales. But it seems to me that the universal resonances, the powerful symbols that I've been discussing, don't do the business for them. They don't feel a shiver of fear at the thought of the great dark forest. They've no desire to right wrongs, to oust the wicked stepmother and restore the status of the displaced child. They do not instinctively see that wolves and foxes are in one camp, little pigs and hens in another. For years, George loved *The Tale of Jemima Puddleduck* (not a folk tale, I know, but with many similarities to one). He had read it and watched it on video time and time again. One day I asked him, 'George, is the fox bad or good?' 'He's good,' said George. 'Why do you think he's good?' 'He's smiling.'

Hampered by such a profound misunderstanding of motive, and indifferent to miracles and magic (when so much of the real world is baffling to autists, how can you expect them to be impressed when a frog turns into a prince?), what's left for the autistic reader of fairy tales? A response to pattern and shape – yes, that's quite strong in both my boys. But it's a desire for pattern for its own sake. A half-told tale might (*might*) irritate George or Sam just because it's incomplete. They won't suffer from the sense of psychological disruption, the feeling that we can't leave Hansel stuck in the cage, that would trouble Jake.

A relish for quaint and repeated turns of phrase – yes, in George's case that's probably what he likes best about these stories. A means of addressing and allaying fears – no, absolutely not. Autistic people do have fears. Sometimes, their lives are dominated by fears and anxieties. But these fears are rarely the ones we commonly share. In his fascinating book *Nature via Nurture* (Fourth Estate, 2003), Matt Ridley discusses common phobias – snakes, spiders, the dark, heights, deep water, small spaces, thunder. He points out that these were genuine perils to Stone Age people but are not things that most of us need to worry about nowadays. And yet we have failed to replace these phobias with more rational or relevant ones such as cars, skis, guns, electric sockets. He suggests that the human brain 'is pre-wired to learn fears that were of relevance in the Stone Age. And the only way that evolution can transmit such information from the past to the design of the mind in the present is via the genes.' Are the genes inherited by autists faulty in this respect? Ridley quotes experiments which indicate that fear conditioning depends heavily on the amygdala, a small almond-shaped structure near the base of the brain. The amygdala has been found to be abnormally shaped in autistic people. Perhaps heritable fears simply don't take root in autistic brains. I'm prepared to be corrected, but I haven't come across an autist who shares any of the Stone Age phobias listed above. Indeed, autists often conspicuously and inconveniently lack a fear of heights or deep water. Instead, autistic phobias tend to be one-offs, like Sam's broken chairs, or polystyrene, or a boy I know who was phobic about fruit, seedlings, and penises.

Of course, innate fears are reinforced by adult behaviour. A mother who screams at the sight of a spider will confirm an incipient fear of spiders in her watching daughter. And as autists have a greatly reduced capacity for imitative behaviour, it's unlikely that they will learn fears in this way, whether rational or irrational. It's interesting that parents can teach a rational fear to a neurotypical child, but only up to a point. They can teach the child to be wary of traffic, but they are unlikely to inculcate a deep, shuddering, giddy-making response to the sight of a car. And if their child's autistic, they'll have a hard job teaching even basic road sense.

Autists feel fear, anger, panic, joy, love. They feel most things, but their feelings are somehow displaced. Press the right buttons, with neurotypical people, and you activate certain feelings. The buttons are in predictable places, as Hollywood knows only too well. Autistic buttons are very hard to find. 'How does it feel?' asks the girl, after she kisses Dustin Hoffman in *Rain Man*. 'Wet,' he replies.

Back to fairy tales. They are unlikely to speak to autistic fears, or autistic desires. The autist is unlikely to identify with a character, because, as we've seen, he lacks a theory of mind, and he exists in the here and now. Jake might well think, I want to be like that prince, strong and handsome, slashing through the brambles and winning the prize. These are social ambitions; Jake, like many little boys, wants to be top dog. George and Sam have no social ambitions. They have no true ambitions at all. They do not place themselves in a social context. Their sense of their own identity is too frail or too rudimentary to be properly projected on to that of any other character, real or fictitious.

That business about story-telling strengthening relationship bonds; that hardly applies, either. I can see a vestige of it. George likes to choose who will read his stories to him, and he associates certain adults with certain stories. But neither he nor Sam has the sense that they are co-adventuring with the adult reader. Jake likes me to make up stories with both of us in them, he in a leading, me in a supporting role. (He likes to have George and Sam in them too – 'But you can make them not autistic, Mum.')

Jake shows a very obvious, very normal, unconscious understanding of the uses of enchantment. His brothers do not.

It almost goes without saying that autists won't pick up on the practical wisdom or the moral of the story. They have a hard enough time generalizing in real life – it doesn't come naturally to them that 'don't tip Ribena down the sink' also means don't tip wine, milk, coffee, Fanta or lemon barley water either. So it's highly unlikely that the body of folk wisdom passed down in fairy tales over the centuries will have any impact on them.

To sum up, then, it seems to me that autistic people fail to respond to the symbols and archetypes that resonate for neurotypical people the world over. What has this got to do with Sam and his regression? Well, what I'm trying to suggest is that behaviour which in a neurotypical person would indicate psychological disturbance does not necessarily indicate any such thing in an autistic person, because the psychology of an autistic person functions so very, very differently.

I have to be careful here, because I don't want to suggest that autistic behaviour never reflects their experience (it does), or that they have no profound emotional life (they do). Sam has a tendency to obsessive-compulsive behaviour, which increases at times of 'emotional' stress. Recently, Ian, our nanny, went to hospital, and was away for three weeks. Sam's obsessive behaviour – opening and closing doors, taking shoes on and off, endlessly retracing his steps – reached fever pitch. Ian returned; the behaviours receded. Sam does care about Ian, and was made anxious by his absence. But I don't believe Sam was worried about what Ian was undergoing. He didn't think about Ian's pain, or worry that the operation would go wrong. He didn't put himself in Ian's place, thinking, 'I hope I don't have to have an operation.' He was reacting to the change in routine, the loss of the 'games' he shares with Ian, the sense of loss of control that Sam seems to feel when unwelcome things happen.

What I'm sure about is that while many autistic behaviours may look as if they have psychological origins, the real cause is likely to be physical or sensory. A normal seven-year-old who smeared faeces over his hair, clothes and bedroom, would certainly be expressing anger or upset. That wouldn't be true at eighteen months, but it would be true at seven. The seven-year-old knows what the social norms are, regarding excrement. He knows that smearing will produce shock, anger, revulsion, in an adult. If he smears, then for some reason he wants to invite those responses. His behaviour is a challenge to his adult caretakers. George, at seven, often smeared. He knew I would be angry, but that wasn't the effect he was after. He was interested in the physical properties of excrement, and it was worth enduring the trivial matter of my outrage to explore these properties to the full. I found him watching an episode of *Pingu* when Pinga, Pingu's little sister (incidentally, one of *the* great characters of children's television) daubs herself all over with paint. George had done the same thing to himself, but with shit. It was the nearest thing to hand.

Where does this leave psychotherapy in relation to autism? That's an important question. Until quite recently, most health professionals believed that autism was a psychosis. It was only in the 1990s – after George's diagnosis – that the genetic component was firmly established. It's only now, in the 2000s, that the structure of the living brain can be examined, and though this study is in its infancy it looks as if autistic brains are structurally, physically different from normal ones. The child is born with autism. That's what I believe, and that's increasingly widely accepted. But in the 1960s, when Clara Park's Jessy was a child, autism, often called childhood schizophrenia, was believed to result from cold, inadequate parenting. Park cites Bruno Bettelheim, who wrote that parental rejection is an element in the genesis of every case of childhood schizophrenia [autism] that he has ever seen. Bettelheim, author of the hugely influential book *The Empty Fortress*, has been much misquoted; I believe that he never actually used the notorious phrase 'refrigerator mother', which has been widely attributed to him. But he certainly saw autism as a result of nurture (or lack of nurture) rather than nature. Kanner himself considered that parents must play a large part in the onset of infantile autism. He summed up the parents of his autistic patients as 'detached, humourless perfectionists, more at home in the world of abstractions than among people'. And Beata Rank, an American psychiatrist, set out as her main hypothesis that 'the atypical [autistic] child has suffered gross emotional deprivation . . . the younger the child, the more necessary is it for us to modify the mother's personality'.

The Parks and the other parents of their generation, in addition to the hard work of looking after an autistic child, had to bear the burden of suspicion that the child got that way because of their emotional inadequacies. Never mind that they had three other happy, bright, sociable children; in the eyes of the doctors, Jessy was living proof of the emotional inadequacies that must lurk behind their façade of normality. I consider myself very fortunate that I came to autism in a more enlightened era. No one has ever suggested to me that the boys' autism is my 'fault'. But this pervasive assumption about the origins of autism of course led to the conclusion that psychiatric intervention, including the techniques of psychotherapy, would help.

When George was five, we had a consultation with Dr Anne Alvarez, of the Tavistock Clinic. She is an intelligent and sensitive person, and she wrote a perceptive and thorough report on George; many of her comments still ring true. She attributes quite a lot to his difficult birth, and tactfully but clearly indicates that she regards our parenting as inconsistent and too indulgent. She underestimates – in my opinion – his echolalia, and the eccentricity of his play. She notes, for instance, that he 'began mumbling . . . the Lord's Prayer to himself', without remarking on the oddness of this choice for a five-year-old child brought up in a non-churchgoing household. (I remember George's version of the Lord's Prayer – it included 'Give us this day our staley bread,' and 'As we forgive those who are pressed up against us.') But she comments accurately and enthusiastically that his grasp on her hand was 'affectionate, controlling and even possessive. He's an intense, probably quite passionately attached little boy when he lets himself go, and he has a very strong will . . . he is not in a fixed state of withdrawal.' She recommended psychotherapy, and we followed this up.

The ideal, in Dr Alvarez's opinion, was three sessions a week. This was beyond our financial means; it would also be impractical, as the nearest suitable practitioner worked thirty miles away. We compromised; George had one session a week, for several years. We gave it up when we started ABA, in the interests of redirecting time and money. The psychotherapy did George no harm, and in some ways it did some good; the therapist realized, for instance, that George over-identified with Sam, and was using Sam as a screen between himself and the real world. She worked, successfully, on decreasing his dependence on Sam. Having any bright, kind, sympathetic adult interact closely with your autistic child on a regular basis is a good thing, so as far as that goes psychotherapy could be of use. But I feel that, as a system, it underestimates the autisticness of autism, and misinterprets symptoms that may well have an organic rather than a psychological origin. I did smile quietly to myself when George pooed in his pants in the therapy room, and his therapist told me that she was 'glad that he felt able to bring something to the session'. Hmm. Beware of geeks bearing gifts.

Thank goodness, no professional has ever, in Beata Rank's chilling phrase, attempted to 'modify' my personality. The extremists of the 1950s and 1960s no longer operate – not in East Sussex anyway – and no one could have been more benign than George's therapist. But I do feel that, as far as autism goes, psychotherapy is based on false assumptions. There's something about autism that makes it more psychotherapy-resistant than any other condition. When it comes to the imagination, the emotions, the operation of the subconscious, there's very little common ground. The usual instincts just aren't there.

10. Mild Peril

Spring 1999. Sam, my Aunt Meriel and I stood in the cathedral cloister at Hereford. Meriel, being the Bishop's wife, lives in the Palace; we had left George and Jake under the supervision of the Palace staff while we nipped out with Sam for a change of scene.

We whirled through the cathedral – Sam's whole-hearted enjoyment of church acoustics keeps such visits brief – and out into the cloister. Sam was with us. We stooped for one second to examine the inscription on a memorial – and Sam was gone.

Sam had often disappeared at home, but I'd worried less about that, because he has an excellent sense of direction. When Sam is 'lost' he's not truly lost, just absent without leave. But this time it was different. Sam didn't know Hereford, not beyond the Palace and its grounds. We were right in the centre of the city. The dangers were real – crowds, traffic, the wide, fast-flowing River Wye.

Calling to an autistic child is pointless, because even if they hear you, they don't usually feel any need to respond. I tend to do it anyway, because it's what mothers do when children are lost. At home, when we're walking on the farm, I can often locate Sam not because he listens out for me, but because I listen out for him. Sam may not say much, but he's rarely silent. He drones, hums, vocalizes and bangs his hands together to the accompaniment of a nasal sound like that of a deep-toned mosquito magnified several thousand times. When he was younger, his noises bore closer relation to 'real' sounds. For instance, he used to do a cheerful and accurate imitation of the torrent of bloodcurdling abuse our neighbouring farmer used to hurl at her sheep. He would imitate a drill, a chainsaw, or the final, climactic shudder of the washing machine. Over time, these sounds have become abstracted from their originals, and now form a flow of white noise, an external tinnitus, which has the useful side effect of enabling me to find Sam even when he is some way off.

Hereford City Centre, however, is crowded with sounds competing for attention. Meriel and I ran round the cathedral precinct for a while, vainly calling, and then I ran back to the Palace and rang the police. It is odd, and infuriating, that when one dials 999 one is asked to supply a full address before any action is taken. I found myself having to repeat a distant postcode – 'No, not M for mother, N for nutter' – while Sam, in my mind's eye, ran towards some distant horizon, ever further from reach.

I went back out to find Meriel. She'd found a young man who had seen Sam heading for the river and had called the police. He hadn't stopped him – but why should he? Sam was seven, strong and agile; it wasn't as if he was a wandering toddler. How could a young man grab hold of such a child without fear of suspicion? And if he had got hold of him, what would he do with him then? No use asking Sam his name and address. It was good of the young man to do anything at all, when there was ample reason not to get involved. 'I thought it was a bit unusual,' he said, 'because he went up to a dog, took the ball out of its mouth, and put it in his own.'

We forged on. I can't remember the exact sequence of events, but before long I was touring the city in a police car, eyes peeled. At last a call came through. A woman had found Sam dancing on the treacherous bank of the Wye. She had taken him to the corner shop at the end of the nearest street. We drove there with all speed. Sam was hopping up and down in the middle of the shop, shouting, 'Lollipop!' We bundled him into the police car and returned to the Palace.

Sam was not hurt, neither was he frightened, or even especially bewildered. The whole episode, which had seemed like an eternity to me, had taken, I think, less than an hour, but it would not have made much difference to Sam if he had been away all day. Sam doesn't get frightened because he lacks the capacity to imagine dangers. He doesn't associate me, or adults in general, with security or with protection from fears, so he doesn't mind not being with an adult. Sam does have fears, but they are not the kind that would oppress the mind of a normal seven-year-old alone in an unfamiliar city. To say that an autistic child's fears are irrational doesn't clarify the matter, because all children have irrational fears as well as rational ones. Jake won't go alone up one of our flights of stairs because he fears that Buzz and Woody (from *Toy Story*) are waiting at the top. And for a long time he made me come to the lavatory with him because, he said, Zebedee from *The Magic Roundabout* might boing up out of the pan. Honestly, Jake, I said, I *know* Zebedee isn't in there. No, said Jake, but when you were four you would have thought so.

But Jake, alone and lost in Hereford, wouldn't have worried about Buzz or Zebedee. He would have prioritized his fears; his main concern would have been to get back to me, and he would have known that explaining his predicament to another adult would have been the best way to effect this. At present, Jake is worried about kidnappers, because of a note his school sent home about the strange behaviour of an individual seen in the village. Jake holds my hand tightly when we're out, and if we see anyone who fits the police description ("chubby, balding, 5'5"") he urges me to ring 999. He is particularly anxious that Sam might be kidnapped, though somewhat cheered by the thought that anyone who kidnapped Sam might reconsider their chosen career path. Sam has no such worries. Sam's fears would remain approximately the same whether he was careering along through crowds and traffic or safe at home with me.

Some autists are gripped, dominated, by fears and anxieties. I remember hearing a very able autistic man, a graduate, eloquently explaining that the sight of a pencil near the edge of a table, where it might roll off, produced in him an anxiety as intense as the news of a car crash. Neither of my boys suffer to this extent. George is more fearful than Sam; his worries are more conceptual, like not wanting to grow up, and at times they do limit his activities, though they eventually recede. Sam sometimes shows distress at unfamiliar surroundings – I've noticed that he's very unlikely to eat anything away from home – but apart from that, the only true fear he seems to have at the moment is of dogs. When we walk in the woods, if a dog approaches, be it a Great Dane or a Yorkie, he will spring into my arms – so it's not quite true that he doesn't use people as protection, though I think he uses me as a physical rather than an emotional refuge. But his fear of dogs doesn't prevent him from going on the walk in the first place. The dogs always seem to take him by surprise.

The Hereford incident was the most worrying, because we were so far from home, but there have been many similar escapes. Police helicopters have been called out on several occasions. When I was enormously pregnant with Jake, and simply couldn't move fast enough, I lost track of Sam on our farm because George was playing near water and I thought it was dangerous to leave him. My search for Sam proving fruitless, I returned to the house. I was on the point of calling the police when the doorbell rang. A neighbour, who lives a mile or so away, was holding a naked Sam. She'd taken off her coat and wrapped it round him. It was January, but Sam, naked, barefoot, and scratched by brambles, had seemed quite cheerful when she'd found him in the woods. A couple of days later, the police called. A walker had found a pile of children's clothes by a stream. A nametape had located our GP. Police and social services made inquires of the GP and of Sam's school, concerning, I imagine, my fitness as a parent.

Sam's youthful passion for oast houses left him with a dominant ambition – to reach a particular oast which stood on the top of a hill about a mile and a half away. When Sam escaped from home I think he was usually trying to reach this Nirvana. Once he succeeded. Its owner, taking an afternoon nap, was startled to be joined in bed by a small boy still wearing his wellington boots.

It wasn't always Sam. Devon police once retrieved George from a pig field near his grandparents' house – he'd gone out at dusk to have a wallow in the mud. George moves more slowly than Sam, who can outrun the wind, but if he gets an idea into his head he's hard to stop. He developed a mini-obsession about Brambly Hedge, a series of books and videos about fancifully dressed mice who live in minutely detailed citadels among twisted roots. He convinced himself that Brambly Hedge could be found in a field opposite our house. This field can only be reached by crossing an extremely busy A-road. He also convinced himself that Danny, one of his school 'friends', dwelled therein. Danny is a solid, sturdy lad; it's hard to think of a less likely resident for Brambly Hedge, unless it might be John Prescott, but George was determined to go and look for him. This caused me considerable worry as George has no more road sense than a hedgehog. Thank goodness, the dream seems to have faded.

Autists have very little common sense. In fact, 'common' sense is exactly what they don't have. They may have survival instincts; Uta Frith, in *Autism: Explaining the Enigma*, has suggested that 'feral' children, such as Victor, the 'Wild Boy of Aveyron', were in fact autistic, and this seems highly plausible to me, not least because autism would explain a) why the children were abandoned in the first place, and b) why they didn't seek human help, even though in some cases they were found close to settlements.

Some of these children survived for long periods using considerable ingenuity, and I don't doubt that tough, fearless Sam would do pretty well left to his own devices, though the vague, limp-wristed George wouldn't last five minutes. So autists do have sense, of a kind. But 'common' sense is closely linked to social sense, and this is something they find almost impossible to acquire. They don't see the way things fall into patterns, they can't generalize from one situation to the next. If his brothers have been painting, Sam will wash up their palettes and brushes, but he'll also wash up their finished paintings. The cleaning-up process is, he knows, a way of getting rid of paint. He doesn't see that paint on paper is desirable, paint on the palette disposable. George wants to go to the shop. 'Put your shoes and socks on,' I say. A while later (he takes ages to do anything) George is standing by the front door, waiting. Are his shoes and socks on? Yes – on one foot.

Few autistic people are able to lead unsupervised lives as adults, almost regardless of their level of intelligence. Many lower-functioning non-autistic people with 'learning difficulties' cope far more effectively in terms of self-care and social integration, because, whatever their problems, they do have some common sense. And they can transfer learned ideas from one situation to another. A non-autistic person of low IQ might well grasp that 'Don't touch that broken glass' applies to all broken glass, not just that particular piece. An autist, even one of high IQ, cannot generalize in this way. 'Don't touch that broken glass' means don't touch that piece, here, now, on the floor in front of you. The instruction will not be retained and applied to future broken-glass encounters.

George has always loved fires. In our big, cold, old house open fires are not an indulgence but a necessity. George sits next to the fire, inching ever closer; every so often I push him and his chair back to where they started from. Once, I was upstairs bathing Jake, and forgot that George and the fire were unsupervised. I belted downstairs to find George, both feet propped on a smouldering log, humming contentedly and gazing at the smoke that curled up from the soles of his shoes.

He finds it hard to resist throwing bits of paper into the fire and watching them flare and die. The trouble is, he's undiscriminating about which bits to use. I've lost important phone messages this way; once my address book was dangled over the blaze, and was only rescued just in time. Sam's much better about fires now, but he, too, had a period of dangerous fascination. He used to throw in large objects – toys, books, cushions. But though this might seem like deliberate naughtiness, and certainly it was accompanied by roguish chuckles, I actually think it was simply what Sam thought you were meant to do with fires. He saw me putting logs on, so he selected approximately log-sized objects. He didn't consider the objects for what they were, nor did he consider that burning them would cause them to disappear for ever. Sam has no sense of the future. Often, the sacrificial victims were things he liked, and I do not feel that he was trying to destroy them. Similarly, when he pours an entire packet of salt into a pan of boiling pasta, he's not setting out to ruin our dinner. He's seen salt go into boiling water; he just thinks that's what you do.

Reading Hermione Lee's biography of Virginia Woolf, I came across Woolf's callous description of her 'backward' half-sister, Laura Stephen, which persuades me that Laura was autistic. 'A vacant-eyed girl,' Woolf calls her, 'whose idiocy was daily becoming more obvious, who could hardly read, who would throw scissors into the fire, who was tongue-tied and stammered and yet had to appear at table with the rest of us.' Laura had odd vocal mannerisms ('a queer squeaking or semi-stammering or spasmodic uttering'). She was 'given to uncontrolled gestures like spitting out or choking on her food', and, to the immense frustration of the whole family, had a 'strange perversity' which meant she disregarded all their reprimands. Hermione Lee raises autism as a possibility; I think it a certainty. Autists ignore requests to stop not because they want to defy you but because they are socially indifferent. They don't mind about upsetting or worrying you – they are largely unaware that their actions affect you. They are driven by a compulsion to perform the forbidden action (like throwing scissors on the fire), and this compulsion is far, far stronger than any tiny amount of social or common sense they might possess.

Constant repetition of 'No' will, in the very long run, have some effect. A short, simple explanation of the reason for the prohibition may also eventually chip away at the compulsive behaviour. Thus George has some respect for 'No, that's dirty' or 'No, that's dangerous', but it has taken years to instil, and is by no means watertight. George no longer smears excrement over his bedroom curtains or over radiators (the heat intensifies the smell). He no longer pulls down his trousers to urinate in public – though he does remove his underpants in public lavatories and stuff them behind the cistern. He knows it's naughty to eat out of the cat's bowl, though sometimes he can't resist the temptation. In such instances, constant nagging has succeeded in rerouting his impulses. Though he can't think things through to their consequences, he does know that certain activities will make me cross, and he doesn't like that.

Sam has only recently begun to care about whether I'm cross

or not. If I really, really yell he looks briefly cowed, perhaps only due to force of decibels. He sometimes shows defiance, which I take to be a good sign, as it indicates a dawning awareness of my reaction. Sam's ABA programme (see Chapter 7) has hugely increased his compliance, so it's now easier than it was to stop him from doing something undesirable, but he still has very few built-in inhibitors. Prevention is still a very important part of Sam-management. There is no still, small voice within telling him not to do dangerous things with matches, scissors and medicines. These all have to be locked away, as does toothpaste, which will be squeezed and smeared, shampoo, which will be tipped down the sink, and cosmetics, which will be crudely applied to his own face and then bitten or finger-painted on to windows. Art materials are also hidden – glue and paint for obvious reasons, felt-tips because their ends will be bitten off, rubbers because they will quite simply be eaten. I have locks on my larder and food cupboard. The lock on my freezer doesn't work, so when I buy a box of ice lollies I hide some in unlikely bags and boxes to make sure he doesn't eat all ten at once. At present, some are in with some frozen coffee beans, others are nestling beneath a pile of 'breaded hoki loins'.

The foods outlawed by his diet, such as 'normal' bread and biscuits, obviously have to be locked up, but he can wreak havoc with many other ingredients. He filled the doll's house bath with runny honey; he grabbed a 1kg bag of currants and ran round the house scattering handfuls as if he were sowing seeds. He hates to eat only a couple of biscuits out of a packet. He'd rather nibble a little of each one and trample the remains under foot. This preference is messy and expensive. Even messier are Sam's occasional forays into cooking. Before I had locks fitted on the cupboards, Sam would pour ill-assorted ingredients into a bowl, stir or whisk them, and then put the whole lot in the oven. He once made a fairly good approximation of a chocolate pudding. I suggested that he put an egg in, so he did exactly that – put in an egg, unbroken. He wouldn't let me crack it. I surreptitiously removed it before cooking as I thought it might explode in the oven. Sam was quite keen to inspect the 'pudding' once cooked, but he didn't want to eat it. He hid it, as I discovered later, under a pile of sofa cushions.

The electric beaters, the food processor and the ice-cream maker are objects of fascination to Sam, the last vestiges of his obsession with things that spin. It is a mistake to leave the ice-cream maker unattended. Sam's additions have resulted in unconventional combinations – strawberry 'n' curry, raspberry 'n' Frosties and banana 'n' plastic dinosaur ice cream.

Some autists are violent. This, I would suggest, might arise more from a weak sense of cause and effect, and a very limited sense of social responsibility, than from an unusually high level of aggression. Most boys fight – most children fight – but they quickly establish rules, even without adult intervention. Biting is outlawed, faces are avoided, opponents are approximately matched for age and size. If such rules are overstepped, playing tips over into bullying, and most children understand the difference. Autistic children engage far less in straightforward fighting than normal children do, because fighting is a version of social interaction, albeit to the adult mind a rather tiresome version. George and Sam rough-and-tumble with each other, and I'm glad they do, because their other play skills are so very limited. When Jake joins in – as, to my surprise, he frequently does – they make no allowances for his size and lack of strength. Again, I welcome this interaction between Jake and his brothers, but I welcome it with gritted teeth, because while I can leave George and Sam rolling interlocked on the floor and know that little harm will be done, once Jake's involved I have to stand there, watching like a hawk.

Autistic violence can be a serious matter. A big, strong girl, intelligent and verbal, who used to be at the boys' school, has had to go to residential school where, I have heard, she has four assistants to keep her under control. She suffered badly from premenstrual tension. Her mother asked the doctor to put her on the Pill to try to reduce the symptoms but was told that to do so would infringe the girl's human rights because she was under age.

Pinches, kicks and bites are common in autistic units – another reason why integration into mainstream is too much for many teachers to cope with. Granny Eva, who works in Sam's unit, wears a padded waistcoat to school which she calls her body armour. Though neither George nor Sam has been uncontrollably violent (yet), both have had phases of pinching or biting. The most serious wounds (not very) have been inflicted on each other, but they bear no grudges, nor ever seem to avoid each other's company.

One of the strongest motives for setting up an ABA programme for the boys was the need to make them more compliant before adolescence struck. Once they were bigger and stronger than me, if they posed real danger to themselves or other people, I knew that I would have no option but to find residential care for them, and I didn't want to be forced into that position. It may be that, one day, residential care is the best option for them. I can't see it at the moment – my strongest instincts tell me to keep them close to me. But if this changes, I want the decision to be made in their best interests, not as a last resort.

Adolescence is only just beginning for George. As I write, he's still a lot smaller than me. I can still lift him up. His voice hasn't broken, though it can't be long now. By the time this book's in print, he'll almost certainly be towering above me. Who knows what furies the hormonal onslaught will unleash? But I'm optimistic that the system of compliance instilled by ABA will be enough to rein in the worst excesses. When George was hurting other children at school, he was given a timer. For every half-hour of pinch-free time, he earned a token. Once a designated number of tokens had been achieved, he could choose his own reward – watching a video, turning on the heater, being allowed to lie on the floor in the quiet room, or whatever. Breaking the no-pinch rule resulted in the removal of a token. This worked well, and it wasn't long before the aggressive behaviour had all but disappeared.

Such a system sounds obvious and commonsensical, but it's taken a couple of years of ABA to get George to a state where he can understand the workings of it. Of course, like every mother, I'd resorted to bribery and barter when the boys were little, including being driven to illogical extremes, as in, 'If you sit down in the dentist's chair I'll give you a lollipop.' But I'd been surprised, and frustrated, at how difficult it was to get them to grasp the concept of a reward, particularly Sam. For children with 'weak central coherence' (see Chapter 11), and severe problems with meaningful sequencing, such obvious dog-training tricks don't seem obvious at all. Sam is only beginning to respond to a 'token economy'; he's way behind George in terms of timers and points systems. But, since ABA, Sam's usual response to 'No' is to stop whatever he's doing, if only briefly. Before ABA, 'No' was little more to Sam than a startling or amusing noise.

Eighteen months ago, Sam's aggressiveness at school was quite a problem. Now, it's almost non-existent. I think this is because ABA has increased his ability to express his desires verbally, which has lowered his level of frustration. His gf/cf diet has decreased his physical discomfort, which obviously helps. And, though most days still include periods of unexplained crying, these periods are short. Sam's range of purposeful activity, which had contracted to almost nothing, is expanding a little. His playfulness and sense of fun, lost for several years, is returning. ABA is slowly making his life more jolly and less boring, so he has less need to liven things up with pinches and bites. And at school, Sam's got things pretty much sorted out. He knows how to avoid most unpalatable demands, and he's adept at risk assessment. When an adult interposes between Sam and his object of desire, I'm told he'll size up such factors as height, breadth and wingspan before making a dash for what he wants.

At one time, Sam's aggression towards Jake was one of our biggest problems at home. The only thing to do was never leave them alone together, even for a second. Now, this aggression has diminished. It will flare up occasionally, nearly always as Sam's response to being thwarted. If Sam's angry with me, he's quite likely to take it out on Jake, by dragging his arm or pushing him off a chair. This is no fun for Jake, but in terms of Sam's development of 'theory of mind' it's quite good news; he looks at me as he does it, keen to see my outraged reaction.

We've had episodes of climbing on the roof and pulling out the tiles, unscrewing light bulbs and smashing them, breaking windows, throwing things out of windows, flooding bathrooms, pushing the television over, tipping up heavy items of furniture. The perpetrator is usually Sam. But the house is still standing, and we're all still alive, not even lightly scarred. I've called this chapter 'Mild Peril', to quote the notes for parental guidance on video boxes, because it's my rather blithe belief that autistic behaviour is not as dangerous as it looks. People do themselves most harm when they panic, and autistic people, like animals, don't panic unless they're cornered. Autists are protected from danger by their inability to think, 'What if?' They also, in a sense, know what they're doing. Their systemizing brains seize on a detail and observe it very, very closely. Watching Sam slice vegetables with a sharp knife strains the nerves, but he manages it with (almost) a chef-like aplomb.

Of course, one cannot be blasé about danger. I have to be extremely vigilant. But I also have to trust my children's balance, surefootedness and concentration on their chosen activity. Autists don't do things half-heartedly, if they've chosen to do something themselves. I take precautionary measures, then I let them go as far as I can without intervening. And I try to relax. I have to believe that they know what they're doing, in a physical sense at least. If I didn't, I'd be a nervous wreck.

11. Blackberries and Tumble-Driers

When Sam was two, he would sit in the bath rotating flannels inside a toy bucket and emitting a loud, continuous drone. A little worry may have flickered through my mind; Sam's noises didn't sound very normal. But once I realized what he was doing, I was reassured. He was pretending the bucket was a washing machine. He was using his imagination – and isn't that what one wants one's child to do?

It took me a long time to recognize that Sam's imaginative play was abnormal. It was limited, repetitive, unshared. Contrast Sam, absorbed in his 'washing machine', with Jake, aged three, manipulating two fronds of bracken, talking to me:

'I'm a mummy wasp. I'm knitting a green jumper for my baby wasp. Mum, you be my baby wasp. No –' as the bracken becomes a steering wheel '– this is the Hungarian Grand Prix. I'll be Michael Schumacher, and you be David Coulthard's brother.'

On the face of it, there may not seem much to choose, in terms of the degree of eccentricity, between turning a bucket into a washing machine and switching in a couple of seconds from being a wasp to being a racing driver. All young children seem barmy at times, which is one reason why autism can be overlooked. But Jake's rapid, flexible thought processes, and his desire to include me in his game, are non-autistic. Sam, rotating flannels in the bucket, was sending his imagination down a single track. It never broadened, it rarely included anyone else, and it never rehearsed behaviour or experiences that would be of any social use to him.

Sam played washing-machine games because he loved washing machines. Like many babies, he had enjoyed being propped in his little chair to watch the spin-cycle. Unlike most babies, he didn't tire of watching the spin-cycle for at least five years. Tumble-driers were just as entrancing as washing machines. We never owned one, which made it a great treat to visit the houses of people who did. Other laundry accoutrements also found favour, though whether by association or as objects of interest in their own right I was never sure. Clotheslines, clothes pegs, the basket I kept the pegs in, irons, ironing boards, soap powder, fabric conditioner . . . Sam would show his enthusiasm by jumping up and down in front of these things, chortling with delight. He talked about them a lot. 'G'anny Ann got red ironing board. Black G'anma [Grandma Hilary, who often wore black] got grey ironing board. Delia got blue ironing board.' By their ironing boards shall ye know them. I drew laundry pictures for him, putting in all the details at his request – 'Dwaw fabric 'dishner. Dwaw pegs.' I usually added human figures to these endless utility-room scenes. 'Here's Mummy,' I would say, brightly. 'Look, here's Sam.' But Sam never requested a person.

He drew his own pictures, too. At four, he could draw a detailed washing machine, with lights, knobs, a door handle, clothes going round inside, and soap powder and fabric conditioner on top. These drawings weren't remarkably skilful – Sam's no Stephen Wiltshire. But they were easily up to standard for his age, and, more significantly, they were by far the best drawings he's ever done. Now, aged eleven, Sam will produce a stick figure if you talk him through it. He never, ever draws unprompted. His pencil control is very poor. And yet, seven years ago, he could draw quite creditable washing machines, because the motivation was there.

Sam's favourite books all had washing machines and other white goods in them. It's surprising how many children's books do feature these things. Sarah Garland's *Doing the Washing* is particularly good because it shows an interesting arrangement of pipes draining out into the bath. We had several of those books for toddlers that encourage naming things round the house – what's in the kitchen, bedroom, bathroom, and so on. The utility-room pages became creased and grimy from much handling – or were torn out, which was the way Sam often treated his favourite things. A video episode of *Old Bear* showed, fleetingly, the edge of a washing machine in the top right-hand corner. Sam rewound the tape until it wore out.

Sam's idea of a good day out was a visit to a launderette. Faced with so many machines, he became so excited he hardly knew which way to turn. When George was doing his Auditory Integration Therapy we spent a fortnight at my brother's house in Islington. That part of London, especially Caledonian Road, was Launderette City. We found a different launderette for Sam to visit every single day.

Once, back at home, I took the boys down a lane to gather blackberries. At that time, George's interest in blackberries was nearly as strong as Sam's laundry obsession, and he spent ages chatting to one particular bush. I failed to look round for perhaps half a minute, and, in a flash, Sam had gone. Dragging George after me, I ran up and down, checking the pond, the little wood, the place where I'd parked the car. No Sam. It was a warm afternoon. The door of the bungalow at the top of the lane was standing open. On a hunch, I looked in. There was Sam, bouncing up and down in front of a washing machine. A very old man in carpet slippers stood staring at him in utter bemusement. I tried to explain, failed, grabbed Sam, and fled.

Sam created washing machines all over the place. He would twist a sock inside a shoe, or chew an apple, spit the bits into a bowl, and shake it, making deafening chuntering noises. Our rocking horse had a round hole under its saddle; Sam filled this with bits of fluff and 'turned it on'. Anything vaguely round would find itself filled with anything vaguely clothy. On his fourth birthday he was given a pink plastic Barbie Laundry Center which was, as one of the party guests remarked, 'almost too successful a present'. Sam had eyes for nothing else, he kept it going all afternoon, hardly pausing even for the cake. His appreciative noises, combined with the Laundry Center's battery-powered whirrings, made conversation difficult.

Sam was famous as the Washing-Machine Boy. At school, his

teacher made him one out of cardboard boxes. Come the Nativity Play, poor Angel Gabriel couldn't find her costume anywhere. She was about to perform, ignominiously, in something makeshift, when the costume was discovered, stuffed by Sam into his cardboard washing machine, wings, halo and all. Washing machines were used as rewards and reinforcers. Sunday supplements and Argos catalogues were rich sources of pictures to be cut out and stuck on to things. I remember the four-year-old Sam watching, open-mouthed, the whole of a documentary about the design of domestic appliances in post-war Italy.

And then there was Mr Bean's visit to the launderette. It has been posited that Mr Bean is himself autistic. He certainly uses autistic logic, as when, packing his holiday suitcase, he finds that a pair of espadrilles won't fit, so he packs only one. He shows autistic delight when one of his little plans works, and like Sam he expresses delight with his whole body. But Mr Bean has a malevolent streak. He enjoys outwitting and discomfiting other people, and this is a very unautistic characteristic.

Sam didn't seem especially drawn to the character of Mr Bean, but he was intrigued by some of his activities. He liked it when Mr Bean drilled through the living-room wall, because drills excited him, and he liked it when Mr Bean caused a baby's nappy to career through a fairground, because he had a thing about nappies, but what he liked best of all was Mr Bean's visit to the launderette. He could see humour in the incongruous objects that Mr Bean put into the machine – a lampshade, a teddy, giant fluffy dice – though when Mr Bean accidentally put on a girl's skirt Sam remained impassive. But the crowning glory of the whole episode was when Mr Bean got stuck inside a tumble-drier. Sam's great ambition was to imitate this feat. He would open the door of the plate-warming oven of our Aga, climb inside, and beg me to shut the door behind him, which of course I wouldn't do. He imitated other actions of Mr Bean's as well. Mr Bean gets a raw turkey stuck on his head, and Sam tried to butt his way into our Christmas turkey. He sometimes imitated other TV characters. He used his Slinky spring as Fireman Sam uses his bullworker, and he stretched his mouth until the corners were sore, in homage to Wallace of *Wallace and Gromit*. But I don't think he ever truly identified with a character. It was more that he mimicked some actions, as George mimicked their turns of phrase.

Mr Bean in the tumble-drier combined two of Sam's obsessions – laundry, and getting into confined spaces. Daniel Shepherd, aged ten, sent me a project he'd made about his autistic sister Rebecca, which included a charming set of photographs of Rebecca inserting herself into the washing machine, the laundry basket, a large flower pot, and so on. Sam used to lower himself into a badger hole in our orchard and sit there in a kind of beatific trance. He was interested in nappies, bandages, life jackets and inflatable armbands; he seemed to like anything which put pressure on the body, whether his own or somebody else's. He visited his Great-Aunt Hilary in hospital and was enchanted by the bandages she had on her legs. That night, I found him lying in his own bed with his swimming armbands on his legs. Aged five, he would pursue female toddlers and lift their skirts to admire their nappies. In one instance this led to his early discharge from hospital. Temple Grandin has experimented extensively with the calming effects of applying consistent pressure all over her body, and indeed has based her career as a designer of cattle-handling equipment on this research.

Washing machines and their ilk reigned supreme, but between the ages of two and six Sam had many other obsessions. Grandfather clocks were sentient beings for Sam; he dreaded them as much as he loved them. At his Great-Aunt Meriel's house, the grandfather clock stood at the foot of the stairs. Sam couldn't get past it to go to bed until it had been covered by a counterpane. But on another visit, he fiddled with the pendulum and broke it. At his Devon grandparents' house he went into the back yard and ran all round the house to the kitchen door, rather than go through the dining room past the grandfather clock. The clocks didn't make him cry, but they exuded a powerful force field that he couldn't cross.

Sam sought out grandfather clocks in books and doll's houses, and, like washing machines, he could draw them quite well. Cuckoo clocks were next best. 'See the hen!' he would shout, longing for the little door to fly open. Alarm clocks were good, too, especially the kind with a pair of bun-like bells on top. The opening sequence of *Fireman Sam* was very satisfactory in this respect. Sam's favourite clock book was *The Day the Clocks Stopped*, about a clockmaker called Timothy Tumblespring. Sam knew this by heart, and would 'read' it at high speed, gabbling the words so they were unrecognizable to anyone not in the know. Alas, he loved Timothy Tumblespring to death. Like so many of his favourite things, including the Mr Bean video, he destroyed it.

He liked barometers, though I don't think he knew what they were for. Come to think of it, I don't suppose he knew what clocks were for, either. He developed special words for his obsessions – to 'yunk' meant to twist the knob on, for instance, a washing machine. 'Stonkers' were the dangly innards of a clock. 'Mushroom hands' were – I think – the bells on top of an alarm clock.

Washing machines and clocks are fairly obvious autistic obsessions. They make noises, they vibrate, they are similar-but-different, and therefore 'collectable'. Sam's passion for oast houses was more unusual. Oast houses are common in East Sussex, where we live. They are cylindrical buildings with cone-shaped cowls on top, once used for drying hops, now mostly converted into desirable residences. Sam would draw them, paint them, make them – he took a measuring cylinder, the kind with 'sago', 'ground rice' and 'gran. sugar' marked out on it, stood it on top of a roll of kitchen towel and announced, 'Oast house!' He liked other odd buildings, too, like windmills and church spires, but his real love was oasts. On the morning of his fourth birthday we drove him round to visit thirty of them.

One of Sam's most idiosyncratic responses was to broken structures. There was a partly demolished oast in a nearby road called Poppinghole Lane. 'Poppinghole' is the kind of word Sam incorporates into his verbal 'stims'; the combination of the name with the glimpse of a 'broken' oast house was irresistible, and I often found myself obliged to make this detour. Sam preferred glimpses to full-on views; he liked to look at things obliquely. A great thrill was to spy bottles of lavatory cleaner through frosted glass. 'Go an' see G'anny blue bockles,' he would demand, so we'd walk up the track to my mother's house and peer at her Harpic. He loved to be lifted up to look in at her kitchen window – 'See G'anny ironing board peeping out.'

Broken clocks didn't appeal, nor did broken washing machines, though he did enjoy seeing these things in inappropriate places. On a Dorset holiday he went into ecstasies over the sight of a washing machine dumped in the River Stour. What really did it for him was an interrupted structure, rather than non-functioning innards. He loved to glimpse an oast through trees, or spot the corner of a grandfather clock behind an open door. On the stairs leading up to our attic stood a chair with a broken back. Sam was drawn to this again and again. He would circle the chair, muttering what sounded like incantations. 'It's as if he sees things we can't,' said one of my friends.

Electric beaters, food processors, ice-cream makers, vacuum cleaners, floor polishers . . . up to the age of five and three quarters it was easy to give Sam presents because he loved the plastic child-sized versions of these things. His birthday presents resembled a wedding list in miniature.

Sam was a great one for visual correspondences. The T-shaped stalk of a bunch of grapes became a folded ironing board; he filled the house with petrol via a trailing loop of jasmine. A head of honeysuckle was a helicopter. He would bend over and shake his long, straight hair until it flew about – another helicopter. I found him crooning over an apple pip – 'No one seems to bother him much, please don't touch.' This baffled me until I recognized it as a song sung about a hedgehog on *Tots TV*, and indeed an apple pip does resemble the aerial view of a hedgehog. When Sam was three, I was in hospital with meningitis. On my return he found a child's plastic brick with a straight line on it, like a subtraction sign. The straight line encased within a square structure was enough to make him say, 'That's Mummy lying down in hospital.' When he was two, objects were designated as helicopters, moons, washing machines or snakes, according to their shape and action. Thus a rotary clothesline was a helicopter, a belt was a snake, a round brooch was a moon, and so on. At the time I thought this a sign of imagination; now I see it as symptomatic of the autistic need to fit everything into a system.

Sam liked animals, though not in the nurturing or anthropomorphic manner of most children. Nor did he have the junior natural historian's love of amassing information about them. As with machines, he enjoyed their sounds and vibrations – the purr of a cat, the beating of doves' wings. A trapped butterfly became yet another helicopter. The butterfly's plight was of no moment.

Poultry was a big interest. Delia, our neighbour, who has been one of my chief helps in bringing up the children, keeps lots of poultry, and both boys liked to be near, or sometimes in, her henhouses. George named the hens, eccentrically ('Stick', 'You're a lovely one', 'You're a no-no'), and relished calling their names, just as he relished the litany of the register at school. Sam liked to crawl in with them, to squat down, cluck, pretend to lay eggs. His imitations were accurate. One day I lost Sam, and, like Tabitha Twitchit, I roamed the house looking for him in every room and mewing dreadfully. I found him inside the airing cupboard, squatting, with an expression of great concentration on his face. 'Go 'way,' he said, 'Sam is sitting on a egg.' Beneath his bottom was a golf ball.

From hens it was but a small step to worms. There seemed to be some confusion over these. Sam always liked snakes, or snake-like shapes. He enjoyed flapping ribbons or ropes or strips of seaweed. Worms came into the snake category, but they also held an association with death. I must, at some point, have mentioned that buried corpses were eaten by worms. Whenever an animal known to Sam died – usually a hen or a hamster, once a peacock, and once a cat – he would intone, 'Worm ate hen' or 'Worm ate Conan [cat]' with what sounded like gloomy satisfaction. He believed that worms lived in the badger holes in the orchard and he would collect 'nutkins' with which to feed them. 'Nutkins', in those days, meant the discarded hazelnut shells lying on the orchard floor; these days, the word is used for any small, round edible object, for instance, Mint Imperials. Sam threw the nutkins into the badger holes as if in propitiation. Was he imagining some vast, devouring worm, lurking beneath the surface?

Unlike high-functioning autists, who are often described as 'little professors' in their desire to find out everything there is to know about their chosen subject, Sam wasn't interested in facts about worms, snakes, washing machines, or anything else. Something about them gave him a buzz – something about their shape or the way they moved. The stimulus for him was sensual, physical, not intellectual. Just because he was interested in some aspects of them, it didn't follow that he had any interest at all in other aspects, any more than the fact that he liked fingering his toy Owly meant that he had any particular interest in owls in general.

This fragmentation of interest is common to all autists, but at the more able end of the spectrum the fragments tend to be larger, and arguably more useful. A high-functioning autist can develop unrivalled expertise in his or her chosen subject, but the fragmentation is still there. It's unlikely that the interest in the special subject will lead on to exploration of areas which, to a neurotypical mind, would seem related. A high-functioning autist might know, say, all the butterflies of Europe but remain indifferent to moths.

What causes this fragmentation? Probably something called 'weak central coherence'. Recent research suggests that differences in the structure and functioning of the autistic brain mean that the autist is incapable of seeing that details are parts of a greater whole. There is a disengagement between central and peripheral devices; the autist can pay sustained attention to one topic, or one aspect of one topic, but whereas the neurotypical brain will instinctively seek to place that detail in a wider context, to relate the part to a whole, the autistic brain confines its focus to the detail alone. In *Autism: Explaining the Enigma*, Uta Frith cites the example of a man who obsessively collected the addresses of juvenile courts. Well-wishers, hoping to expand his horizons, provided him with information about courts of other kinds. The information was rejected. When asked why he didn't want to know the addresses of non-juvenile courts, the autist replied, 'They bore me to tears.'

Fair enough. When George was about six, he became attached to a poster on the wall of the staff room of his primary school. It was a poster issued by the County Council, headed 'East Sussex Advisory, Inspection and Training Service'. It showed the photographs, names and telephone numbers of forty-eight County Council officers – the Appraisal and Assessment Adviser, the Business Education and IT Adviser, the European Links Officer, and so on. George displayed such a passion for this poster that he was allowed to take it home with him. I still have it. I do not understand wherein its appeal lay, but I'd bet that a similar poster of, say, workers for Connex South East, or the Hastings Police Force, would have bored George to tears.

This fragmentation is both the autistic problem and the autistic strength. The intensity of the interest, the phenomenal powers of close observation, give rise to the exquisite chromatic paintings of Jessy Park, the incredible architectural drawings of Stephen Wiltshire, the virtuoso piano playing of Glenn Gould, the advanced mathematical powers of Richard Borcherds (see Simon Baron-Cohen, *The Essential Difference*, Chapter 11). But the other side of the coin is the endless repetitiveness, the insistence on sameness, the refusal to explore and experiment. And this extends to all areas of life. If a child enjoys, say, Cadbury's Flakes, the neurotypical assumption would be that he would also like Galaxy Ripples. But no. It's quite likely that the autistic child will reject Galaxy Ripples, perhaps not even recognizing them as edible. It's also possible that if Cadbury's decided to change the design of their Flake wrappers, then these, too, will be placed beyond the pale.

Autistic interests nearly always seem bizarre. But in most cases it's not the subject itself that's bizarre (*pace* Sam's lavatory cleaner) but the narrowness of the focus. It's not odd to be interested in cars; it is odd to be interested in Peugeots to the exclusion of all other cars, or in only the hubcaps of Peugeots. It's not odd (well, not very odd) to save theatre programmes, or tourist brochures, or even tickets associated with expeditions of special significance or enjoyment to the collector. It is odd to save till rolls. George likes till rolls. At a National Trust shop, he made a sudden plunge across a counter of fudge and tea towels and decorated ginger-bread. He'd seen a piece of till roll lying on the floor beyond, and this was far more attractive to him than anything else in the shop.

George's obsessions were never as all-powerful as Sam's, and in many cases they seemed to be more closely linked to a normal child's play, or to more human concerns. This corresponds to the difference in their characters; Sam is, by and large, socially aloof, more interested in mechanical objects than in human behaviour, whereas George has strong social instincts, which fit Lorna Wing's category of 'active but odd'. Many of George's obsessions have involved characters from children's books or films. I've described his attachment to Pinocchio and Bashful in Chapter 5; he also had a big Mickey Mouse phase. This was when he started primary school, aged four and a half. He was the Mickey Mouse Boy; the other children, who were attracted to George and wanted to be friends with him, bought him many Mickey-related gifts. He would smile shyly at the children when they handed these over. He liked to have a few Mickeys on the table where he worked, or beside him at lunchtime. Mickey became something he could hide behind – he often seemed to use characters in this way, including going through a phase of claiming to be Sam – but I think he was initially attracted to the large eyes and the wide, unequivocal smile. George, atypically, has always been interested in facial expressions, though sometimes he finds them overwhelming. He both likes and fears strongly delineated features; if he sees a picture of Cherie Blair in the newspaper he'll pile lots of things on top of it. Her dark, wide-apart eyes and pillar-box mouth are just too much for him. His fear of men with beards arises, I think, because he finds their faces confusing. They look as if it wouldn't make much difference which way up you turned them.

George also had his Thomas the Tank Engine phase. An admiration for the works of the Rev. W. Awdry is almost a diagnostic requirement of autism; Thomas was chosen as the icon for Autism Awareness Year in 2002. It's easy to see why the engines appeal to a systemizing brain. They each have a name, a number, a colour (though sometimes, alarmingly, they go for a respray), a similar-but-different shape, a designated function. They are predictable; the pattern of their behaviour is interrupted by small mishaps, but these can result in interesting visual variations – Percy's face reflected in a pool of water, James's red paint smeared with coal dust. Their faces are broad and clear, their range of expressions limited and well defined. It's easier for the autistic child to see that Gordon is cross or Percy is mischievous than it is for him to judge the moods of his own mother.

George liked all these features of the engines, but because use of language particularly excited him he also latched on to the Rev. Awdry's characteristic turns of phrase. '"Stow it, you two," protested Bert.' '"I don't know whether I'm standing on my dome or my wheels."' George used to chant these and other phrases constantly, and they still occasionally surface to this day. He developed a particular liking for one of the engines, but, being George, it couldn't be one of the main players, like Henry, Edward or Thomas himself. No, it had to be Douglas.

Douglas is Scottish, and his speech is heavily accented ('"Then awa' wi'ye, Donal', an' tak' yon guids"') which meant reading his dialogue aloud was jaw-achingly tedious for me. He is also relatively obscure, and appears in only a handful of stories and video episodes. In the early 1990s, images of Thomas and friends abounded, but could you purchase a T-shirt, mug or pasta shape in the image of Douglas? You could not.

Douglas is also a twin. Donald is No. 9 and Douglas is No. 10. They are both black, always an important colour for George. Apart from their numbers they are identical, at least as far as I can see. But George only liked Douglas. He wasn't interested in Donald. Donald bored him to tears.

Despite his singling out of Douglas, George usually liked twins, or pairs. He was intrigued early on by the twin-ness of his cousins Will and Kate. My friend Elspeth gave birth to identical twin boys, and George found them enchanting, as indeed they were. He liked to carry round pairs of things – two toy engines, 'James' and 'Mike', a bottle of shampoo and a matching bottle of conditioner, a pair of wooden cutouts of boys playing football, which he named 'Adam' and 'William'. He also developed mild obsessions about colour, and at one stage would only wear black or red. At the moment he favours pink, which isn't that easy when you're dressing a thirteen-year-old boy. He decided that Sam's colour was green, and luckily Sam seemed to concur. If asked to choose something for Sam, George will still usually select something like a green lollipop for Sam, and a pink or red one for himself.

He designated a balloon of a different colour for each of the people in his life. These balloons were imaginary; he would sometimes draw them. He would chant, 'A red balloon for George, a green balloon for Sam, a blue balloon for Mum, a yellow balloon for Delia . . .' Sam enjoyed this recitation, and joined in. When he ran out of colours, George would introduce a 'stripey' balloon, or a 'spotty' one. By and large he would eat only red food, and to this day he uses ketchup to mask unwelcome colours.

I call his colour obsession 'mild' because I've heard of far more extreme cases. George always retained some measure of flexibility. Even at the height of his red/black craze, he would consent to wear his school uniform, which was royal blue and grey. For a while, he liked to carry a small red object – a brick or a car – but it was never hard to separate him from these. I've come across children whose colour obsessions rule their lives, and those of their families.

Some of George's obsessions seemed to develop from fears. It was as if he could master the fear by dwelling on it, never letting it out of his sight. He had a great interest in sea life, particularly whales. He had several factual books with titles like *Creatures of the Deep*, and he would require me to read every word of these aloud, over and over again. 'The ocean is the most varied habitat on earth . . . The different kinds of plants and animals living at various depths have adapted themselves to their surroundings in astonishing ways . . .' I don't believe he understood much of this sort of thing, but he liked hearing it. Whales were tops, followed by dolphins, which fulfilled the criteria of being similar to whales, only satisfyingly different. George invented a third member of this group, the 'wophin'. He talked about wophins with such conviction that his teacher checked on their existence in an encyclopaedia.

He was very frightened of sharks and stingrays. When I reached passages in the books that dealt with these, he'd clap his hands over his ears and make loud 'la–la' noises to drown out the dreaded words. But he didn't want me to stop reading. His love of whales and dolphins arose partly from his dread of sharks and rays. By poring over the one, he could reduce his terror of the other.

The sea-life obsession was also linked to his fascination with water, which had been present from the beginning of his life. I dreamed, once, that George was rocking astride the branch of a pine tree just outside our house. The branch transformed into a dolphin, which bounded off into the twilight, George safely on its back. The dream felt peaceful, and appropriate. I've just watched a friend's old home movie, which shows us in the gardens at Sissinghurst. George, aged six, lies down without warning on the path and stares into a pond, keeping his eyes as close to the water's surface as he can. He remains in that position for some time. People walk by him, even step over him, but he remains oblivious. We took him to garden centres so that he could stare into tanks of tropical fish. I considered buying fish for him, but decided that his love of dropping small objects into water would make life too scale-raising for them.

A strong reaction to water – either for or against – is common in autists. With their highly developed sensory responses, sparkles, ripples, bubbles or crashing waves are experienced more intensely

by them than by the rest of us. Only yesterday, Sam was trans-
fixed by raindrops splashing on to the surface of a horse trough;
he stood watching the circles spread and fade, unmindful of the
fact that he was soaked to the skin. George used to spend hours
muttering by the edge of the pond on our farm. One evening
he wanted to walk there, but I explained that it was too late,
we'd have to go in the morning. The next day he said, on waking,
'The waterlilies have opened their eyes now.' This was his way
of saying, 'It's morning, remember what you promised.' He was
four.

It did seem as if waterlilies had characters for him, or at least
sensate life. He never seemed clear about the difference between
things that could feel and things that could not. I remember him
rebuking me for ironing; 'Too hot! Poor shirt.' Blackberries
became important to him, almost to the point of obsession. He
endowed them with semi-human characteristics. He would stand
in front of blackberry bushes, repeating phrases over and over
again until he'd shaped them into a kind of poem. I noted down
one of these 'poems', composed when George was four years and
eight months:

> Just look at all those blackberries.
> They want them to pick
> And they want them to grow.
> They want them to pick
> And they want them to grow
> The blackberries smiled.
> Pick them down to the ground.

This seems to express his rather Keatsian ambivalence about blackberries. He liked eating them (the only fruit he did eat) but didn't
like them to be picked – he used to urge me to 'stick them back
on the white sides', i.e., the white patch left when one is picked.
There was also a lot of chat about the berries as though they
were people. 'The blackberries have woken up. They come downstairs. They put food in their mouths.'

Nature – weather, seasonal changes, atmospheric effects – held George in thrall. He loved dawn and dusk – we saw rather more of dawn than I might have wished. He made up several twilight 'poems' – 'The sky is washed. The sky is clear. The prickly leaves are turning black,' was one. Another was:

> The light is fading fast.
> All the beasts can talk in the night,
> 'Brm brm,' called out the silver car,
> 'All is ready for the morning.'

Once, waking to find a late fall of snow covering the daffodils, he said, 'We're lost because the spring has gone.' Such remarks were not addressed to anybody, and he had no interest in recording the 'poems'. He would repeat them over and over to himself, not to me, and he always knew when he'd finished with them.

The 'poems' contained phrases from his usual sources – books, songs, videos. The one about the silver car, for instance, owes much to *The Tailor of Gloucester*. But he would customize these sources, rework them until the sound and shape gave him satisfaction. He tried to do this to most things that caught his attention; he seemed to be constantly trying to reshape the world the way he wanted it. He had a mini-obsession with lions and other big cats, which arose, like the sea-life obsession, out of fear. For a long time the *Sainsbury's Book of Big Cats* was a favourite, but unacceptable passages had to be altered. Thus 'lions often kill zebras' became 'lions often play with zebras' and 'Pumas leap on to the backs of animals they want to kill' became 'Pumas leap on to the backs of animals they want to see.' In other stories, the changes were not so obviously made for the purposes of consolation. In Arnold Lobel's *Frog and Toad* stories, George simply reversed Frog and Toad. (These stories were great favourites, because Frog and Toad were a pair, one green, one brown, the-same-but-different.) Often, a minor character would be promoted to a major role. I did my best to follow George's instructions, but I drew the line when his championship of

Moppet and Mittens led him to demand that *The Tale of Tom Kitten* be read without reference to the eponymous hero.

It's hard to know when an interest becomes an obsession, and when an obsession becomes a 'stim'. Everybody has interests, and the existence of a great and dominating interest does not in itself indicate autism. But what the autist does with his interest, what function it fulfils for him, is, I believe, qualitatively different from, let us say, my Uncle Norman's interest in dragonflies. Norman enjoys dragonflies for many reasons, but he does not enjoy the isolated fact of them. Quite the reverse. To Norman, dragonflies demonstrate the importance of biodiversity, and for Norman, as for many people, understanding the need for biodiversity is crucial to understanding human existence. Our survival depends on biodiversity; our moral sense, the sense of responsibility which is a by-product of civilization, obliges us to respect it. Norman has concentrated on dragonflies, but they are the gateway to profound, far-reaching ideas. His interest in them connects different parts of his mind and character, sensual, intellectual, aesthetic, moral and emotional.

As far as I can tell, autistic interests never provide this kind of connection. The obsession seems to assuage the rage for order, or to satisfy some almost physical craving for stimulus. It never unlocks a morality, a philosophy, a world view. This may explain why autistic interests disappear as quickly as they arrive. Norman's interest in dragonflies is only the most specialized part of the love of natural history which has been observable in him since early childhood, and which has directed his career, his choice of dwelling place, his holiday destinations, even, to some extent, his choice of clothes, food and furniture. Barring some catastrophic brain injury or disease, it's inconceivable that he will ever lose interest in dragonflies. Not so with autistic interests. Clara Claiborne Park describes how Jessy reached degree level and beyond in mathematics, but has now lost all interest in the subject except in totting up the cheques she receives for her paintings. Other autists seem to experience the same cut-off. Tree frogs one day, manhole covers the next.

George, who is less deeply obsessive than most autists, now has a few mild interests – dogs, their gender and breed; poultry, ditto; vehicles – when is a truck a lorry, when is a coach a bus? These are the subjects he most often mentions, but they don't dominate either his life or mine. Sam has no interests. The washing machines, cuckoo clocks, oast houses, fabric conditioners, fell from grace in the autumn of 1997, and have never been replaced. Their disappearance marked the beginning of Sam's huge regression. He seemed to move into a world of physical sensation. So distracted was he by the humming and buzzing inside his body that he seemed incapable of thinking about anything at all. I never thought I'd say this, but I miss washing machines. At least they were something you could talk about.

12. Ketchup with Everything

I like food. I consider my relationship with food to be uncomplicated. Unusually among my female acquaintance, I've never been on a diet. I'll try new dishes with alacrity, and I'm a reasonably adventurous cook. By choice, I eat quite healthily. I particularly like vegetables, and I'm not tempted by junk.

It seems to me indicative of the power of autism, therefore, that the diets of both George and Sam are eccentric, unbalanced, nutritionally impoverished and strongly orientated towards junk. I started out with the usual middle-class intentions about feeding my children. Breast was best; solids should be introduced slowly; fruit and vegetables were important; additives, salt and sugar should be kept to a minimum. I was far from fanatical. I had no objection to the odd biscuit, and happily used jars of baby food to save time, particularly when I was working. But during their babyhoods I was careful to introduce a range of tastes and textures, and though I wasn't prepared to eat my evening meal at half past five I did try to be with them and talk to them while they ate.

I would have been astonished, and horrified, if I could have seen into their nutritional future. This morning George breakfasted on six After Eights and some lemon barley water. I was pleased – *pleased* – because lately he hasn't been eating anything at all. Sam had no breakfast. This is common. I set out some Frosties (dry) and a beaker of orange juice, but he tipped the juice down the sink, and ignored the Frosties. The only thing he ate before the school taxi arrived was a sugar mouse, which was the bribe I used to get him out of bed.

Sam takes a packed 'lunch' – a bag of plain crisps, some gluten-free biscuits, some raisins, an apple, a bag of Whizzers (dairy-free Smartie wannabes) and a small marzipan cat made by my mother.

He will eat about half of this. Guess which things he'll leave. George doesn't have a lunchbox, because at the moment he chooses to deny that he eats anything at all. So I smuggle supplies into his taxi on Monday mornings. On arrival, Pat, the taxi escort, conveys the supplies to George's teacher by similar sleight of hand. They are kept in the classroom in a drawer to which George has unrestricted access. Most days he won't eat unless nobody's looking – or until everybody's pretending not to look. The drawer contains Twiglets, crisps, Aeros and Bourbon biscuits – George is not on the gf/cf diet. Some days he gets through quite a lot of these, but today was not one of those days. The note in the home–school book says, 'G. has eaten nothing except a small tube of Parma Violets.'

I don't think Parma Violets count towards the recommended five daily portions of fruit and veg. For years I've been mentally straining to accredit goodness to the horrid things my children eat. Crisps are only potatoes, really, I tell myself; ketchup is a vegetable. It had better be, because it's the only one George eats.

When George is in eating mode – and after five or six days of starvation he'll usually have a kill, like a python – he eats meat smothered in ketchup. Burgers, sausages, bacon, ham, mince, casseroled lamb, sometimes roast meat, chicken curry; he covers all these, including the curry, with ketchup so thick that you can't see what's underneath. Occasionally, chips or potato waffles or even roast potatoes will get the same treatment. I slip a few slivers of vegetable matter in with the mince or the casserole, but as often as not these will be removed, even from deep within the ketchup, wiped clean, and left in a neat row on the kitchen table. George eats no fruit except, in season, blackberries. He does like lemon sorbet, and if he's on top form he'll eat fromage frais in those little pots, raspberry flavour only. Jake gets tired of having to finish up their strawberry-flavour conjoined twins.

There are a few other foods which enjoy bursts of favour – Coco Pops (dry), toast and Marmite – but meat is George's staple, and always has been. It isn't the limitations of this diet that concern me most. I've heard of worse – indeed, I've experienced worse, like the period of several weeks when the only solid food to pass Sam's lips was the top part of Jaffa Cakes. (I threw the pallid sponge bases out for the birds. They bounced, and the birds weren't keen.) More worrying, to me, than the restricted, protein-heavy, over-salted range is the pattern of semi-starvation that has been going on for the past eighteen months.

George's attitude to eating has something in common with anorexia. He has linked eating with growing; well-meaning adults, myself included, have made the usual remarks along the lines of 'Eat that up, it'll turn you into a big strong boy.' But George doesn't want to be a big strong boy, and he certainly doesn't want to be a man – 'I won't be a horrid man with a big black beard.' Eighteen months ago, George changed schools. Like most autists, he finds it hard to cope with change. He wanted to put things back how they were, and as he knew that the new school was for 'big' children, he decided to stop growing.

He has now accepted the change of schools as irreversible, and no longer wants to return to the old one. But the obsession with staying small has remained. Daily, he begs me to tell him that he will not grow up. It's tempting to lie to him in the hope that this will make him more relaxed about food, but though lying may be a successful short-term strategy it stores up trouble for the future (as well as being, well, wrong . . .). His teachers and I attempt to reassure him that though his body will change, the 'George-ness' of him will not. He doesn't find this wholly satisfactory, but it's the best we can do.

When George is in starvation mode, he fights for control over his hunger. 'No tummy, stop rumbling,' he says. 'Be quiet, my tummy. You're not hungry.' He woke me this morning at five-thirty, weeping, demanding, 'Don't cook for me! Never cook for me again! Take that bacon back to Sainsbury's!' He tries to control what others eat, too, putting food in the place where Sam sits at table, or saying, 'Those are for Jake, not for me.' When the food phobia first emerged I did the thing which childcare experts tell you not to do, but which suggests itself naturally to mothers: 'Eat that, and then you can have this.' In George's case the 'this' was

Refreshers or Softmints. The strategy not only didn't work, it backfired. George began to refuse Refreshers and Softmints, and came to regard them with fear and loathing. I then decided to remove all pressure, and offer George no food at all, ever. I made sure that food was left out in places where he could reach it, but I never set it near his place at table. I stopped asking him to sit down. I tried to make no reference whatsoever to food.

This was more successful. Like a shy animal, George would inch towards the food and take a nibble before darting away again. I made no comment, and pretended I hadn't noticed. But one can't instruct other people in all the niceties of one's apparently barmy autism strategies. 'Hello, George,' say cheery visitors. 'What are you eating? That looks delicious. Do you like it?' Piercing shrieks from George. 'It's not mine! I don't like it! I'm not eating!' Food pushed aside; down the snake he slides, back to Square One.

It's not clear to me just how damaging the boys' eating habits are to their physical health. Not very, the evidence suggests, at least in the short term. Both boys have less than their share of minor illnesses; they almost never have a day off school. Sam has had only one course of antibiotics in his whole life, George only three. Admittedly, this is partly due to the difficulty of getting them to take medicine, but I've never felt that they've missed treatment they desperately needed.

Their hair is thick and glossy, their eyes clear and bright. Sam is small, but he still has his splendidly delineated musculature, and he has enormous stamina. George is exceedingly thin. He was last weighed in April 2002, when he'd been denying himself food for about four months; he weighed four stone three, which for a twelve-year-old boy about five feet tall is very, very little. It was round this time that I asked the doctor to look at him. 'He's thin,' he said, 'but he's not in danger. Give him another month, and if he hasn't started eating we'll take action.'

He did start eating, and the only legacy of this, his most prolonged fast, was constipation, which took a few days to sort itself out. On non-eating days, George is floppy; bursts of activity are followed by slumps. He becomes irritable and sleeps badly – but that's been true all his life, the not-eating isn't wholly to blame. At nearly thirteen, he's poised on the brink of his big growth spurt, and I'm hoping his appetite will win the battle with his neuroses. But I can't be sure.

Sam's eating habits and problems are very different to George's, but they're just as hard to correct. Sam was my heaviest toddler by far, and up to the age of two he ate pretty consistently, in his placid, undiscriminating way. The first peculiarity I noticed was when he refused to be spoon-fed, well before his first birthday. He managed his own spoon quite well, ate lots of finger food, and glugged away at bottles of milk, so I didn't see it as a problem. Much later, I realized that this spoon business was not so much a manifestation of independence as his deep dislike of having his head touched. He just couldn't bear the sensation of having someone poke a spoon into his mouth.

At two, Sam rejected all meat, fish, eggs, cheese and vegetables. Increasingly he would only tolerate dry, crispy food – toast, biscuits, crisps. He didn't want milk on his cereal, though he drank it in huge quantities via his bottle. Milk and fruit juice; I told myself that he must be getting the nutrients he needed, even though he no longer ate 'proper' food.

The number of acceptable foodstuffs steadily dwindled, until we reached the tops-of-Jaffa-Cakes-only phase, which must have been when he was about four. He had an appointment with a dietician around this time. She asked me to keep a food diary for four days, to record absolutely everything he consumed, and what it weighed. The diary got off to a flying start: 'Monday. Breakfast – one chocolate-flavour shape out of Advent Calendar. Weight –?' Whatever the dietician's advice was, it didn't come to anything. You can take an autistic child to broccoli, but you can't make him eat.

Like George, Sam has been through phases of eating virtually nothing, but whereas George has powerful psychological motives for starving himself, in Sam's case I think it's mainly a physical problem. Sam seems to find chewing and swallowing difficult.

He'll gag and spit things out, even desirable things like sweets. Sam enjoys quite a wide range of flavours. He'll bite into most kinds of fruit, and even into raw vegetables if I leave them on a chopping board rather than offering them to him directly, but the textures seem to defeat him, and he won't swallow them. Fruit can only be ingested in the form of juice or ice lollies.

It's common among autists to favour certain textures. Sam's preference for crisps, Frosties and Japanese rice cakes is typical – thin, dry, crispy, yellowy-brown is often preferred. As one might expect, autists want sameness in their food; one of Leo Kanner's two defining characteristics of autism was 'desire for the preservation of sameness'. Sam likes food that's the same all the way through, like Pringles or popcorn. He also likes food that comes in a packet, and he hates to leave the packet half finished. But he can't manage a whole packet of, say, biscuits, so he'll take one bite out of each. He likes food with a clear beginning, middle and end. The textural surprises of something like a casserole are anathema to him.

When Sam was tiny, he would drop food from his high chair, as most small children do. As soon as he was released he would scramble under the high chair and eat the bits he'd dropped. Crumbling and scattering food has been an abiding feature. He'll nibble round the edge of a cracker, then break it into little pieces and sweep them on to the floor. He takes little snatching bites, very fast; for him, food is an enemy that needs to be subdued.

On the rare occasions when Sam will eat a sausage or a burger, it has to be smoking hot. Like many autists, he has a high pain threshold; he snatches burgers out of the frying pan with his bare hands. Then he will lick the fat out of the hot pan. He eats ice cream with his fingers, and likes to dab blobs of it all over his jumper. For years he wouldn't use cutlery; we're currently working on reintroducing spoons. Again, a dislike of cutlery is quite common. Thérèse Jolliffe, a very able autistic woman who became a university researcher, says that she has never been able to see the point of cutlery. She made the conscious decision to conform to the inexplicable habits of the neurotypical world where possible, so she has trained herself to use cutlery. Sam has made no such decision.

Once he outgrew his high chair and its constraining straps, it became more and more difficult to persuade Sam to sit down to eat. Again, this problem is widespread. The dilemma for the mother is, do you prioritize social training and 'manners', or do you just try to get food into the child by hook or by crook? I went for the latter, which I now regret. At one stage Sam ate so very, very little that if he opted to eat anything, anywhere – on the floor, in the garden, in the bath – I tended to concur. He liked to sit on top of a large court-cupboard in the kitchen. He was often naked; he would take his Rice Krispies up there and rain them down like some kind of hobgoblin. For years he most commonly ate while sitting on top of the Aga.

Just as I lost control over *where* Sam ate, so I felt powerless about *what* he ate. I am very far from being alone in this. At gatherings of families with autistic children there will always be several parents holding Tupperware boxes containing cold toast and Marmite, or beakers full of a certain obscure brand of herbal tea which is the only fluid their child will accept. George once had a craze for a kind of cereal called Bran Buds – like All-Bran cut up into tiny bits. Bran Buds were not readily available, so family and friends were under instructions to buy up stocks whenever possible. Em, George's godmother, came across them in Nine Elms Sainsbury's. She filled her trolley. At the checkout, the assistant gave her a pitying, inquiring look. 'Oh, they're not for me,' she hastily explained. 'They're for my godson.' Autistic children are very powerful and controlling. Most of the mothers clutching strange specimens in Tupperware boxes have other children who eat an unexceptional balanced diet, and have no special provision made for them.

I've never met an autistic person who ate completely normally, although some come close. Most are extremely picky, but a few go to the opposite extreme and eat indiscriminately, without stopping. Obesity can become a problem in such cases, but many of the 'faddy' autists are noticeably thin. Typical fads involve number

– it has to be five sausages and ten chips; colour – only red foods will do, and by red we're not, alas, talking about tomatoes, peppers and red mullet, but red Smarties, red jelly, Hula Hoops in a red packet; utensils – food can only be eaten off a Thomas the Tank Engine plate; shape – pointed chips must have their ends squared off, toast must be cut into squares of equal size; brand – 'He'll only eat Bird's Eye fish fingers, and, yes, he can tell the difference'; packaging – the whims of food manufacturers, who endlessly alter their packaging, are the despair of many mothers who've relied on frozen lasagne that looks like *this*, and find it won't be touched now it looks like *that*.

Many seem to like extreme flavours – in George's case, curry and ketchup; in Sam's, lemons (biting into the peel), marzipan, and ferociously salty foods. Some will eat most things as long as they're coated with the preferred flavour. Saskia Baron's brother, Timothy, ate little apart from lettuce, until it was discovered that the vinaigrette dressing was what really attracted him. Now he has a good mixed diet because he'll eat most things if they've got vinaigrette on them. Many eat, or at least taste, substances which aren't food at all – soil, coal, soap, paint. George used to raid the cat's bowl. I had a brainwave, and offered him mashed sardines, which to me smell similar to cat food. It worked, for a while.

The best outcome is when an autist can be persuaded to eat certain foods because of their healthy properties. This cuts no ice whatsoever with George and Sam, but I have come across intelligent, hyper-logical people with Asperger's syndrome who will diligently consume the recommended balance of protein, carbohydrate, unsaturated fat, fruit, vegetables, and so on. The Asperger brain likes to systematize things; if applied to diet, this can be good news. Asperger eaters like this are likely to be odder in their eating habits than in their choice of meals. Thérèse Jolliffe, for instance, dislikes 'mixed-up' food, or disguising sauces. She eats one thing at a time; carrots, then meat, then potatoes. The neurotypical habit of loading a fork with several different items seems to her unnecessary and unpleasant.

Drinking is nearly as fraught as eating. It's only recently that the boys have begun to drink plain water, unless you count bathwater. As a toddler, George was addicted to Ribena, which had a bad effect on his mood and behaviour. When I bravely removed the Ribena and substituted red grape juice he improved to the extent that I thought his difficulties were at an end – this was when he was about two and three quarters, pre-diagnosis. Sam can't drink anything without spitting some out and tipping some more down the sink. If given straws, Sam blows bubbles. If allowed to pour his own drinks, he fills the cup until it overflows. Sam likes wine. If I set my glass down for a moment, he'll take a swig, swill it round his mouth, and spit it back into the glass. A flyer arrived advertising a local wine-tasting event. Jake drew my attention to it, earnestly suggesting that it would be something Sam might enjoy.

Many normal children are, of course, faddy eaters. My cousin Henry went through a stage when he would eat only sieved raspberry yoghurt and Kraft cheese cut into the shapes of First World War bi-planes. Such peculiarities should not be taken as symptomatic of autism unless there are similar eccentricities in other areas. Four-year-old George would ask for a boiled egg, weep when the shell was broken, demand that I 'put the bits and pieces back on', eat the egg, then turn the empty shell upside down so that it looked whole. Jake, at the same age, cried when I threw crusts to the hens, 'because we'll never see that poor toast any more'.

In Chapter 7, I described Sam's gluten- and casein-free diet. Life with and for Sam has changed immeasurably for the better since I implemented this. His 'stimming' has reduced, he is far more sociable and playful, his ability to process what is said to him is much better. I intend to keep him on the diet for the foreseeable future.

More information about this diet can be found via the addresses and reading list at the back of this book. The 'opoid excess theory' on which it is based is, at time of writing, only a theory; no scientific studies have, as far as I know, proved or disproved it. I have no scientific ability, and I don't want to make the diet into a soapbox issue. All I can say, in common with many parents, is that Sam's pre-diet behaviour fitted the description of a child suffering from 'opoid excess', and the improvements following the diet have been obvious to everyone who knows him. The theory, in brief, argues that the guts of some autistic people cannot properly break down gluten and casein. The fragments of these proteins – peptides – pass through the wall of the gut; autistic gut walls are more likely to be damaged than most. The peptides travel round the body, damaging the central nervous system and the brain. The gluten peptide is gluteomorphine and the casein peptide is caseomorphine – as the names suggest, the action of these peptides is similar to morphine, which is why the pre-diet behaviour of children like Sam can resemble that of a junkie.

My assumption is that the unsuitable foods slowly harmed Sam throughout his early life until at nearly six he overloaded. It took me a while to get the diet going – I had to cross all the usual mental boundaries, thinking it was too difficult, too expensive, too time-consuming, not nutritionally balanced, and so on, but once I'd actually started, improvements were evident within a few weeks.

So, what can Sam eat? In theory, any meat, fish, fruit or vegetable. Eggs, rice, maize, potatoes, nuts, pulses, beans, tofu, soya . . . the permutations are endless. The snag is, of course, that Sam doesn't recognize most of these things as foodstuffs. At the moment he relies heavily on rice crackers, gf breakfast cereals, extremely expensive gf biscuits, and 'potato products'. The 'best' things he eats are eggs, in the form of a bi-weekly omelette, and gf sausages and burgers – maximum once a week. He eats a daily vitamin tablet, but won't touch the special nutritional supplement provided by the dietician. But I don't feel guilty about the low nutritional value of Sam's diet. In nearly every respect, it's nutritionally superior to the junk he ate when he was free to choose.

Sam now sleeps soundly. His stomach is flat, he never screams (though he does still cry, usually once a day), he can sit down and concentrate, and his bitten hands have nearly healed. He still likes sweets, but this terrible restless craving has gone. Why, if this diet works so well for Sam, have I not implemented it for George? Partly cowardice. George, being so much more vocal than Sam, would put extreme pressure on me were I to interfere with his eating arrangements. Partly because George has a little bit more of a social life than Sam, and it's much harder to say 'No, you can't have that' when you're eating outside the home with other people. Partly because George has such a complicated psychological relationship with food that I don't want to risk rocking an already unseaworthy boat. But most important of all, I don't believe that George has the same digestive problems as Sam. He has never had a swollen stomach, loose stools or screaming fits. He has never exhibited any junkie-type behaviour. He has never mutilated himself; his pain threshold seems to be much lower than Sam's. In the case of diet, as in most other things, they're worlds apart. Two very different boys; same diagnosis.

13. Education, Education, Education

When George was diagnosed by Dr Gilly Baird, she told us that the right education was the only effective 'treatment'. Chapter 7, on interventions, makes it clear that I consider several other treatments worthwhile, but in essence I agree with Dr Baird. No diet or vitamin supplement is going to magic away true autism. You use diet, or supplements, or AIT, or whatever, to get your child as well as you can, and that will help them to learn as well as they can – but that may still be not very much.

What is the 'right' education, though? That's a subject of much debate. At the time of writing, national and local government favour a policy of inclusion; special-needs children should be included in mainstream schools if at all possible. I believe this policy to be wrong; wrong as in misguided, and in some cases wrong as in immoral. I also believe that current practice is storing up enormous problems for the future.

All case histories are different. But I feel able to speak with some authority, because I've tried both mainstream and special education for my boys. George, as outlined in Chapter 6, started in a mainstream nursery school, aged three. At that time, pre-diagnosis, we were hoping that the routine of school and the contact with other children would iron out some of his peculiarities and antisocial behaviours. Of course it did nothing of the kind. It was a lively, well-run nursery, one I'd have warmly recommended for any normal child. And George was not so 'lost' that he couldn't get something out of it. He enjoyed some of the activities, shied away from others. He learned to write his name, very large, on two sheets of A4 Sellotaped together. After the trauma of the first few weeks he seemed quite happy; he learned new songs and rhymes and reproduced these at home with pleasure. He memorized the register, and seemed to relish the fact of the children's names. He even seemed to single out a couple of children as 'friends', though these friendships didn't extend as far as inviting anyone home for tea. On sports day, when George's autistic lack of competitiveness and team spirit were clearly apparent, he cheerfully allowed himself to be towed up and down by one of those kind-but-bossy little girls who in later life will run the PTA with aplomb.

I don't think that George's mainstream nursery experience harmed him, except that by keeping him there we deprived him of special help, of the kind of intensely structured, individually tailored learning that would have targeted his deficits and smoothed out some of the bumps in his intellectual and social development. But such specialized nursery teaching is not easy to come by, and besides, by the time George was diagnosed he had less than two terms left before he reached the age for 'proper' school. If we'd been very, very clued up, we'd have either found him a special-needs nursery or started a home programme for him ourselves, but for a long time we'd believed that our son, far from being handicapped, was in fact exceptionally bright. It would have taken a great leap of imagination to look at George aged three and declare, this child is wholly unsuited to mainstream education.

The educational psychologist assessed him, and judged him ready for mainstream primary school, starting in the Reception class at the age of four and a half. He received a Statement of Special Educational Need – these are, I gather, increasingly hard to obtain – which meant that he was entitled to a certain number of hours per week of extra help. His helper was Ruby Cruse, who worked at the school as a dinner lady and classroom assistant. Ruby continued as his helper throughout his time at the school, and once our ABA programme was running she became one of his tutors. She was a great friend to George and a huge support to us all. She died of cancer a couple of years ago, and her loss was deeply felt.

We chose our village school, where my brothers and I had been pupils in the baby-boom 1960s. In those days the classes were huge – up to forty children, with just one teacher, and no assistant. We sat in rows and trilled 'London's Burning' on our recorders as our free milk stood in a crate by the radiator, the cream rising unappetizingly to the top of the third-of-a-pint bottles, each lid pierced by a paper straw. We learned our joined-up handwriting in great loopy swirls, rows and rows of fs and gs of almost Elizabethan elaboration. Girls and boys separated for needlework ('binca') and woodwork ('balsa'). The playgrounds were segregated, of course, and the lavatories were all outside; the boys peed against a wall into an open drain. In Assembly we sang our way through *Hymns Ancient and Modern* and recited the Apostles' Creed. I was put in a corner for whispering during a tracing lesson. Even aged five, you could be rapped on the knuckles by a ruler, and for grave misdemeanours the older children were hit by the headmaster, who kept a slipper for the girls, a cane for the boys.

It was a happy school; we took the cane and the slipper (which were sparingly used) absolutely for granted, in the way children do. I daresay much of the teaching was fairly humdrum. Maths was still mainly about a farmer taking his wheat to market to sell at sixpence ha'penny a bushel; if he sold nine bushels, then . . . We wrote it all out in laborious columns. I remember being forced to insert adverbs into a story I'd written, and being aware, even then, that they were injurious to my prose style. But the work didn't concern me much; I lived for the life of the playground. I spent six years there, and they were rich and vivid.

So I was pleased, for sentimental reasons, to be sending George to the same school. It had changed a great deal. By the 1990s, primary schools had become much more child-orientated. The classes were much smaller – I think there were only twelve in George's year. The old hierarchies had gone. The staff were more affectionate and involved with the children, and the older children had a lot more to do with the younger ones. The three Rs were still taught effectively, but in interesting and creative ways. There were computers, a library, a cooking area. There was more to art teaching than the three pots of primary colours and the single sheet of paper bulldog-clipped to an easel that had characterized the Friday afternoons of my childhood.

Of course, the school wasn't perfect. But it was pleasant and busy and it had a positive atmosphere. The headmaster hadn't come across autism before, but he was keen to learn, as were the other staff. When I described George's condition, the head asked whether he was likely to wander off, perhaps try to walk home? I said it was a possibility. 'Then come and look at our locks,' he said. 'If there aren't enough to keep George safe, we'll have more put on.'

George started at the school surrounded by goodwill. This continued to be the case. I can't fault the teachers in terms of their attitude towards him, nor of the effort they made. George has always been an attractive child, and the other children were disposed to like him. Many made particular efforts to be kind to him. There were some disagreeable moments; there always are, with children. There was some teasing, and I'm sure George was called 'mental', not that he would have noticed or minded. But there was no sustained bullying, and George was carefully watched and protected by adults.

Bullying is usually a problem when autistic children are included in mainstream schools. Autists, with their naivety, their odd mannerisms, their failure to understand social rules, are obvious victims. And when they are bullied, they have no idea of how to deal with their aggressors. At best, they won't notice or care; it'll be water off a duck's back. But, more often, they *will* notice; they will be hurt and frightened. They won't understand the nature of the attacks, whether verbal or physical. They won't know how to alter their behaviour to make themselves more acceptable. And above all – and this has to be borne in mind in every instance of mainstream inclusion – it won't occur to them to tell an adult what is going on. Remember, they don't know that the adult doesn't already know.

Luke Jackson, in *Freaks, Geeks and Asperger Syndrome*, is unequivocal. 'All my life I have been bullied,' he states. 'I never knew why. Everything at school was so loud and so complicated.' What was bearable at primary school – just – became unbearable at secondary. Luke ran away, never to return to that school. Clare Sainsbury, in *Martian in the Playground*, quotes many high-functioning autists on the subject. The conclusion is inescapable; for a pupil with an autistic spectrum disorder in a mainstream school, being bullied will become a fact of life.

Luke Jackson says that the ASD child is an easy target, as well as an obvious one, because he is often alone. He reminds his readers of the literal-mindedness of the ASD child – 'Bullies don't actually say, "Now I am going to bully you." Therefore your child may not realize that the torment they are suffering is bullying.' He also points out that 'there is another side to the bullying problem . . . some bullying may not actually be bullying! AS kids don't always realize when friendly messing about is actually friendly stuff.' Most of us know that fighting and the exchange of insults are part of the bonding mechanism of male teenage friendships. Controlled, playful aggression is an acceptable disguise for affection and intimacy. But this kind of behaviour has specific and subtle rules, and the autistic child, who finds it so hard to pick up social rules of any kind, has no hope of learning these, which flourish in a subculture largely untouched by adults.

I started this digression by stating that George was not bullied at school. Nor was Sam. But they left mainstream school when they were eight and six respectively. I have no doubt that if they had stayed, they would have become victims, as their contemporaries grew more powerful, more concerned about what is or is not socially acceptable, and moved further away from adult control.

However, during the boys' period at the village school, bullying wasn't something I had to worry about. On paper, if any mainstream setting was appropriate, then it was this one. Small classes, dedicated support workers, intelligent, well-intentioned teachers, a supportive head, a short journey from home to school . . . the set-up was benign and cosy, and communication between home and school was good. The teachers paid home visits and discussed strategies with me. And yet the school could not serve the boys' needs beyond a certain point. Why was this?

I need to back track here, to include Sam. As mentioned in Chapter 6 Sam was lucky enough to go to a special nursery-assessment unit from three and a half to four and a half. Here he prospered, to the extent that at four and a half the gap between his accomplishments and those of a normal child of his age seemed really quite narrow. Socially, too, it was a good time for Sam. He joined in group activities. He particularly liked songs with actions, and a kind of mini-aerobics exercise; he would come home and practise his movements. To say he made friends would be putting it too strongly, but he noticed the other children, and sometimes mentioned them at home. (Only the other day, seven years on, he started talking about 'Treesa'. Teresa was a girl who shared his taxi to the nursery. I asked Sam a couple of questions and his answers indicated that he was, indeed, remembering that child.) He got on well with the staff, and had a particular favourite, Maureen. He named his hamster after her.

Sam was cheerful and equable and he enjoyed school. This, coupled with the fact that he co-operated with the assessment tests – cutting, sorting, drawing, and so on – led to the conclusion that he was suitable for inclusion in mainstream. This turned out to be a mistake, but it would have been hard to see that at the time. And besides, there was no special provision for autistic children at that time. If the boys hadn't gone to mainstream, they would have gone into a school that catered for a variety of special needs, many of them not remotely similar to autism.

So in September 1996, the term Sam turned five, he joined George at the village school. He, too, received a Statement of Special Educational Need, entitling him to a certain number of hours with a helper. Kim, like George's Ruby, was a classroom assistant and dinner lady. Like Ruby, she stayed in touch after Sam left the school, and became one of his ABA tutors.

From the start, Sam's integration was trickier than George's. Despite Sam's apparently sunny nature, he was much less aware of other people than George was. George showed some desire to do what the other children did – he'd sit at his desk, get his work out (though he'd only complete it under strict surveillance), sing in Assembly (sometimes), sit on the mat at story time. Sam didn't. Sam has never compared himself to anyone. He never got into the rhythm of classroom life. He just did his own thing. His teacher would set aside time in which to pay special attention to Sam, and then find him intractable. Without the careful, unvarying structure of the assessment nursery, Sam's progress slowed and then went into reverse.

In common with many parents, one of my complaints about the system of 'statementing' is that the hours of help the child receives don't cover playtimes and lunch breaks. That arrangement would be appropriate for a condition where the problems are primarily academic. But it cannot be emphasized strongly enough that autism is a social handicap more than it is an academic one. The most social parts of the school day, such as the dinner hour, are the times when the autistic child is likely to be most at sea. Sam's dinner-time behaviour became so wild that, for his last term, I had to collect him every day, take him home, and return him an hour later.

Yes, it would improve matters if the statemented child had a dedicated helper for every minute of the school day, though few authorities would fund it. But that wouldn't address the underlying problem about mainstream inclusion, which is that very little of normal school life is appropriate for or applicable to an autistic child.

When I came to choose a primary school for Jake I looked for a caring, supportive atmosphere above everything else. But I also looked for liveliness, variety, bright wall displays, music and drama, outings, links with the local community, sporting opportunities, playground games. I wanted – and got – an environment that would be visually and mentally stimulating, teaching that would be enterprising and imaginative. Nearly all of this runs contrary to the needs of an autistic child.

When George and Sam started school, I had underestimated their sensory abnormalities. Having now read many accounts by adult autists, I know how difficult and distracting the physical features of a school environment can be. Strip lights flicker, radiators hum, the chatter of other children is bewildering and incomprehensible. The walls are covered in a confusing jumble of colour and sparkle. Classrooms are rearranged – you've just got used to one layout when you have to start all over again. Smells of cooking or cleaning fluid, or even the teacher's perfume, are overpowering. You can't take in the teacher's instructions – she talks too fast, and her earrings jangle.

The ideal autistic environment looks dull to neurotypical eyes. Plain, pale walls; floors evenly covered without changes in carpet or tile design, to help those who, like Sam, have problems with depth perception. Displays, whether of art or of information, kept to a minimum – the autist often inadvertently notices every tiny detail, which can lead to 'overload'. Soft, non-neon lighting. No harsh bells marking the end of a lesson. Ideally, no abrupt end to the lesson at all, which should finish when the task is completed. As few transitions as possible from one room to another. A simple, coherent timetable, presented in pictogram form; deviations from the timetable to be kept to a minimum. Plenty of space between the work area of one child and the next. No disruption of routine for sports days or Christmas shows, events that are important to neurotypical children, but meaningless to the autist. All this would be on my wish list.

At George's present school, each child has his own workstation, a V-shaped structure where the child works facing the wall, with his back turned on the others. The aim is to cut down distraction, to aid concentration, rather like the blinkers on a horse's harness. But isn't this just strengthening the child's isolation? No. It's creating a feeling of calm and security which puts the child in a better frame of mind to cope with the social demands that will, inevitably, be put upon him.

The environmental needs of an autistic child, then, are not compatible with neurotypical needs. Academically there will be a little more overlap, but even so the differences will be profound. As we've seen, the intellectual profile of the autist is characterized by peaks and troughs. All teachers have to cope with a wide range of ability within the same class, but in the case of an ASD child she could be faced with, say, mathematical skills approaching A-level standard in a child who can neither read, write, nor wipe his own bottom.

Good mainstream teaching makes links between subjects. In primary schools, project work dominates; you choose a subject like 'The Romans' and from it develop exercises in all the disciplines. Creative writing – imagine you are a galley slave. Maths – calculations using Roman numerals. Geography – a map of the Roman Empire. Technology – make a scale model of an aqueduct. Art and craft – DIY mosaics with squares of coloured paper. Even cookery – there may be no larks' tongues or honeyed dormice to hand, but let's find out how the Romans made their bread. A good teacher can turn a single subject to endless use. The children learn that the past affects the present, that one culture gives birth to another, that you can combine using your imagination with your practical skills and your powers of logic, that the world is wide.

To the autist, this fluid, creative approach may well be baffling. Autists like to compartmentalize. They are likely to prefer the certainty of traditional, rigid, academic boundaries. Just as the ideal autistic environment looks plain and boring to us, so the repetitive sheets of sums or lists of memorized facts in which some autists delight may seem dry or sterile. These comments don't particularly apply to my sons, who have never achieved much academically, but the nearest equivalent would be George endlessly colouring in the same photocopy of the Seven Dwarfs. Isn't that getting boring? Wouldn't he like to colour something else? No, and no.

I'm not suggesting that the autistic student should be endlessly indulged in his taste for repetitive exercises. New subjects, new skills, have to be introduced. But what I am saying is that the swift changes of subject, the creativity, the diversity, of good mainstream teaching is likely to be so bewildering to the autist that he may withdraw altogether.

One argument often put forward to support the inclusion policy is that ASD children will benefit from the example of mainstream behaviour. Well, if these children could learn by example, they wouldn't be autistic. When autistic children imitate others, they do so only in the most superficial and transient ways. They don't relate behaviour to the underlying social structure. George's time in mainstream was far more successful than Sam's, but he still never learned in any meaningful way from the play of the other children. This isn't surprising – if you think about it, most autistic children have had a 'mainstream' home life, and they haven't learned from that.

Thérèse Jolliffe, an autistic woman who has become a university academic, has written a brief account of her life. She states,

I hated school. Parents of autistic children should never think about sending their children to ordinary schools, because the suffering will far outweigh any of the benefits achieved . . . Although ordinary schooling enabled me to leave with a dozen or so O-levels and a few A-levels and then to obtain a degree, it was not worth all the misery I suffered . . . I was frightened of the girls and boys, the teachers and everything there. I was frightened of the toilets and you had to ask to use them, which I was not able to do, also I was never sure when I wanted to go to the toilet anyway . . . When I attended a place for autistic people, life was a little more bearable and there was certainly less despair.

This was a girl with spectacular academic gifts who didn't have the social skills or the word-finding ability to ask to use the toilet. That's autism in a nutshell.

Am I suggesting that inclusion in mainstream is always wrong? Not quite. But I do believe that the cases where it works well are hugely outnumbered by the cases where it fails. At the heart of the government's inclusion policy are two fundamental misunderstandings. One is that normality rubs off on abnormal people, to their benefit. It doesn't. The other is that intellectual ability is a more important educational criterion than social ability. It isn't.

Many parents will disagree with me. I would have disagreed with myself, when the boys were first diagnosed. Like the majority of parents of autists, I believed, for a long time, that I had normal children. Autism isn't like Down's syndrome, which is identified from physical characteristics in the first few hours of life, if it hasn't already been picked up by prenatal screening. The parents of a Down's baby can't fully imagine what life's going to be like for them or their child, but at least they will never harbour the mistaken belief that their child will have the same needs as everyone else's. They can make decisions about the child's education from a position of some knowledge.

When 'autistic' parents come to choose the first school for their child, it's likely that they will not long have received the diagnosis. It can take years for the full import to sink in. It's hard to shift that bedrock expectation, that illusion that nothing is wrong with their beautiful, healthy, loveable child. When George and Sam were first diagnosed, I think I saw their autism as a kind of cloak, a covering of their true selves that might one day fall away. I didn't recognize that they are autistic through and through.

So, when the educational psychologist or the person from County tells you that your child is suitable for mainstream, you're happy to believe it. I've often heard such authority figures say, 'We always try to put the parents' wishes first.' Fine – but how does the parent know what their child's needs are? Giving birth to an autistic child doesn't make you an instant expert on the subject. Parents at this stage are vulnerable to suggestion. They jump at the chance of mainstream, thinking that it means their child's difficulties are superficial, curable. When the boys were four, it was impossible for me to foresee that they were as deeply handicapped as has proved to be the case.

This is a sensitive area. It would be wrong to come down heavily on the parents, to tell them that their child will inevitably be severely handicapped, that he has no hope of functioning in the 'real' world. Autism is a highly unpredictable condition, as we've seen. My boys, to date, have done far less well than would have been predicted, but there are plenty of cases where the reverse is true. What does need to be explained carefully to parents is that autism is an all-pervasive condition. Whether high or low functioning, there isn't one aspect of the child's life that won't be touched by it. And most mainstream schools are not adapted to take account of autism *in any way*.

It was really the deterioration in Sam's behaviour that led me to take both boys out of mainstream. George could have carried on. True, he wasn't learning very fast, but he didn't learn much faster after the move, either. George, in contrast to his infant precocity, was on an intellectual go-slow from which he is only just beginning to emerge. But at the age of eight, when he left mainstream, he was quite manageable in the class. He needed Ruby, his helper, but with her support he didn't cause undue problems for the teacher or the other children, except on the odd occasion, as when he pulled up a hedge, newly planted to commemorate an important date in the school's history. But increasingly he was a satellite to the activities of the others. As their work and play became more sophisticated, there was less and less with which he could join in. The move would have come sooner or later, but George was quite happy; it wasn't a matter of urgency.

Sam, though – Sam's position at the school had become untenable. During his first year there he had been blithely impervious to instruction, restless and unfocused, but jolly enough, motivated by washing machines, and with the odd flash of responsiveness. In his second year, the great regression happened. As I suggested in Chapter 8, his inappropriate educational placement may have played a part, though I suspect that the causes were mainly physical. But Sam's huge shutdown, his loss of all motivation, his seesawing between torpor and wildly destructive behaviour, was too much for the school to cope with. As for peer-group interaction, Sam no longer had anything in common with the rest of the class other than that they were all housed under the same roof.

My instinct has always told me to keep Sam and George together. They've always been close, perhaps because they are the only people in the world who put no pressure on each other. The bond between them will be important to them throughout their lives; a decision about one involves a consideration of the other. I hope I'd be flexible enough to respond if their needs diverged sharply. But when it became obvious that Sam had to leave mainstream, I decided to take George out as well. George's move, I realized, was going to happen one day; why hang on and watch him fail?

Luckily for us, autistic provision in our area had improved. Torfield School, a special-needs school seven miles away from us, in Hastings, had opened an ASD facility, where no more than eight children were taught by experienced staff. There was a part-time in-house speech and language therapist, and a high staff:pupil ratio. The boys would be able to stay in the same place until they went to secondary school, aged eleven. And they would be together.

So in September 1998, aged eight and nearly seven, that's where they went, and that's where they remained. George has moved on to a similar arrangement, a facility attached to Saxon Mount, a special-needs secondary school. Sam will join him there very soon. They'll stay there until they're sixteen and then – well, who knows?

The experience of the last few years has convinced me that an autistic environment is the right environment for them. There have been plenty of problems. George took ages to adjust to the change to secondary school, and became aggressive and semi-anorexic, but now loves school and is settled and manageable. Sam is still resolutely unteachable – as Mark, the classroom assistant, says, 'No one is better than Sam at being autistic.' He has a knack of deflecting all attempts to coerce him into constructive and meaningful activity. But he feels secure at the unit; he runs out to his taxi every morning with alacrity. Removed from the bewildering pressures and mental and sensory overload of mainstream life, he is calmer, happier, and less destructive.

And the boys need that high staff:pupil ratio. All autists do. Most of them can't learn anything in a group. Everything has to be presented to them individually. Indeed, learning to tolerate sitting in a group at all, even for the register, is difficult. They can't be expected to follow any kind of generalized curriculum. Only an individual education plan makes sense. Ideas about what an average ten-year-old (or whatever) should or should not be learning just don't apply. And the comments I made about autists failing to pick up the 'good' habits of mainstream children applies in reverse as well. Parents fear that their child will learn to be 'more autistic' from being in a class with other autistic children, but this doesn't seem to happen. Autists take so little notice of each other. Neither George nor Sam has ever imitated a new 'autistic' habit in anything other than a fleeting, superficial way.

It's lucky for me that both boys are sufficiently handicapped to qualify easily for special-needs provision. It's much harder to find an appropriate placement for a more able autistic or Asperger child. Sadly, the common pattern is that the more able child more or less makes it through mainstream primary school, where smaller numbers and a more protective attitude among the staff give the 'different' child some degree of shelter, only to find everything falling apart once they move on to a comprehensive. That big change at eleven, from a smallish, cosyish school where you are taught by the same teacher for nearly everything, to a large, split-site comprehensive with a complicated timetable and a different teacher for every subject, is daunting for most children. How much worse it must be for the ASD child, with his impairments of communication and social interaction, let alone his anxieties and hypersensitivities. It's like parking a child in a wheelchair at the bottom of a steep flight of stairs and expecting him to climb them.

Arguably, the whole concept of school is wrong for children on the spectrum. Any school, even the most specialized, involves some degree of social co-operation and space-sharing. One of the motivations behind home education programmes, such as ABA, is the impossibility of finding any school environment in which an autistic child can thrive. Luke Jackson, now at a gentler, more tolerant school, still has many difficulties, and takes comfort from the knowledge that, if things get really bad, home-schooling is a legal option.

I think schools can be adapted or created to suit ASD children. Opting out altogether has its own pitfalls. The current provision is woefully inadequate, and I could go on for pages about necessary improvements, but I'll confine myself to main targets.

Firstly, all special-needs children diagnosed before the age of five should have access to special-needs nurseries with trained staff. Nursery education is hugely important. With autistic children, it'll be much easier to work with them later on if they have been expertly diverted away from their rigid routines and anti-social behaviours at an early age, before these get 'stuck'. It's not realistic to expect the parents to do all this. Sticking an autistic child in an ordinary nursery is often pointless and can terrify the child and confirm his isolation.

Secondly, local authorities should be prepared to fund home therapy programmes such as ABA for families who feel that their children are not suited to any kind of school setting. If, as its most devoted practitioners claim, ABA given young enough can turn an unreachable child into one ready for gradual integration into school, then it's money very well spent.

Thirdly, the provision for high-functioning autistics and Asperger children is worst of all. Such children need academic teaching, in some cases to a very high level. They also need careful and sensitive teaching in social skills and self-care. It's vital that the authorities recognize that a high IQ has very little to do with common sense or the ability to communicate. A unit attached to a mainstream school might be a good option, where the able pupils can access the academic expertise of the main school, but where they are also protected from the hurly-burly of school life, and where they can be given help in their specific areas of weakness. The current 'sink or swim' attitude to inclusion is extremely harmful.

Fourthly, the government needs to invest in training teachers to work with autistic children. The odd half-day course here and there isn't enough. Teaching autists is very different from teaching mainstream, and requires almost opposing skills. Teaching autists can also be a rewarding, interesting and important job. If the current estimates are correct, and nearly one in a hundred children are on the spectrum, then we need a huge expansion in expertise.

Autistic children don't need much in the way of special equipment. They need computers, but then who doesn't, these days? Most of them are physically healthy. A sizeable minority suffer from epilepsy, but apart from those, few cost the state in terms of drug treatments. What they do need is man and woman power. It's ironic that this most unsocial of conditions is best tackled by constant input from a large number of people. No man is an island, though most autists would probably think otherwise, were they capable of conceptualizing in that way. These little would-be islands need to be surrounded by bridge-builders who know what they're doing. People cost money; there's no getting away from that. But effective input early on may lead to savings in the future. The better, the more purposeful, the child's early education, the more likely he is to achieve some degree of independence in adulthood. The current inclusion policy dooms many children to failure, and in the long run, failure is expensive.

14. Did You Sleep Well, Dear?

The last time I could rely on an unbroken night's sleep, the Berlin Wall was tottering, Nelson Mandela was still (just) on Robben Island, and Dirty Den held sway at the Queen Vic the first time round. If anyone had told me then, at the end of 1989, in those last restless nights of late pregnancy, that I would not be allowed to sleep through the night until well into the twenty-first century, I'd have – well, what would I have done? Simply not believed them, I expect.

I'm writing this in February 2003, and the sleeping's a whole lot better than it's ever been. Sam now goes to sleep before eleven, and never wakes before seven. George retires at about ten-thirty; most mornings he joins me in bed at about three, but he usually falls quickly back to sleep. Sometimes he even stays in his own bed all night. Jake, asleep by eight-thirty, crawls in with me at about two, tells me his dreams, and then sleeps again until seven. It's rare for me to wake alone in my bed in the mornings, but it does sometimes happen.

It would be tedious to recount all the variations of nocturnal disturbance I've encountered over the last thirteen years, but I'm by no means the only sufferer. Sleep is a problem for many autistic children – or rather, it's a problem for their parents, since the children don't seem to care. It's certainly the aspect of life with the boys that wins me the most sympathy, though it's not the one that bothers me the most. 'Oh, I just couldn't do without my eight hours,' people say, considering my plight with pity and horror. I might well have said something similar myself, pre-children. But of course you can do without your eight hours, or even your six hours, if you have to.

I can't say exactly why autists should sleep badly, but as they do nearly everything differently, it seems unlikely that their sleep habits would conform to ours. They are often highly tense, anxious, over-stimulated people; relaxing isn't usually part of their repertoire. Their heightened senses may mean that they find it difficult to block out intrusions of light or sound. They are often dependent on rituals, and the disruption of a ritual may prolong wakefulness. Jacqui Jackson, four of whose seven children are on the spectrum, says that Ben, her youngest, is very hidebound by routine. If he's missed his pudding, he'll scream for it in the middle of the night, not because he especially wants the pudding in itself, but because he can't bear to have his routine altered. And of course, having defective social wiring, autists fail to conform to the sleep pattern society expects of them, just as they may fail to conform to the pattern of greeting people on arrival, wearing warm clothes in winter, or wiping their bottoms after they've been to the lavatory.

Very new babies don't seem to distinguish between day and night. They feed, sleep, feed, sleep, feed, have a little look around, feed, and then sleep again. However, it doesn't take long for the normal baby to be nudged into the habit of sleeping more during the hours of darkness, and having its wakeful, playful times during the day. Even poor sleepers – and Jake was (is!) one – soon follow this pattern. It's common to find a six-month-old who wakes several times a night, much less common to find one who is fully alert, playful and ready for action at all times of the night. By this age most babies have settled for a longish night and two naps a day, even if the night is not as long as the parents would like, and of a somewhat ragged texture.

I have already described the newborn George's super-wakefulness, and the lack of pattern or coherence to his sleeping, even after many months. George really didn't seem to know night from day. His sleeping and waking remained entirely unpredictable, and unpredictability is very exhausting.

Like all new mothers, I had listened with a kind of smug horror to tales of other people's sleepless nights, and had privately decided that my baby would be different. My baby would sleep through from early on, because I would do all the right things. I had, of course, reckoned without the baby's force of character, and my own lack of resolution; if giving it yet another feed and taking it back into one's own bed is the only way to grab a few more minutes' sleep, then that tends to be the path one takes.

As George grew older, the problems changed. He did, at last, accept the difference between day and night, but he would become very uptight at bedtime. He had to fall asleep in our arms; we could never just lie him down and leave him. And when he woke during the night, he could never put himself back to sleep without our help. I remember doing feeble things like buying cot sheets with little pictures on them in the hope that he would occupy himself with looking at them, but George was not to be fobbed off with anything like that. As soon as he could pull himself up to stand, at six months, he devoted his energies to working out how to escape from his cot. At ten months, he succeeded. I remember with a shudder the rattle, the thud, and the pad of tiny footsteps hurrying towards our room.

Sam seemed to be a sleepier baby than George. Certainly, you could put him in his cot and leave him; it wasn't until I went on holiday and had him in the room with me in a travel cot with transparent sides that I realized what a lot of time he spent awake, fingering Owly, staring at the ceiling. Unlike the social George, he didn't call for me, but he didn't sleep, either. Once Sam had graduated from a cot to a bed, things became a lot worse. It dawned on him that he had no need just to lie there any more, so he didn't. He ran up and down the corridor, chuck-ling. Putting him to bed in the evening was the worst part. We tried to do what the baby books suggest – return him to bed, cover him, reassure him, make a decisive exit. We did this over and over again – forty, fifty, sixty times. Often, the evening would end with one of us taking him out and driving him round in the car; another failure.

The sleep issue probably caused more friction between me and Min than any other. Since I've been on my own, I've changed my attitude, and nights have improved. I never try to stop them from coming into my bed any more. Night time is full of fears for any child; how much worse for one who can't express his terror? If George finds comfort in the pressure of my inert back, then why should I deprive him of it? In *Nobody Nowhere* Donna Williams writes about her night terrors: 'I had become literally terrified of falling asleep and then, frightening as my mother had become, I would go into her room and stand there watching her sleep, feeling secure in the knowledge that if anything was to get me it would have to get her, too, and she knew how to fight . . . Unknown to my mother, I lay stiff and silent under her bed, almost too afraid even to breathe.' Donna Williams's mother was a violent drunk, and yet Donna still sought her as a refuge. How can I possibly deny my children access to my bed?

Having children in bed with you isn't great for a marriage, but the loss of evenings is worse. Sleepless autistic children can be with you for eighteen hours a day; the lack of adult, child-free time is more of a deprivation than the lack of sleep. Now, I'll often choose a late night, reading or going out with friends, over extra sleep. I read stories to George and Sam, sit with them until they finally subside, fall asleep on the sofa in their bedroom, then wake an hour later, read for an hour, then sleep again. When I go out, I stay up later than is strictly sensible. I need the mental space, the change of scene, more than sleep itself. Since I've been single I've been able to suit myself in this respect, and it works much better. Experts are divided about how much sleep we actually need. I suspect most adults need less than they think. You get used to it. I don't think I'm any more haggard or less energetic than my sleep-fulfilled friends.

Acceptance is the key – for me, anyway. Once I'd let myself stop fighting the boys' sleep habits, everything improved. One should set oneself realistic targets. I put Jake to bed at eight-thirty because I know I can. Plenty of children of his age go to bed at seven. I know he and I can't manage that, so I don't try. Ten-thirty to eleven has become feasible for the other two, so that's what happens. It's not too bad.

The worst time of all was when Jake was a baby, and waking for breastfeeds at all-too-frequent intervals, and Sam was at the height, or depth, of his regression, the strange physical and mental disintegration from which he is still not fully recovered. At midnight Sam would still be racing up and down, whirring, humming, hooting and flapping. His hands were bloody from being bitten, his fingers were swollen like sausages from being banged repeatedly against hard objects. Once asleep – often with the aid of a car ride – he would jump up as if woken by an electric shock seven or eight times before morning. Each time he would drink a bottle of milk or juice before going back to sleep. When I had to get him ready for school in the morning, he would be a lowering zombie, groaning, barely conscious. Astonishingly, he never wet the bed.

Desperate times, desperate measures. I'd already, years before, begged the doctor to give me a sleeping drug for him. At last she handed over some Phenergan, with the warning that, in a small percentage of cases, it had the opposite effect. Well, guess which category Sam fell into? I laced his bedtime bottle with Phenergan, and his head hardly touched the pillow. Autists seem to have an ability to override conventional medication. When Sam had a general anaesthetic, he was up and running minutes afterwards. It's an interesting area, and one into which there's been little research.

My experiment with Ritalin, the hyperactivity drug, is described in Chapter 7. Once the Ritalin was in the bin, I knew I could no longer delay what I had been dreading – the removal of gluten and casein from Sam's diet. This is also dealt with in more detail in Chapter 7; here, suffice it to say that nights improved pretty quickly once the diet was under way. Sam is now the soundest sleeper of the three.

I'm not the person to ask for advice about sleepless children, but I suppose I do have some views about what not to do. I do think that past early babyhood it's a bad idea to give them drinks at night. For years I was tyrannized by horrible, scummy feeding bottles lined up in the corridor outside the boys' room. I'm pleased with myself for never putting a bottle (or a dummy) into Jake's mouth. He went from breast to beaker, and once he was off the breast he never, ever had another nocturnal drink. It's easy to be smug about doing without a dummy, but I have to admit that Jake's thumb was in his mouth from the word go. But the great thing about thumbs is that they don't get lost.

Giving children bottles at night does send them back to sleep, but it's habit-forming, and I suspect that it messes up their appetites and makes it harder to stick to a three-healthy-meals-a-day routine. It's also bad for their teeth, of course – though Jake has managed more cavities than the other two, despite no bottles and a relatively healthy diet. Bottles are depressing and squalid and oppressive, but in dealing with sleepless children, it's hard to reject instant assuagements and take the long view.

Personally, I wouldn't bother with books about how to make children sleep. I had a horrid book called *Healthy Sleep Habits, Happy Child*, which just made me feel worried and inadequate. I would also ignore, or heavily edit, advice from friends and family, especially from the older generation, who often recall the infancy of their progeny through a rosy and inaccurate glow. The main thing is to get in tune with yourself, with what you can and can't tolerate.

Having a reason for a problem helps a lot. Once I knew the boys were autistic, I found it much easier to accept their unsleepiness. It was a symptom of their condition, not a failure on my part. Once I'd given up any expectation of a good night's rest, I found it didn't affect me as badly as I would have expected. Luckily, I'm a good sleeper; I don't lie awake worrying, and I can usually get back to sleep quickly after a disturbance. If I've had a truly terrible night, I try to snatch a nap of five or ten minutes during the day. One of the very few things for which I'm grateful to Margaret Thatcher is the concept of the 'power nap'.

When I was an undergraduate, my preferred modus operandi was to go out in the evening, come back late, write an essay in the early hours and then sleep until noon. I was outraged at being expected to attend a tutorial at nine in the morning; it felt like an abuse of human rights. These days, I couldn't sleep all morning even if I got the chance. I like early mornings now – this morning, yellow leaves and crimson berries glowing through furry frost, and the sun, shorn of its rays, a giant red eye bouncing up through the orchard. Intimately acquainted as I now am with every stitch in the weave of the twenty-four hours, I've grown fond of the declining moon, of foxes barking at midnight, of the pre-dawn crowing of the cocks. Would I swap all this for a solid, predictable eight hours a night? Well, perhaps I would – but I'm not quite sure.

15. What Do They *Do* All Day?

Five in the morning. George is up, and has been for some time. He's longing to jump on Sam, but I'm not going to let him. So I put a video on. After eleven years, it's still the most reliable way of keeping George out of trouble at times when I'm prepared to give him rather less than full attention.

He chooses *Kipper the Dog: Looking after Arnold*. Kipper is designed for four-year-olds, but George doesn't know that, and if he did, he wouldn't mind. No normal thirteen-year-old boy would be able to watch Kipper (or Teletubbies, or Tweenies, or Bob the Builder) other than in a spirit of irony or nostalgia, but irony and nostalgia are strangers to George. Irony depends on playing off one point of view against another, but George can only ever hold one point of view in his head, which is, of course, his own. Nostalgia requires that you look at the past and make a misty-eyed comparison between yourself as you once were and yourself as you are now. For George, time past and time present are the same thing. He's troubled by suggestions that he was once different, or that change is in store in the future. He can remember the past – he remembers everything. For most of us, the operation of a shared culture externalizes memory, edits and shapes it. George undergoes no such sorting process. His memories seem almost as present, as real to him, as what's happening here and now. When he started school, there was a little boy in his class called Adam Perry. Not long after, Adam left the school. George asked about him frequently, bothered by this disruption in the register. Two years later, Adam returned to the school. 'Here's Adam Perry!' said George, as if Adam had never been away.

This idiosyncratic sense of time may be one reason why George returns to the same videos over and over again. *Looking after Arnold*, this morning's choice, might have been selected during any of the intermittent Kipper phases which have recurred throughout the last six or seven years. George has 'customized' his video-watching in the same way that as a three-year-old he customized his books; he selects certain key moments (not complete enough to be called scenes) or snatches of dialogue, and rewinds them. At other moments he'll enact the video – if a character falls he might cast himself off the chair (or push Sam off), or if Kipper switches off the light, George will do the same. And then at other times he'll run out of the room. You'll think he's lost interest; he's sitting on top of the Aga, or on the garden wall, twiddling a flapper. But if you turn off the video there'll be a shriek of protest. Running out during certain scenes is not a sign of lack of interest, it's all part of the elaborate choreography that video-'watching' has become for George.

His treatment of his videos goes beyond any normal interest in narrative and characters. It's hard to explain what he gets out of them, because I don't exactly know. Of course, repetition of any kind is soothing and reassuring. George likes to know that you only have to press a button to see, for the umpteenth time, Kipper blowing out his candles, Arnold sucking his lollipop. But there's more to the endless rewinding than a simple desire for repetition. An American author, Robert Hughes, has written a memoir of life with his autistic son, Walker (*Running with Walker*), another champion rewinder. Hughes presents Walker's favourite videos as if Walker himself had written a guide to them for other autists, including 'great rewind ops.': 'Highlight: The scene where Cinderella's cute little creature friends sing "We Can Do It" . . . All those friends! All that happiness! It's a terrific rewinding moment!' Hughes believes that, for the largely non-verbal Walker, the most rewound moments are passages of special emotional significance. He may well be right. It's possible, as I suggested in Chapter 5 that George identified with Pinocchio, for instance; that he, like Pinocchio, yearned to be a 'real boy', and that he rewound bits of the film in order to learn how to do it. It's also possible that he made no such connection.

George was less than two when he received his first video. It was *Pingu: Barrel of Fun*, and it was given to him by his godmother, Em, whose daughter Sophie was just ten months older. 'You'll love me for giving him this,' she said, and I did. *Pingu* hollowed out a forty-minute oasis of calm in George's highly coloured, energized, chaotic world. I bought it for several friends expecting second children. I didn't really see how, without *Pingu*, one had any chance of breastfeeding a new baby.

Pingu seems to have fallen from favour with the general public, but he was very big in the early 1990s. He is an animated Plasticine penguin who lives with his parents and little sister, Pinga, at the South Pole. He's a brilliant creation – a funny, mischievous, sometimes insecure little boy penguin whose adventures are rooted in domesticity without ever being dull. Each five-minute episode deals with one of the mini-dramas of a young child's life. Pingu tips his chair over backwards, pretends he's brushed his teeth when he hasn't, spits unwanted vegetable matter into the lavatory, fights with his sister, eats too much popcorn, wets himself. His parents are sentimental, quarrelsome, inconsistent and slow-witted, just like real parents. An astonishing amount of personality is conveyed by each twitch of a flipper, each prod of a beak. Pingu and his companions converse in a kind of quacking gabble, with all the rhythms and intonations of real speech, but with hardly any recognizable words. Despite this, each narrative is entirely comprehensible. Anyone interested in linguistics would do well to study *Pingu*.

Barrel of Fun was followed by many other Pingu tapes. Sam joined George in adoration. ''Gu! 'Gu!' Sam would demand, aged two, and both would solemnly imitate the penguins' actions as they watched. As usual, different aspects appealed to each of them. Sam enjoyed spotting his objects of desire recreated in Plasticine – a cooker, an ironing board, a washing machine. George was fascinated by the quacky language. With his good ear for mimicry, he became completely fluent in Pinguese, and would quote large chunks of 'dialogue'. It's hard to tell whether he attached meaning to the sounds he was hearing, but my guess is that he did.

Pingu certainly had emotional significance for George. Sam was indifferent to scenes of naughtiness, jealousy, punishment or affection – though he did find some things funny – but for George, all that was important. There's a character called Mui in Timothy Mo's novel *Sour Sweet*, a Chinese woman newly arrived in 1960s London, who watches *Crossroads* intently in order to learn the social habits and moral values of Westerners. For George, *Pingu* fulfilled a similar function. George, with his socially-active-but-odd variety of autism, was intrigued by social behaviour, even though he didn't understand it. Here, the rewinding comes into its own. Rewinding helped George to learn at his own pace. In real life, people won't rehearse their emotions for your benefit. Videos gave George time to sort out the action in his own mind. Pingu's mummy's cross. Yes. Why is she cross? Better check. Rewind. Because Pingu broke a plate! Hmm. Thought so.

Rewinding can also be used to create stimulating visual effects – stimulating to autists, that is; numbing to neurotypical viewers. Both boys went through a stage, early on, of preferring the credits to any other part of a film. Sam, aged three, would imitate this effect by holding a sheet of paper with writing on it close to his face and moving it quickly upwards, rolling his eyes at the same time. He found a tiny, tiny label with the Disney logo on it, and this, too, he ran upwards in front of his eyes, 'singing' as he did so. Some of the boys' videos were made by a company called Pickwick. At the end of the tape, the viewer's eye would be directed as if into a keyhole, then the solid white letters of PICKWICK would disperse and whirl through space. This was one of Sam's 'great rewind ops.' He would also re-enact the whirling of the letters using his own hands and body and his long, flying hair – 'I a white Pickwick,' he used to say. Yes, he sometimes used the first-person singular in those days.

There is a remarkable consensus of opinion among the autistic 'community' about their viewing matter – remarkable because, unlike neurotypical children, they rarely converse with one another and are highly unlikely to give each other recommendations. Casey Junior, the steam train struggling up the hill in *Dumbo*, is a favourite autistic rewind. So is the 'pink elephants on parade' sequence – a surreal dance hallucinated by a drunken Dumbo. Will and Kate, the boys' twin cousins, got frustrated when George kept rewinding the pink elephants – for them it was the dullest part of the film, because they, with their neurotypical plot-and-character motivations, wanted to get on with the story. Finding out what happened was rarely of interest to George and Sam. I remember observing the twins and George as they watched *Dumbo* together, and thinking how different they were. They were three at the time; this was before George's diagnosis. The twins cuddled together and wept when Dumbo was parted from his mother; George, oblivious to suffering, danced with delight in front of the psychedelic pink elephants. At that stage I didn't realize quite how profound the difference was. I recalled this years later when Jake, also aged three, watched *Dumbo* for the first time. 'They've taken his mummy away,' he sobbed in outrage and disbelief. 'This can't be for children.' It was another year or more before he felt brave enough to watch to the end.

Pingu was quickly joined by various Beatrix Potters, *Rosie and Jim*, the unavoidable *Thomas the Tank Engine*, *Spider in the Bath*, which particularly excited Sam, and *The Magic Roundabout*, which provided George with some of his best lines: 'This will make Ben Hur look like a vicarage tea party!' he would exclaim, at the sight of me and my friends drinking tea. 'This will make Ken Russell spit with jealousy!' he declared, spitting on the floor. Some of these lines are still in use. 'I've been let down by the government,' George recently told his trampoline teacher, who was startled by the apparent profundity of the remark, not knowing that it was borrowed from Dougal.

There was *Fireman Sam* – during that emotional half-light through which mothers of toddlers grope their way, I remember idly wondering which was the more fanciable, Fireman Sam or his side-kick, Elvis Cridlington. *Noddy* had a burst of favour, and for George, the dire *Tots TV* was enormously influential. The three ragdoll tots live in a cottage, a sort of care-in-the-community arrangement, where they witter and fuss all day about spillages and breakages and whose turn it is to use the bathroom.

Sometimes they totter out on their woollen legs to have educational encounters with harmless animals. This was absolutely on George's level. Their banal, repetitive exchanges resemble much ordinary human discourse; they provided useful conversational models for George. Later, *Bananas in Pyjamas* reared their ugly skins; 'Big blana! Big blana!' Sam would shout. George became addicted to a strangely mesmeric set of glowing balloon bears called *Jellikins*, each of a colour linked to a personality type. Pepper was red and assertive, Denny was blue and dreamy, Coral was pink and vain.

You'd be hard put to find an 'autistic' family which wasn't in thrall to the Disney empire. I have reservations about Disney, myself, and I've tried to minimize Jake's intake. I dislike the way faces and emotions are stretched out of shape, the way the dialogue has one knowing eye on the adult audience, the way ancient myths and folk tales are remodelled to express middle-American values. I find the colours unsubtle, the wisecracking unfunny, the romance unstirring, the pathos misplaced. And I've never been able to find cartoon characters cute. But I'm also grateful to the Disney Corporation for the hours of entertainment it has provided for my hard-to-occupy children. I know most children like Disney – most adults, too – but there does seem to be something about it which is particularly attractive to autists. Perhaps the exaggerated emotional responses are easier to understand. Perhaps the swooping, swirling movements provide special visual stimulation. The music is certainly important; no one knows better than Disney how to make a tune stick in your head, and autists tend to be even more responsive to this than the rest of us.

Whatever the reasons, you'll rarely come across an autistic child who hasn't had some kind of Disney fixation. In our household, the front-runners have been *Dumbo*, *Snow White*, *Pinocchio*, *The Aristocats*, *Fantasia*, *Beauty and the Beast*, *The Jungle Book* and, for Sam, some of the early Silly Symphonies, especially 'Pig-Net Machine' (*The Three Little Pigs*) and a marvellous sequence about Easter Bunnies painting chocolate eggs. In all of them, the most rewound moments involve an intriguing visual effect, like

Mowgli's eyes mesmerized by Kaa, the Fantasia fairies colouring the autumn leaves, or Snow White peering at her reflection in the wishing well.

The more recent, more sophisticated Disney:Pixar productions, like *Toy Story* and *A Bug's Life*, are more acceptable to adults – well, to this adult, at any rate. They're too complicated for Sam, but George was very taken with them, even going so far as to experiment with some limited pretend play with toys modelled on the characters. But the play never went beyond re-enacted fragments. I've never known George improvise on character and motivation. I think he is, at last, able to recognize Flik the inventor ant as a goodie and Hopper the cruel grasshopper as a baddie in *A Bug's Life* (or *Three Bugs Full* as the toddler Jake used to call it), but it would not occur to him to invent his own acts of aggression for Hopper or heroism for Flik. Nor does he display any fear of the one, or admiration of the other. George's response to favourite videos is enthusiastic, but essentially dispassionate.

Toy Story and *A Bug's Life* are the nearest to age-appropriate that George gets. Attempts to interest him in feature films about 'real' children – even *Harry Potter* or *Chitty-Chitty-Bang-Bang* – have largely failed. He is interested in real children – he loves the activities of children on *Teletubbies* or his various nursery-rhyme tapes, and likes to know their names. When he was younger he wanted these children to step out of the television and join him. My attempts to convince him that this was impossible were thwarted when we went to a friend's house and met another visiting family. The sons, Oscar and Felix, were the very boys who George had watched over and over again as they read 'The Gingerbread Man' in an episode of *Teletubbies*. George recognized them at once. 'Here are Oscar and Felix!' he trilled, delighted. The encounter gave him food for thought. If Oscar and Felix could turn up in a Sussex garden, then clearly I was wrong about the non-transferability of TV or fictional characters. 'Mum, The Cat in the Hat *can* come to our house,' he stated on the journey home.

So, George is far from indifferent to seeing 'real' children on screen – indeed, they exert considerable fascination. But it's difficult to interest him in a full-length feature film with child stars because he has no curiosity about what happens to them. They talk too much and too quickly, and one's understanding of the film is too dependent on listening properly to what they say. And again, there's this failure to identify. Normal children cast about constantly for role models. When Jake was three, he was gripped by Shirley Hughes's books about a little boy called Alfie, because Alfie was very like himself. Alfie had a security blanket, Jake had his hankies. Like Jake, Alfie wanted to go to parties, but found it difficult to let go of his mother's hand. Alfie admired a more boisterous child – 'rough, tough Bernard' – but his admiration was tempered by shock. Alfie reflected and enlarged upon Jake's own experience. His mild adventures led Jake's imagination just a little further than it had been before – a few steps beyond the garden gate – and gently expanded Jake's sense of his own potential. Aged five, Jake now happily identifies with a range of characters from books, videos and real life. Whether it's Harry Potter, Michael Owen or Danny, the John Travolta character in *Grease* (yes, I'm afraid so), he can annex aspects of other characters to explore facets of his own personality.

George has very little of this capacity. Sam has none. Nor do either of them use television, as Jake does, to find out about the adult world. Jake is a big fan of quiz shows. 'Mum, I support the clergy,' he called out the other day, which baffled me until I realized he was watching a special edition of *University Challenge*, the clergy versus the lawyers. When he was three, he would arrange his toy engines in a semicircle, and announce that he was playing 'The Leakest Wink'. He fired questions at the engines (Q: 'What does get brown when you do wee on it?' A: 'Grass.') and dismissed them with scorn when they gave the wrong replies. Just the other day, he memorized the telephone number to apply for *Who Wants to be a Millionaire* and rang it. ('Mum, I'll just ring Chris.') I heard him talking to the recorded message: 'My mum could be on your show. Then we could afford a new kitchen bin.'

It doesn't matter to Jake that he can answer few, if any, of the questions. He likes quizzes because he likes scoring, he likes winners and losers. And he is fascinated by adults, their concerns and preoccupations, the way they interact. He watches quiz shows, and *Top of the Pops*, and *Neighbours*, partly because, he thinks, they allow him an enticing sneak preview of his own future. To George, thinking about the adult world is difficult and disturbing. For Sam, it's simply irrelevant.

Other parents of autists report similar viewing habits to those of George and Sam. Videos are always preferred to television. Short, simple episodes, prefaced by a catchy theme tune, and peopled by a small predictable cast, form their foundation of video-watching; *Postman Pat* and *Bob the Builder*, it seems, can be enjoyed any time, any place by most autists, regardless of age or IQ level. Regardless of gender, too; the teenage Walker Hughes's favourite Disneys include *The Little Mermaid*, *Cinderella* and *Alice in Wonderland*, whereas a neurotypical male Disney enthusiast would surely be shy of confessing to such preferences after the age of, say, seven. Indifference to gender is a common autistic trait, and yet another example of how autists don't perceive the same patterns that give life its coherence for the rest of us. George can always tell the difference between men and women, and is interested in categorizing male and female animals ('Is that a daddy cow?'), but he chooses a pink Barbie cupcake at the baker's, and has little idea that some toys, sports or activities are associated with one gender or the other. Sam doesn't seem able to tell the difference between the sexes. ('What is Grandfather Clive, Sam?' 'A mummy.') He uses 'he' and 'she' indiscriminately.

The boys' taste in books is even more infantile than their taste in videos. At three, George's appetite for stories and poetry was prodigious and precocious. It hasn't progressed much since. There's a cycle of old favourites which never seem to weary him. At the moment we're back on the tank engines (the black twins to the fore again, but this time with a more prominent role for Donald). Other hardy perennials are the Doctor Seuss books, some Beatrix

Potters, Eric Carle (highly coloured, highly patterned books, usually about insects), Arnold Lobel's *Frog and Toad* stories and Allan Ahlberg's *Funnybones* skeleton family. Then there are a few oddballs, like *Rumples and Tumbles Go to the Country*, which is so dreary that the author has declined to put his or her name on the cover. Rumples is a pink toy rabbit, Tumbles a blue one. They spend a day in the country learning facts about wildlife. This little volume has exerted a powerful hold over both boys since early childhood, and is now so patched with Sellotape that it has swollen to twice its original size.

The fact that the rabbits are a not-quite-identical pair appeals strongly to George. He is almost equally devoted to an Enid Blyton book called *Bimbo and Blackie*, about a pair of kitten cousins, one white, one black. The best bit is when they change colours – Blackie gets covered with flour, Bimbo with soot. George's love of pairs has been a consistent theme throughout his life, and is in some way linked to the way he sees himself and Sam.

Sam is much less likely to request a book than George, though if I put a selection in front of him he'll leaf through them with some slight interest. If he were able to select a favourite author, it would be Doctor Seuss. *Green Eggs and Ham* would be found under the palm tree on his desert island, along with the Bible and Shakespeare. Sam appreciates bouncing rhythms and rhymes, and Doctor Seuss is good at both. Sam also finds these books comical. When I first started reading about autism, the received wisdom was that autists had no sense of humour, but this isn't true. Humour was one of Sam's strongest characteristics from the earliest age. Of course, autistic humour isn't the same as ours, but that doesn't mean it doesn't exist.

Nursery rhymes have been important to both boys, perhaps most markedly to Sam. When Sam was at his very worst, veering between hyperactive and destructive one minute and catatonic the next, nursery rhymes and their accompanying tickling games ('This Little Piggy', 'Round and Round the Garden') were one of the few remaining ways of making contact with him. He still likes to climb on my knee and play 'This is the way the ladies ride', he's small for his age, but all the same, it's getting tricky to manage. He knows a great many rhymes by heart. He'll rarely repeat a whole one, but if I pause in my recitation, he'll supply the missing word, or an approximation. This may not sound like an impressive skill for a boy of eleven, but it's way ahead of many of Sam's other attainment levels.

I love nursery rhymes, too. I'm fascinated by their mysterious power to restore the equilibrium of a fractious toddler. When a two-year-old wakes, cross, after a nap, there's no better way of bringing him or her round than to sit together for half an hour reading nursery rhymes. Something about them operates on a level below consciousness – it's akin to the soothing experience of sitting near a fountain, or listening to the wind. For normal children, nursery rhymes operate on many levels. The vocabulary, imagery and characters stock the store cupboard of our imaginations and continue to nourish us throughout our lives. They are a kind of quintessential poetry – the best possible words in the best possible order. They provide us with an immense wealth of shared experience. It's extraordinary, given how short the rhymes are, how strong a sense we all have of the personalities of Little Jack Horner, Miss Muffett, Bo Peep, and so on. 'Hey Diddle Diddle' is the essence of a good party, 'Humpty Dumpty' expresses the randomness of disaster, and what could be more melancholy than the second verse of 'Polly Put the Kettle On'?

I'm not at all sure that Sam and George tap into this. I don't know whether they see anything in their mind's eye when they hear nursery rhymes recited. George, with his greater interest in people, may have some degree of response to Bobby Shafto or Mary Mary as characters, and his love of phrases may mean that the words resonate for him in an almost visual way, but for Sam, I have a feeling that they don't operate at this level at all. I don't know that Sam sees Humpty Dumpty as an egg, or can imagine what skipping over water and dancing over sea would be like. The impact of nursery rhymes, for Sam, lies in their rhymes and rhythms and pleasing word sounds, which is not to say that they are any the less intense for him than they are for normal children.

As with books and videos, neither boy has any inkling that nursery rhymes are inappropriate for their age. Sam doesn't know what his age is. I have no evidence that he's aware of being younger than George or older than Jake. He just doesn't fit himself into any frame of reference. Much of the boys' taste in music would seem to be age-appropriate, but if so, this would be purely by chance. Both of them like a range of rock and pop, but neither has any idea of what's hip or cool (which is just as well, because it means that I can impose my very uncool tastes upon them) and neither makes any connection between music and clothes, hairstyles or modes of behaviour. Most autists seem to be strongly affected by music; perfect pitch, which George may have, is not uncommon. Neither boy plays an instrument, but listening to CDs is an important part of their day. As a way of keeping them entertained, music is on a par with videos, and far more important than books. At school, music therapy has been, for them, one of the most successful parts of the curriculum.

George segues effortlessly from his nursery rhymes to Bowie, the Police, the Rolling Stones, Elvis, the Beach Boys et al. He loves *Peter and the Wolf*, and a few classical pieces – for a while he was gripped by Stravinsky's *The Rite of Spring*. He likes the blues, especially Robert Cray, and he loves Christmas carols performed by cathedral choirs. He goes through periods when he wants to hear the same CD over and over again – it's the Bee Gees at the moment – and finds it difficult to tolerate anybody else's choice. He posts unwelcome CDs down behind the bookcase. His aversions are strong. He abhors Queen ('Bohemian Rhapsadaisy', as Jake calls it), which is a pity as Sam is quite a fan. Sam has cruder tastes than George, and enjoys anything with a thumping great beat. Status Quo would be exactly Sam's thing, if I could bear it. Both boys like reggae and ska – Desmond Dekker's 'Israelites' would be one of Sam's desert island choices.

Both boys 'dance' as they listen; their dances are quite like running on the spot, and have no reference to anyone else, either as a partner or as an audience. George shrieks at me if I try to dance with him. He can recognize all the tracks on any of his CDs from any part of them, and is just as likely to be heard singing the bass line as the melody. He also likes lyrics, and sometimes quotes them, as when I told him to hurry up and get into bed, and he replied, 'I can't, I'm a rock 'n' roll suicide.' Sam has less musical subtlety than George, but he does distinguish between tracks. He can't ask for them by name, but he reserves his most energetic dancing and his loudest participatory squeals for a few particular songs – Cockney Rebel's 'Come Up and See Me', Jimmy Cliff's 'The Harder they Come' and Elvis's 'Long Tall Sally' among them.

One might assume that George's musical ability meant that he could join a choir or a dance class, or at least learn to play an instrument properly. But that assumption fails to account for the disconnectedness of the autistic experience. Being able to sing well doesn't mean that you want to sing with other people. It doesn't mean that you want other people to hear you singing, or even that you want to sing at all. George has a good voice, but he can go for months without using it. Besides, joining any class or group requires a basic acceptance of the rules of herd behaviour. It would be possible to train a child like George to conform to these rules, but it would take a long, long time, and the training process would be disruptive to the rest of the group. George can learn a new song after a couple of hearings; to learn to follow a choir leader's instructions would take him a couple of years.

What about an instrument? Many autists become proficient players; why not George? Given the right teacher, that should be possible, and it's something we'll try one of these days. It would be hard for George to read music – it's been hard enough to teach him to read words – but his musical memory is so good that he could probably learn by ear. So, why didn't I start him on an instrument years ago? There are two, linked, reasons. One is motivation. George, as a rule, resists learning *any* new skill. As Clara Claiborne Park describes in *The Siege*, the autistic child

finds its contentment, its Nirvana, in nothingness. Jessy Park spent
hours circling a spot on the carpet. Any attempt at redirection
was a disruption of her inner peace. I'm reminded of Malvolio
in *Twelfth Night*: 'Let me enjoy my private.' Jessy's parents' difficult but ultimately successful task was to lay siege to the walls
Jessy had erected to protect that core of nothingness. George was
never as sealed off as this. He was, as I've described, a highly
proactive baby. But, past babyhood, George's behaviour did often
display large 'Do Not Disturb' signs. I was wary of introducing
new skills and ideas because I didn't want to prod the over-
sensitive George back into his shell. Autistic children overload
quickly. Once they crash, the restoration of harmony can take a
very long time.

Alongside this lack of motivation, there's a problem best
described by Jessy Park herself as the feeling of 'too good'. Some
things are experienced too intensely, enjoyed too acutely. Pleasure
tips over into pain. Music, for George and for Jessy Park, can
become 'too good', and then it can no longer be borne. (This
doesn't seem to be an issue with the more phlegmatic Sam.)
There is some kind of self-protecting mechanism at work. Music,
painting, even some people; once they begin to overwhelm, they
need to be put away. Attempting to participate in George's activities is the surest way to precipitate shutdown. If you praise George
for his singing, or admire his painting, he'll swiftly retreat from
both.

There are signs, though, that George's skin is growing thicker,
and it may soon be possible to introduce 'proper' music lessons.
He enjoys music classes at school – in fact he takes charge of
them, telling the other boys what to do and what their favourite
song should be. He seems happy to sing alongside familiar people.
He goes to a mainstream trampoline club; he still has to be
supervised, but he is now able to follow the teacher's instructions almost as well as the other children. In the past, painting
was a private activity for George, but now he'll allow his tutors
to sit by him and make suggestions as he paints. It's encouraging to hear from older parents that learning doesn't seem to have

a cut-off age for their autistic offspring. Some of the skills and experiences missed in childhood can, it seems, be recovered or introduced in later life.

George started painting 'properly' when he was five. Not drawing; it puzzled me, early on, pre-diagnosis, that my amazingly intelligent child showed little interest in or aptitude for drawing. George's early drawings of people were all in bits. He'd draw eyes, legs, hands, and so on, separately, scattered across the page. Neurotypical children's drawings develop in a remarkably consistent way. Drawings of people by Chinese four-year-olds, I gather, look very similar to drawings by American four-year-olds. First there'll be a circle with eyes and legs; later there'll be an ellipse for the body, and the addition of hands, fingers, hair, ears, and so on, will all happen in the fullness of time. I've never come across another child who failed to link up the features as George did.

When Sam was three and a half, I asked him to draw a picture of Grandma. He'd never attempted to draw a person before *at all*, but he immediately drew a fully fledged figure, with features like hair, fingers and toes. 'Draw Grandfather Clive,' I said. He complied. On request, he added Lulu the dog and Vinnie the cat, and the tumble-drier. The dog and cat were different from the human figures, and different from each other. Sam had missed out all the developmental stages in infant drawing; from nothing, he produced a drawing that was easily age-appropriate. I tried to get him to reproduce this feat on other occasions, but he never would.

Now, at thirteen, George will draw on request or command, but never spontaneously. His figures have a certain energy and charm, but his skill level barely exceeds Jake's, and he rarely places his figures in any sort of context. His paintings, however, absorb considerable amounts of thought and care. I don't think they are ever intentionally representational, or at least, they're not planned as such. If asked, George may say that he's painted a storm or the sea, but I have a feeling he's being wise after the event. All his paintings are explorations of colour, and always have been.

Both boys have always been strongly responsive to colour,

George especially. Both of them could name every colour well before their second birthdays. I remember George, aged two and a quarter, in his pushchair, looking at a donkey. 'What colour is the donkey?' I asked him. 'Grey. No, browny-grey. No, pinky-browny-grey,' he replied. This acute colour sense is shared by other autists. Jessy Park, now in her forties, uses colour ranges in her minutely detailed paintings where the gradations in shade are so subtle as to be almost invisible to the neurotypical eye.

At five, George painted round discs of colour, some free-floating, some overlapping. He limited his own colour range. In one painting, he would work his way through every combination of red, white and yellow; in another, he'd stick to blue and green. The discs would be joined by a few vertical stripes. He painted on a little easel; he'd walk round it, peering at his work from every angle. Then he'd lie on the floor looking up, apparently admiring the way the light glinted on the fresh paint. He always knew exactly when he'd finished. This wasn't when the paint ran out, or when some alternative activity suggested itself; it was when he'd done whatever he felt he had to do to the painting. After that, he lost interest. I stuck his best ones on the wall, but he didn't look at them again.

He then abandoned paint for a couple of years, perhaps in reaction to too much praise. I can't remember why or how painting crept back in, but the pattern in recent years has been a burst of intense interest followed by a fallow period. Since the discs, he has been through several 'styles': stormy Turneresque vortexes, thick Van Gogh coils of ridged, textured colour, late Kandinsky battlefields of converging stripes and dashes. He goes through phases of preferring different media – poster paints, powder paints, acrylics, heavy finger paint (always applied with a brush), thin paintbox water colours. One summer, he switched to felt-tips, which he mixed with pencils and wax crayons to create dense 'scribble' pictures, the colours converging on, or radiating out from, a dark centre. Occasionally he'll use something other than a brush, like a potato print, and he'll sometimes turn his brush round and make scratchy patterns with the end of the handle.

Today marked a new departure – graded colour, from pale green to deep crimson, crossed by regularly spaced black horizontal bars. This, George declared with more certainty than I'd heard him use before, was 'a sunset'.

Poor deluded woman, my readers must be thinking. Only mother-love could turn these splotches and dribbles into Turner and Kandinsky. Yes, of course I'm biased, and George is not a phenomenal autistic artist like Stephen Wiltshire, Jessy Park or David Braunsberg. But he does have a real affinity for colour and, to a lesser extent, texture. He works with great purpose and concentration, he always seems to know what he's doing, and, like a true expressionist, he incorporates drips and other minor accidents into the overall scheme. And despite the fact that he's usually working with basic children's materials, the results have a depth and brilliance of colour that I, for one, couldn't possibly achieve.

Sam still eats paint. He loves mixing colours, and he splats his brush on to the paper with relish, but he has little awareness of any visual effect. Leave Sam alone with paints for thirty seconds and the kitchen will have been redecorated. He has a similar attitude to Play-Doh or cooking ingredients; it's almost impossible to get him to concentrate on the end product. Handling materials, squidging, slicing, smearing is what interests Sam. Since the demise of his obsessive interests, Sam has been much, much harder to occupy than George. I'm writing this in the middle of August; the summer holidays can seem very long indeed.

For Sam, strenuous physical exercise is important to fill the time as well as keep him fit. He has the physique and stamina of a sportsman without any of the team spirit or ability to practise techniques. It will never be possible for either boy to participate properly in a game like football or cricket; they will never develop the capacity for social co-operation that such activities require. Luckily, neither of them shows the least interest in team games. Solo activities, like trampolining, swimming or riding, are usually a better bet for autists. I'd certainly advise any family with a big enough garden to invest in a proper trampoline if they can possibly afford it. It's been the single most important piece of play equipment for my boys, though a swing runs it close.

During the holidays Sam gets taken for a long walk every day, like a dog. We go to woods, beaches, parks or public gardens. Sam can outwalk anyone; I've never known him run out of steam. When he was fifteen months old, he walked unaided to our blue-bell wood, a distance of about three quarters of a mile. George, though not quite so sturdy, was also an uncomplaining walker. Before Jake was born I would spend hours out with the pair of them, enjoying their enthusiasm for the wind in the long grass or the ripples on the water's surface as they threw acorns into the pond. George and Sam were the most undemanding compan-ions on these walks, completely absorbed as they were in the physical experience of grass, trees, water and mud. I was free to watch them and to think my own thoughts. Jake, alas, has all the normal childish reluctance to walk unless there's a specific end in view. More than two fields' worth of walking is usually accom-panied by demands to be carried and a litany of complaints about physical discomforts.

Sam runs as much as he walks – dog-like, he covers about five times as much ground as I do. I like walking too, so when I'm out with Sam I'm happy to be looking at beautiful places, albeit at high speed. It's hard to judge whether or not Sam has a sense of natural beauty, but he certainly seems internally calmer and happier when he's charging along a woodland path or leaping back from crashing waves. And he always knows exactly where he is. He won't necessarily be able to name the place, but his behaviour shows that his sense of direction and ability to recog-nize landmarks is extremely strong.

We take the boys on lots of trips to castles, children's zoos, rare breeds farms, steam trains, and the like. We need to fill their days; they are very much more aimless than normal children, and left to their own devices will quickly revert to 'stimming' – hand-bashing, stick-twiddling, or the tearing up of valued garden plants. Their social life is limited, and almost entirely engineered by me.

There are no sleepovers, no camping expeditions, no chats on the telephone. But neither are there the grumbles and clashing schemes that accompany normal childhood occupations. A couple of weeks ago, George announced, 'I'm so bored' – it was the first time any of my children had ever said such a thing. George himself looked startled, even as he said it. I don't mean to suggest that autism and boredom are strangers to each other. Far from it – I think autists often suffer from ennui without knowing what the feeling is or what to do about it. But they don't have the neurotypical preconceived ideas about what's boring or uncool. Almost no conversation means almost no arguments, and speaking as a parent, that's not entirely bad.

16. God and the Tooth Fairy

When George was four, we asked him what he wanted for Christmas. 'Aphids,' he replied. His kind godfather provided a box of stick insects as an approximation. The stick insects did attract George's attention – he liked to watch their moon-walking progress from one side of their box to another – and they lived for several years in a corner of the bathroom in seeming contentment. But I now realize that George hadn't actually been asking for aphids at all. When asked what he wanted, he had replied 'aphids' simply because he associated the word 'aphids' with the word 'want'. This was because in Eric Carle's story *The Bad-Tempered Ladybird* the protagonist repeats the phrase 'I want those aphids.' George's 'request' showed that despite his apparently precocious vocabulary and speech patterns, he profoundly misunderstood the intention behind much of what was said to him.

It also showed that he had little, if any, concept of what Christmas was all about. This wouldn't have been because he couldn't remember the previous Christmas. George's memory is extraordinary; I sometimes think that he's never forgotten anything at all, and that his lack of an ability to edit or organize his memory is one of his main problems. No, George certainly remembered Christmas. He didn't understand the standard 'What do you want for Christmas?' question because he hadn't cottoned on to the giving-and-receiving idea. He didn't know what presents were for, either practically or symbolically. He didn't have the slightest notion of what he was supposed to want.

Never is the difference between the autistic and the neurotypical child more pronounced than at Christmas. Neurotypical children pick up the Christmas behaviour patterns – the rituals and traditions – really, really fast. By four, all neurotypical children understand presents. They enjoy the expectation, the novelty, the surprise; the act of unwrapping is in itself a pleasure. They know that a particular present comes from a particular person; they are capable of rudimentary gratitude, and some appreciation that a gift is a token of affection or goodwill, though they may not be able to mask their dismay if the present doesn't satisfy their expectations. They are just about old enough to enjoy giving something in return, and they are gratified by the expressions of delight on the part of the recipients. They are also old enough – just – to feel envy if another child has received something more desirable. And they will have no difficulty in distinguishing their own new possessions from those of their siblings. Jake's capacity to distinguish one trifling item from another – say, the bottle of bubble mixture found in his stocking from the one found in Sam's – never ceases to amaze me.

Autistic four-year-olds have very different reactions to presents. Some – usually lower-functioning, like Sam – will sniff each package and if it smells of chocolate will rip it open regardless of who it's intended for, social rules blithely ignored. The more able may be worried by presents. This was certainly true of George. They may come to like the toy inside, though with their restricted play skills it's harder to find toys that will appeal. But they won't like the element of surprise. They won't see the point of wrapping paper, unless they enjoy the physical sensation of tearing it off. Most of them would much rather be handed their *Thomas the Tank Engine* video in an unceremonial, straightforward manner. And if they understand the connection between present and donor at all, they'll be bothered by the pressure of expectation. Some sort of social response is expected of them. They don't understand which response, or why. The whole business makes them agitated and confused.

It's hard for an adult to accept this reaction. It's deeply ingrained in us that children want *things*, that acquisition is central to every child's enjoyment of life. Many adults aren't confident of giving pleasure to a child, or being liked by a child, unless they have brought them something. This is a pity, but it's common. The autistic child's indifference to, or active dislike of, being given things is yet another barrier to forming relationships. My Uncle Norman, on a recent visit, wanted to give each boy a five-pound note. Their reactions were entirely characteristic. Jake wanted to put his into his piggy-bank straight away. George squealed, 'No, Norman, I don't like money.' Sam simply threw his back across the table. Norman, who is used to the boys, was more than able to cope with rejection, but for less well-prepared adults such a reaction could be surprising and upsetting.

I couldn't quite believe, myself, the depth of George's antipathy to Christmas presents. (Sam, as usual, was more indifferent than hostile, and besides, in the days of his obsessions it was relatively easy to find things that would give immediate satisfaction, like toy helicopters and rubber snakes.) When George shrieked with horror at the sight of a parcel, or clapped his hands over his ears – which is what he still does if he wants to evade social demands – I would often conclude that he must be ill, or overtired. No child, surely, could be *frightened* of presents? And there were plenty of things he liked – some books, some toys, some videos. Could he really be so bitterly opposed to getting more?

Yes, he could. Or rather, I failed to recognize that what George was objecting to was the ritual, the social palaver, that surrounds present-giving, rather than the toy inside. If I unwrapped his presents myself, and left them lying about, getting a little battered and becoming part of the landscape, they eventually became acceptable. Then, perhaps, in an off-hand manner, I would introduce the concept of giving. 'Grandfather gave you that,' I might remark, weeks after Christmas; 'Caroline chose that for you.' Depending on mood, such comments might be met by a quick shriek of disapproval, or by quiet acceptance, even interest.

What should you do about a child who expressly rejects presents? You could, I suppose, ask family and friends not to waste their time and money on buying them anything at all. But this doesn't take into account the fact that most adults want to give things. People want to be kind, and the more handicapped the child is, the kinder they want to be. You could ask them just to give the cash equivalent, so that you can choose something acceptable, but this seems too functional and joyless. The best way, I think, is to explain the child's likely reaction, and ask people not to take it personally when a proffered gift is dropped straight into the wastepaper basket. (This has happened!) It's hard for feelings not to be just a teeny bit hurt, but, well, they're adults.

I think that people should go on giving presents, and the parent should stage-manage their distribution in whichever way is appropriate. Despite their negative reactions, nearly all the toys, clothes, books, videos, CDs, tapes, and so on, that give the boys real pleasure have been given by one generous person or another. I rarely have to buy them anything. Over the years, grandparents, godparents, aunts, uncles and cousins and friends have shown great ingenuity in the presents they've found for the boys. I'm very grateful. I can't pretend that gratitude is a concept that George and Sam have grasped as yet, but I like to think we're inching towards it. It's unusual that I, as a parent, have to train my children to learn to tolerate presents, but if they can master it, it'll bring them a few steps closer to inclusion in the 'normal' world. For the same reason, we celebrate their birthdays in a fairly conventional way, with guests, presents, cake and candles. By making the celebration predictable, the boys have learned to do more than just cope with their birthdays – they actually enjoy them in a mild way.

Donors who have been discouraged in the past by the boys' less-than-gracious reaction to their offerings should take heart. Because, in autism, play skills are delayed, many toys are still in use which would ordinarily have been consigned to formless ruin of oblivion. When Aunt Caroline gave the infant Sam twelve wooden men in a boat, who could have foreseen that he'd be doing his maths with them at age eleven? Who could predict that thirteen-year-old George's preferred reading would be inscribed, 'To George, with love from Granny Eva, Christmas 1993'? The boys' condition dispenses with ideas of what age – or gender – is appropriate. If they can use it, then it's very welcome, whatever it is. Jake, going through a toy box recently, said, 'I've grown out of this rattle. I think I'll give it to Sam.'

It's not only present-giving that makes Christmas different or difficult for autistic children. Most people's Christmases involve increased sociability, more visitors, noise and chatter that will be incomprehensible or even alarming. Few autists understand the point of conversational exchange in its own right. Then there's the special food and drink, which may appeal to some, but for most, Kanner's 'desire for the preservation of sameness' will not be waived for Christmas fare. As a family, we go in for Christmas dinner in quite a big way. Stuffings, sauces, home-made pudding and mince pies, a different wine for each course ... our Christmas meal takes no prisoners. But there's nothing on the groaning table that Sam actually wants to eat, except the outsides of the sugared almonds, and the icing on the cake. For most autists, their idea of a satisfactory Christmas meal is whatever they usually have; three fish fingers cut into quarters, dry cornflakes in a green bowl, orange squash with two bendy straws, or unrestricted access to a tube of Pringles.

Is that sad? Not necessarily. I see no need to deprive the neurotypical members of the family of their feast. Sam's enjoyment of his Alphabites won't be enhanced if we all eat them with him. I try to make him something that looks a little festive – say, a jelly decorated with a few sweets – but by and large, his social aloofness is quite handy. He doesn't begrudge us our gourmandizing, doesn't feel excluded because none of it appeals to him. He's got his eye on that cake icing; nothing else matters much.

Some aspects of Christmas do appeal strongly to the boys. They like decorations – glittery, sparkly ones, but also the branches of holly and yew, the trails of ivy and swags of bay, which we use to transform the house into an indoor forest. The boys, by autistic standards, aren't particularly resistant to change of this kind – perhaps they can see it's only temporary. George loves the Christmas tree. One year, in October, he sat himself down in the room where we normally put it, and announced that he was going to stay there until the tree arrived.

For George and Sam, Christmas is a pagan festival of light, heat and colour. They both love fires and candles and bits of ribbon and tinsel to flap. If the weather is icy or stormy, so much the better; both of them respond to elemental extremes. As a parent, I have to say that there are some advantages in the autistic attitude to Christmas. Alone among my friends, I'm not beleaguered by requests for expensive rubbish advertised on television or discussed in the school playground. I don't have to cope with the covetousness, disappointment, and hysterical overexcitement that so often tempers the normal child's genuine enjoyment.

George is capable of accepting some changes in routine as exciting. Sam is more troubled by the disruption, but even for him, there are aspects of Christmas that he welcomes. Not Father Christmas, though. Like most mothers, I introduced the idea of Father Christmas early on. George was appalled. A man with a deep voice and a beard? Like that terrifying individual who came to service the boiler? In *his* bedroom? At night? 'No, Father Christmas is NOT coming to George's house,' he stated. The terror has lessened over the years, and now, at thirteen, he shows some mild enthusiasm for Santa. He even wrote him a letter. 'Dear Father Christmas. I would like a stick of rock and some firewood. Love from George.' Sam remains impassive. When F.C. visits his school, he hardly reacts. Why should he? It's just another incomprehensible adult.

If I'd known the boys were autistic, I don't think I'd have let Father Christmas into their lives in the first place. The point of him is to give delight, a delight that comes not just from the bulging stocking, but from the magic and mystery, the sense of a benign presence who is ungraspable, but who has the child's best interests at heart. Autistic children don't want to be singled out by a bearded stranger, and they don't collude in magic because it involves the use of mentalizing skills they simply don't possess. A normal one-year-old doesn't understand magic either, because she hasn't yet grasped the concept of shared belief. In this respect many autists never progress far beyond that one-year-old level. To appreciate magic, you need a firm grasp of what's normal, what's expected. Autists, who see the world in disconnected detail rather than as a coherent whole, lack that overview of normality.

Now, we continue with Father Christmas mainly for the benefit of Jake, who at five is still a staunch believer. He'd be outraged if his brothers didn't get stockings. It's taken me years to train the boys to put their hands into their stockings. For a long time, they never thought of hunting for anything that wasn't on view. Out of sight was out of mind. If a favourite book was in a different place on the bookshelf, they couldn't find it. They never rummaged through a toy box (though they did, and do, rummage through handbags in the reasonable expectation that they will find Polos and chewing gum). So it was with their stockings. Father Christmas would leave a lollipop sticking out of the top. They would pull these out, grin, and eat them. But it wouldn't occur to them to look further. I must be one of the few mothers in the land who is still urging her children to pull things out of their stockings well into the New Year.

The Father Christmas business also raises the problems of instilling beliefs into autistic children. In a normal child, the gradual waning of belief in Santa is a rite of passage. I've never come across a child who felt cheated or deceived by finding out the truth. The child seems to understand instinctively that the whole thing is a friendly deception well suited to infancy. Children are not deeply rational; they want to believe in magic, but, at a certain stage, guessing the truth gives them a pleasing sense of importance. They recognize that the nature of their collusion with adults has changed. They recognize that to expose the deception to a younger child is unkind and unfair. But none of this applies to an autistic child. A more able autist, with typical literal-mindedness and regard for accuracy, may object to having been told a lie. The less able will simply accept whatever they're told without question. George's early fear of Father Christmas didn't prevent him from believing in him. George believes everything he's told. His intellectual passivity, his very limited ability to question things, may mean that he never will stop believing that Father Christmas rides on a sleigh and comes down the chimney.

What of the other big issue of belief – the Christmas story itself? Whatever your own beliefs or non-beliefs, if, as I have done, you send your children to C. of E. primary schools, there's no avoiding the 'true meaning of Christmas'. Nativity plays bring a mist to the eyes of the stoutest atheist, and it's a stern parent indeed who throws cold water on his five-year-old's enthusiasm for Baby Jesus. 'He who mocks the infant's faith/Shall be mocked in age and death,' wrote Blake. I'm an agnostic, but Jake is devout, and I'm happy for him to be so. Never are the consolations of religion more obvious than when one attempts to explain the mysteries of life and death to an anxious child. Jake has curiosity about the numinous, the intangible; he wants to know what happens beyond the here and now. Besides, his understanding of culture, history and politics would be terribly diminished if I withheld religion from him. I tell him Bible stories, and though I do punctuate discussions about the afterlife with riders along the lines of 'Some people think . . .' I try to leave his core beliefs intact.

For George and Sam, it's a different matter. When Sam was at the mainstream primary school, he received a report which simply said, 'Religious knowledge: Not Applicable.' How do you approach the idea of an afterlife to a child who seems unable to think outside the present? How do you explain the central moral tenets of Christianity – or of any faith – to someone who does not relate their behaviour to that of anyone else, someone who cannot commit an altruistic act because he cannot think himself into the position of another person? Even the most rudimentary religious understanding involves contextualizing. It involves curiosity about the origins of life, the nature of death. It involves using one's imagination.

I'm not saying that all autists are incapable of religious experience or religious instinct. Some, I expect, would appreciate the way a religion provides a clear code of conduct, a set of rules to organize behaviour. Others might enjoy the ritual of religious ceremony, a pleasingly reliable pattern with room for those slight variations which seem to fascinate some autists so much. And there may well be an element of aesthetic response. Both George and Sam like going into churches and cathedrals. George looks up at the ceiling and says 'Wow!' and Sam tests the acoustics with his verbal stims, which means our visits tend to be brief. George likes 'church music' (including 'You Can't Always Get What You Want' by the Rolling Stones, because it features choir-like chanting) and, to a limited extent, he likes the reliable cast of characters who turn up in paintings or stained-glass windows – he's certainly able to identify Mary, Joseph, shepherds, kings, and so on. But the normal range of childish questions about who made the world and where we go when we die remain unasked.

Jake and I have just been on holiday in Italy. A great thrill was putting a coin in a box and lighting an offertory candle. It took Jake no time at all to grasp the concept of asking God for something special, and he knew that 'something special' didn't mean a new GameBoy, either. I remember Sam, at a similar age, spotting the bank of candles at the end of a church in France. With a roar of 'Cake!' he ran the length of the church and blew the whole lot out.

God, Father Christmas and the Tooth Fairy worry and baffle George and make almost no impact on Sam. The Tooth Fairy we can dispense with; the boys don't want money, and besides, I've hardly ever seen any of their milk teeth once they're out. I think they must have all been swallowed. With Father Christmas it's a case of 'I've started so I'll finish,' though I do feel it might have been better never to have started. As for God, I feel wary of attempting to introduce an idea which, if it were grasped at all, would be swallowed whole. Belief in God has many uses for Jake, and I'm happy to concur with him. When he's older, he'll have a sufficiently broad experience and understanding to make his own mind up, and I hope I'll respect the faith, or lack of faith, he chooses. Belief has no uses for George and Sam – though this could change with time – so I leave it more or less untouched.

If I were a firm believer, would their imperviousness to religion worry me? I don't think so. Autists present a fascinating challenge to the theologically inclined. Their absence of altruism, their underdeveloped moral sense, is balanced by an absence of malice, an almost prelapsarian innocence. George once said to baby Jake, who was crying, 'Jake, Tinky-Winky created you for good, but you've turned out evil.' This sounds profound, but it is in fact an adaptation of a line from *Wallace and Gromit*. George does not truly understand the meaning of good and evil, nor is he (as yet) capable of implementing either. Most of the Ten Commandments are easy for the boys to keep. The Seven Deadly Sins are largely an irrelevance. The boys might covet their neighbour's ox – or their neighbour's ice lolly – but the desire would be purely for the ox or ice lolly itself, unaccompanied by any desire to get one over on the neighbour. Any temptations they feel arise from their overriding private preoccupations, not from the kinds of torments which neurotypical flesh is heir to. I met a very intelligent Asperger boy in his late teens, who was a fanatical Lib Dem (if that's not a contradiction in terms) and followed the workings of Parliament with close attention. At the time, a number of sexual scandals among politicians of the Chelsea-strip variety were coming to light. This boy, who wanted to become a politician himself, had the answer. 'I know how to avoid a sexual scandal!' he announced. 'If somebody said they wanted to suck my toes, I'd just say, "No, thank you."'

Wise words. This boy would not have been remotely tempted by any of the usual pitfalls, though when it came to resisting the temptation to recount everything there is to know about the Russian Revolution, he was as weak as water. What would a Christian theologian make of George and Sam's absence of sin? Though the Ten Commandments would pose few problems for them, Jesus's most important commandment – that one should love one's neighbour as oneself – would be impossible for them to attain, having so little sense, as they do, of what Uta Frith calls the 'last visible self', the tiny homunculus who oversees all the executive operations of the brain.

In the instance of religion, as in so many other ways, autism challenges our assumptions about what it means to be human. Christopher Smart in his poem *My Cat Jeoffry*, describes his cat as 'an instrument for the children to learn benevolence upon'. Perhaps this is the most comfortable way to consider the boys, from a Christian point of view. Good and evil may be closed to them, but they can be instruments for us to learn benevolence upon; unwittingly, they provide a yardstick for neurotypical moral behaviour.

17. Wear and Tear

I'm making a visitor a cup of coffee. 'Sugar?' I ask, silently willing the answer to be 'No.' 'Yes, please,' comes the reply. I fish my
tangle of keys out of my pocket, move quickly to the cupboard
and unlock it, trying not to attract the attention of George and
Sam. I fail. They leap down from their vantage point on top of
the Aga and bound across the kitchen. I reach for the sugar, keep
the boys at bay with swift jabbing movements of my elbows,
spoon the sugar into the coffee, and return the bowl to the
cupboard as if I were a wild dog protecting a zebra haunch from
a swarm of hungry rivals. In an autistic household, the physical
and emotional effort involved in performing the simple acts of
everyday life can be considerable.

What would happen if I do what normal people do – leave
the sugar bowl on the table, or on a shelf, or in an unlocked
cupboard? Well, the boys would help themselves to it, sometimes with spoons, sometimes with their hands, sometimes sticking their tongues straight in. What they didn't eat would be
scattered far and wide, so there'd be a patina of stickiness to
clear up, as well as no sugar left for anyone else, and a pair of
buzzing, hyperactive boys. My hypothetical visitor may be startled by my defensive elbow action, but he'd be even more startled, and disgusted, by the sight of the boys licking spilled sugar
direct from table or floor. And he wouldn't know about the
advances I've already made with coffee-making. Time was when
the coffee and milk would also have been locked up, not because
the boys wanted to eat them, but because they loved tipping
them over the floor or down the sink. I now have a shelf next
to the Aga on which jars of spice and bottles of oil are placed
in full view. That's progress. I still shudder at the memory of
the gallon can of olive oil that Sam up-ended; I came into the

kitchen to find it creeping across the floor, an advancing golden tide.

Both boys have a habit of putting things into an approximation of the right place. One of them – I don't know which – filled the kettle with orange juice. Liquid does go into a kettle, doesn't it? I didn't realize and switched it on. The air filled with the aroma of cooking marmalade. I sometimes dry out wet boots and shoes in the very coolest oven of the Aga. George popped his trainers into the roasting oven. The stench was indescribable.

I'm so used to the need for constant vigilance in small matters that I no longer feel the strain of it. It's the same kind of vigilance that any parent of toddlers needs to exercise, but in our case the 'toddlers' are strong and agile, and the need to supervise them will continue indefinitely. Though it has to be said that they're much easier than they were. They'll still appear as if from nowhere when they hear the click of the food cupboard being opened, but they're far more responsive, post-ABA therapy, to the word 'no'. They have no conscience, no inner voice to tell them that they mustn't touch this or that, but if an adult's there to give commands, they'll usually desist. The hundreds of tiny rules and tricks that have to be observed in order to keep home life from degenerating into chaos have become second nature to me and to the other adults who spend a lot of time with the boys. Visitors, however, constantly underestimate their speed and cunning. 'I'll just put my tablets out of reach,' they say, putting their little phial of poison on a shelf a couple of feet up, not realizing that Sam has the climbing skills of Spiderman. 'I didn't think he saw me put it there,' they confess, referring to George, whose eyesight would put the average eagle to shame.

I can't think of any aspect of daily living that hasn't been encroached upon by autism in some way, at some time. Take the car. George used to jump up and down on the roof, making huge dents. Both boys like sitting inside the car. Sometimes, to give myself a few minutes' peace, I'd leave them in there for a bit, but if I didn't remember to remove any cassettes, I'd come back to find them all eviscerated. Once, Sam ripped up the tax disc. I painstakingly pieced it back together, but was told that mosaic-effect tax discs weren't recognized by law. Then there were the more obvious hazards of letting children play in cars, like lights left on and twisted mirrors. And once or twice I've come back to find the seat smeared with excrement, though this hasn't happened for ages.

What a useless mother, you're thinking. Why did she let them play in the car at all? Well, because they wanted to. And because at the stage when they were wreaking most havoc in the car, they'd have been wreaking equal amounts of havoc in the house, and I prefer my house to my car, by miles. Smearing excrement, for instance, could happen anywhere. It's a popular hobby within the autistic community, especially at the lower-functioning end of the spectrum. I met the mother of a severely autistic sixteen-year-old, and asked her, nervously, about the problems of adolescence. 'Oh, masturbation's a godsend,' she replied breezily. 'It's so much better than smearing.' Oddly, it was the more superficially social-ized George, rather than Sam, who had the more passionate engagement with faeces. Touch wood, he's left that stage behind, but I still have to check the lavatories regularly. There are messy seats to be wiped, blockages caused by over-enthusiastic bottom-wiping to be shifted. Sometimes George uses a whole, unravelled, roll of paper to wipe his bottom, and then replaces it. Hand towels can also be used for this purpose. Donna Williams explains that it's easy for the autist to confuse the functions of slightly similar items. If it's whitish and squarish and lives near the lavatory, then it'll get used as lavatory paper. Alien objects are sometimes inserted into the pan. George put the video of *A Bug's Life* down the lavatory the other day. '*Why?*' I bellowed. 'Because I didn't want to watch it,' replied George, only mildly abashed. Well, ask a silly question.

Sam went through a phase of flushing underwear away. It was hard to prevent this. My usual answer with Sam is to keep things locked away out of temptation, but it's not realistic to lock up every item of clothing, and you can't lock lavatories from the outside, because if the boys can't gain immediate access to them, they'll use something else instead. Sam has had periods of weeing in alternative receptacles just for fun – tooth mugs, toy boats, that kind of thing. Unfortunately, his choices are often insufficiently capacious. This habit is clearly not one to encourage, so the lavatories needed to stay unlocked. Like most of Sam's 'challenging' behaviours, the interest in underwear disposal ran its course. When he was down to his last pair of pants and socks, he stopped doing it. Months later, when we had work done on the drains, the builders were surprised to find a couple of binbags' worth of stagnant undies.

I do now lock the bathroom from the outside. There are just so many enjoyable activities, from flooding to squirting toothpaste and shaving foam to running a bath and getting in with all your clothes on. George likes to wash his trainers, which involves immersing them in water and rubbing them with a bar of soap. He doesn't always take his feet out first. If he can't get into the bathroom he'll perform this operation in the washing-up bowl or the garden water tank. Then there are medical supplies. George once dressed a small finger wound with forty plasters. They made a rather neat globe, like a harvest mouse's nest. Sam once ate one hundred vitamin pills. I rang the hospital; apparently it doesn't matter as long as they haven't got iron in them.

Small irritations are more characteristic of life with the boys than major panics. Luke Jackson says he can quite understand why his younger brother Joe takes the laces out of everybody's shoes, and the batteries out of their toys – Joe enjoys chain reactions, and holding a battery is like holding 'a little piece of power'. I suspect there are reasons behind all the strange things the boys do, although George can rarely explain, Sam never. As I write, I'm looking through the window at George, who's in the garden. He's picking bees out of the fennel and holding them by their wings. He knows about bee stings. He's been stung in the past. Now I feel it's up to him. George likes insects, but I shouldn't think the feeling's mutual. The other day he came in with round green blotches all over his face, looking like a cartoon alien. He'd been stubbing out caterpillars on himself, like cigarettes. There's no malice involved; he doesn't set out to hurt caterpillars. It's just that he can't understand that squashing them causes them pain. His mentalizing powers don't extend even that far.

Now he's come in from the garden, and into the room where I'm working. He's chewing a bit of kitchen roll. This is one of his most harmless habits, but for some reason it's one that particularly annoys me. He sorts through the pile of receipts I'd put out to send the tax man, and he's turning some of them into flappers. They're not much good. He's moved on to a Jiffy bag, and he's tearing a strip off it. It never crosses his mind that I might have a use for those receipts or that Jiffy bag, or that he's disturbing my work. He's not thinking about me at all. His entire mental energy is focused on finding something satisfying to flap.

Both boys leave a trail of minor destruction in their wake. Flower heads may be snapped off, especially juicy ones like tulips. Drinks may be spilled – one of the most irritating things George does is turn 'empty' cups and beakers upside down when he's finished with them. Of course, there's always a drop left, so they leave a sticky ring. Sam tears the round bits off jigsaw pieces. They both snap sticks – I've just had to mend a broken flagpole brought to me by a distraught Jake. If there's a small hole in a sheet or a garment, Sam will enlarge it. He doesn't like buttons, and bites them off. As I write, he's come through the door, chewing the raised Harry Potter lettering off the front of his T-shirt. Sam's not destroying his T-shirt because he's angry. He's doing it because he is either annoyed or attracted by the rubberiness of the lettering, but he often does vent anger in physical ways, like tearing a book or breaking a toy. Despite George's apparently greater social awareness, it's more likely to be Sam who uses destructive behaviour to express emotions. George is almost never defiant, but Sam will have one eye on me as he launches an assault on something he believes I value. I have to be quick off the mark to make sure that thing isn't Jake.

As I hope I will by now have made clear, the autist can have an abnormal response to absolutely anything, be it never so mundane or apparently inoffensive. And the responses won't remain constant; the boys can change their minds and reverse their opinions. Take anything – take shoes. George was at one stage always barefoot, at another he would wear wellingtons on the hottest day. He put his shoes on the wrong feet every day for a whole term, and it didn't make any difference my swapping them over, because as soon as I wasn't looking he'd swap them back. He wore slippers (huge, shaped like leopards) everywhere – in the snow, to the shops, on the train. Then he went off slippers completely. At one time only shoes with laces would do, at another laces were anathema. Whatever his preferred footwear at any time, his decision is absolute. This summer, the very hot summer of 2003, nothing would induce him to wear open sandals. Last year, they were all he would tolerate. I don't know what criteria George uses when fussing about his shoes. The one thing I'm sure of is that ideas about fashion or looking cool are never, ever an issue.

Autistic minds run along single tracks. This means that the mental force they bring to bear on achieving their goals is immense. At any time, my mind is trying to cope with hundreds of things at once; persuading George to wear sandals is only one of them. At the same moment, all George's mental energy is concentrated on avoiding sandals. It's easy to guess who wins.

Both boys have 'issues' around nearly everything they eat, wear, sit on, watch or touch. Pyjamas are another case in point. When he was very young, George wanted to control the pyjama-wearing of the whole family. He would set his choices out on the bathroom radiators, and become distressed if we didn't bend to his will. He still tries to control Sam's pyjama-wearing; it's not worth putting Sam to bed in pyjamas that George deems 'wrong', because in the middle of the night George will rip them off him. Sam used to find it immensely difficult to get out of his pyjamas and into his clothes, so much so that I used to send him to school in his pyjamas, and press a bagful of clothes into the hand of the waiting teacher. Then I changed tack, and put him to bed in his school uniform, minus the shoes. I just didn't have the two hours needed every morning to get him changed. This was one of the many 'issues' that his home tutors have successfully addressed. He still takes a long time to dress in the morning, but it's half an hour now rather than two.

You need to be healthy in body and mind to deal with children like mine. You need energy, strength and stamina; it's a hands-on job. Like many parents, I'm irritated by the over-cautious attitude towards physical contact in schools insisted on by current legislation. I don't believe it's sensible or desirable to look after any young children without touching them, and for children with any sort of handicap it's impossible. There are times when George and Sam just have to be grabbed or restrained, for their own safety or the safety of other people. Any medical treatment will require a degree of physical coercion; the boys are impervious to reason, cajoling or even bribes when it comes to taking medicine. All their normal, routine physical care is difficult – I still have to straddle Sam's chest if I want to brush his teeth properly. Hair-washing and cutting, finger and toenails, headlice, foot-measuring, the application of suncream, the dressing of wounds – the boys aren't going to submit willingly to any of it. You need speed, cunning and, sometimes, moderate force. Thank goodness their adult teeth have come through reasonably straight and well-spaced; orthodontic treatment is something I'm happy not to have to tackle. The ABA/VB therapy addresses these areas, and there has been progress. A few weeks ago Sam, accompanied by Delia and Ian, went to the barber's in Battle for a triumphantly successful haircut.

Touch wood, neither of them has been seriously ill. They don't complain about minor ailments, so these tend to go untreated, and I can't see that any harm has been done. They seem to have many fewer minor illnesses than most children, which suggests to me that the link between minor illness and thinking about illness is strong even in young children. It never occurs to George and Sam to be ill, so they're not.

Of course they do occasionally need treatment. Both have had general anaesthetics to remove rotten teeth – dental work without a general anaesthetic wouldn't be possible. Given their poor diet and the difficulty of inserting a toothbrush between their gritted lips, I'm surprised they haven't had more decay. The last extraction was about eighteen months ago. George was at the height of his food-refusing phase and perhaps pain from the bad tooth contributed to it, though he never mentioned it. This was also a time at which he was reluctant to leave the house at all. I had to get him to the (unfamiliar) hospital for the operation. His quasi-anorexia worked in my favour in carrying out the nil-by-mouth instructions, but coaxing him into the car was no easy matter. I allowed two hours for the twenty-minute journey, and we needed it. Once in the car, we drove round and round Bexhill listening to Bach. This had a soothing effect; eventually George, wearing wellingtons, agreed to enter the hospital. He sat in the waiting room, shrieking and refusing to be weighed. In the end I had to stand on the scales with George in my arms, and have my weight subtracted from the total. Again, his self-imposed starvation came in useful. It's not every mother who can easily scoop up her gangly twelve-year-old son.

. He wouldn't tolerate the pre-med. I could see that no amount of plea-bargaining was going to work; the gentle approach was only prolonging the agony. I asked the hospital staff to hold him down and administer the anaesthetic by mask, not by needle. Brutal as that may look, it's quicker and therefore kinder. Six adults were needed. The struggle wasn't pleasant, but the tooth had to come out.

In the waiting room, the other parents and children had been staring at us, horrified. In the recovery room, roles were reversed. The other children moaned and groaned, and extorted huge promises from their parents about game cubes and PlayStation Twos. George sat up, spat out some blood, drank some water and said, 'Let's go home now, Mum.' No fuss, no whingeing. The only thing he insisted on was taking his bloodstained hospital blanket home. The nurse gave us his vast diseased molar, blackened and craggy like a citadel torched by barbarians. She presented it in a sweet little bag decorated with a pink fairy and blue elf, perched on a crescent moon.

★

The house is full of small signs of autism. The locked doors and cupboards are the obvious ones, but there are others, if you know what you're looking for. Any framed photographs have been placed face down by George, who finds photographs of people too much for his nerves. A search through the kitchen bin will reveal evidence of Sam – a T-shirt he's ripped up, the chewed-up tyres off one of Jake's toy lorries, a bowl and plate that he's thrown away along with their rejected contents. I usually give Sam plastic tableware, for this reason. Whenever I take the rubbish out, I have a quick check to make sure that Sam's definition of rubbish has coincided with my own.

Despite the mess he creates with food, paint, felt-pens, and so on, Sam has a tidy mind. Boots and shoes will always be placed neatly in pairs. He stuffs his socks down into the toe of his shoes. He doesn't like to see coats or jumpers lying about, and will always present them to their owners. He picks up stray toys and puts them away, though rarely in the right places. Sam's tidying-up techniques have refined themselves since the days when he used to throw everything out of the window.

A few months ago, George's main interest in life was sweet wrappers – only certain kinds, of course. He collected these and left them in little patterns around the house – seven yellow lollipop sticks in a fan shape, blue Softmint wrappers draped along the top of the radiator. It was quite hard to explain to helpful visitors why 'having a bit of a tidy-up' would send George into a hysterical frenzy, just as it's hard to persuade people not to say to George, 'Goodness, haven't you grown!' ('I won't! I won't! I'll stay little for ever!') The mini-obsession with sweet wrappers disappeared as quickly and suddenly as it came on, to be replaced by a tiresome habit of posting things down behind bookcases and radiators. Milk bills, bank statements, photographs, school reports, all disappear unless I whisk them quickly away. He'll give up on this soon, I expect. It's always been the pattern with both boys that one habit or fad disappears, to be replaced by another. It keeps me on my toes.

★

Autism directs the way I lead my life, in big things and in small. I say 'directs' rather than 'dictates'; I try to work round the obstacles that restrict my freedom, though I have to accept that many of them are unmoveable. Unlike most parents, I can't foresee a time when my children will be independent of me. For the foreseeable future, their needs will come first in any plans I make. I'm fortunate in that, as a writer, I can work from home, and fit my working hours round their timetables. I'm also lucky in that I live in the place I like best. Moving house would, I imagine, be traumatic for most autists, change-resistant as they are, but I don't want to move, now or ever. My travel opportunities are limited, though I do get my breaks. I don't feel I can leave the boys for more than a week, more out of consideration for the exhausted babysitters than for any other reason. But I do manage to get away without them for a few days a couple of times a year, which is more than most parents of normal children manage. I can't travel much with George and Sam. It's the journey that's the most difficult thing. I did take them to France a couple of times when they were younger, but George really hated being on the plane (I think it was the noise) and the airport was not an ideal environment. 'Whose child is that?' I heard someone say, as I struggled with the buckles on Sam's pushchair. I felt I could guess whose child it was. I wheeled round, just in time to see George's feet disappearing through the curtain on the luggage carousel.

At the moment, foreign travel for them isn't worth the disruption and stress. We manage a few days with family in Dorset or Devon (long car rides aren't a problem) and then Jake and I go abroad for a week with friends, leaving the other two at home. They may dislike my absence, but they're not capable of feeling that Jake's being given preferential treatment, any more than they would notice or mind if Jake's Christmas present was more expensive than theirs. They can't imagine what it would be like to be in a place they've never visited, and if they could, that wouldn't make them curious to go there. East, west, home's best, as far as George and Sam are concerned.

So, I accommodate my life to theirs, but I still retain a good deal of scope within it. The petty restrictions are, if anything, harder to tolerate than the big limitations. At home, I can't have things just how I want them. I love the sight of a pretty china bowl piled with fruit, but if I leave such a thing unattended on the table, each piece of fruit will be bitten, and the bits spat out. Whether there are three apples in the bowl or thirty, they'll get the same treatment. I'd be happy if the fruit was eaten properly, actually digested, but it isn't. This annoys me, but I remind myself that it's only quite recently that I've been able to leave vases of flowers round the house. In the past, the water from the vases would have been tipped up or drunk, the flowers shredded. Now flowers are largely unmolested, so perhaps one day I'll be able to put the fruit bowls back out . . .

I'd like to be able to have a bath without anybody else joining me in it. I'd like to open my handbag without finding a bitten-off lipstick or a capless, leaking pen. I'd like to be able to leave a pot boiling on the stove while I answer the door, without finding that an ingredient I hadn't bargained for has been added in my absence. I'd like to be able to watch television; usually I can't, because the boys go to bed late, and while they're up, they often want a video. Buying a separate TV for myself wouldn't be an answer, because George and Sam still have to be supervised. I can't sit in a separate room and concentrate on something else while they're still rampant.

I'd love to be able to get on with anything – reading, writing, gardening – secure in the knowledge that my sons are all safely and constructively occupied without my constant vigilance. I'd like not to have to load the washing machine twice a day. I'd love to be able to do what my friends do – act spontaneously, pile their children into the car and say, 'It's a lovely day. Let's go to the beach' or 'We're all going to spend the night with the so-and-sos.' But this is just how life is, and I don't waste time or energy fretting about it. One good thing about having children like mine is that they don't leave you much spare time for gloomy ruminations.

18. Compensations

Have I made life in an autistic family sound like hell? That hasn't been my intention. There are moments of extreme stress, but isn't that the case in most families? Our tensions, our flashpoints, are different from those of your average family, but who's to say they're more intolerable?

Perhaps this life would be hellish if I riled against it. Hell – my definition, anyway – is a place where you don't want to be, and from which you can't get out. When you have autistic children, there is no respite, either for them or for you. When they were younger, I used to watch them sometimes, and ask them, silently, look, couldn't you stop being autistic for a bit? Just for one day? I mean, a joke's a joke, lads, but this one's gone far enough . . . But I've long since settled into a fairly calm acceptance. They are what they are. That's all there is to it.

Our family life has its own rhythms, its own compensations. Every day, the boys make me feel bored and irritated; equally, every day they provide me with delight, amusement and joy. The sight of them at supper last night, for instance . . . They all sat down at table together: good. Time was when that would have been an impossibility. But I still can't serve them with the same meal. Last night, Jake had pizza, carrots, sugar snap peas, grapes, a plum and a mug of milk. Sam had a bowl of Day-Glo coloured cereal called Rainbow Drops, most of which lived up to their name and dropped to the floor. George had the carcass of Sunday's roast duck. He hauled this out of the larder himself, and tore at it with his teeth, like Obelix devouring a wild boar. The duck was still on its serving dish. George chomped on the skin and licked up the fat. To many, this would not have been a pretty sight, but I found it funny. Of course, on one level I wish that George and Sam would eat the carrots and the sugar snaps, but

I can't worry about that all the time. What makes me smile is the way that every single thing they do is so utterly characteristic. Never imagine that a child who doesn't talk or play much lacks character. Autism is an umbrella term; the condition in no way reduces individuality. The boys express their characters in their every tiny action, and individuality is something I'm inclined to celebrate. When George had finished slavering over his dead duck, he said to me, 'Thanks, Mademoiselle.' A little later, he asked, 'Can you get spaghetti from an owl?'

As a rule of thumb, as long as the boys are happy, I'm happy. There have been times – there still are times, perhaps always will be times – when they are far from happy. Sam, in particular, has frequent periods of distress, though these are not as prolonged or as intense as they once were. His agitation, his tearless crying, the noise that Clara Claiborne Park calls the 'banshee wail', still cuts me to the quick, every time. It's difficult to be the mother of a child who can't explain what's bothering him. It's as if I'm fighting an unseen enemy. Is he in pain? Is it something he's eaten? Is he frightened? Has he misunderstood something he's heard us discussing? Sam's shrieks could mean anything, from appendicitis to the fact that I've put his biscuits on a green plate instead of a blue one. The field of possibilities is dauntingly wide. It goes against the basic instincts of motherhood to raise children who can't be calmed, or comforted, or even properly fed. But the bad periods do seem to be growing shorter. The smiles, the social overtures, are becoming more frequent.

I learned, long ago, that loving children like these had to be unconditional. That's true of loving all children, actually, but with autism you quickly learn that you can't look for gratitude or reciprocity. You can't expect them to consider your feelings or share your interests. This wasn't a hard lesson to master. Loving them is the easy part. They're very loveable. Luckily, I'm not the only person who feels this. Some people may be alarmed or repelled by them, but others are attracted; both George and Sam have always had a secure fan base. Why should this be? As children go, they're unfriendly, indifferent, aloof. When Granny Eva fell downstairs and hurt her hand quite badly, she called out, 'George, can you help me?' George trilled, 'No, I can't,' as he ran gaily past. How loveable is that?

Part of their charm lies in their incorruptible innocence, which underlies even George's apparently callous response to his stricken grandmother. She asked a question – he supplied an answer. He doesn't mind what she thinks of his response. He doesn't mind what anyone thinks. It's not, exactly, that he doesn't care, it's that he hasn't got the capacity to consider the issue. The inability to think about the feelings of others has a positive side – George and Sam can never exploit or deceive. Soon after George was diagnosed, I described his condition to a friend. 'Well,' he said, 'at least he won't be a nasty child. It would be worse to be the parent of a bully, wouldn't it?' I think he was probably right.

It takes a while to understand just how deep that innocence is, to accept that autists don't mean anything personally. In *My Family and Autism*, the BBC documentary about the Jackson family, Luke Jackson's non-autistic sisters try to explain to him why a question like 'Does my bum look big in this?' should not be answered truthfully, or at least that the truth should be softened. Luke, articulate speaker at conferences and author of two published books before the age of fourteen, just doesn't get it. He's literal-minded; surely you should just tell the truth? It's unnerving when an intelligent, verbally able person makes a personal remark unmodified by social awareness. This hasn't yet arisen as a major problem with George and Sam because they don't often make any kind of comment about people. But George often tells visitors, 'Time for you to go now.' I would never be able to persuade him that this is rude. For him, it's just a statement of fact. Sam's equivalent is a simple 'Go a-way.'

The people who get on best with autists are those who can put their own ego to one side. Once you get used to it, and stop worrying about what the autist thinks of you (which is probably hardly anything at all), it's actually quite relaxing to be around people who ask so little socially, whatever they demand of you physically. I'm writing this in the garden. George is by my side.

He's completely happy with the September sunshine on his back and an empty Minstrels packet to flap. He doesn't require that I chat. Every now and then he makes a statement, which he wants me to corroborate or refute:'Wolves are usually black';'Helicopters have fires inside them'; 'There's nothing in the oven'; that kind of thing. As long as I supply the right answer, I can go on writing. I couldn't possibly do this if Jake was around, with his unquenchable thirst for interaction, but Jake has gone into Hastings with Ian to buy his first-ever pair of shin pads. Sam's safely in therapy. Sam demands no more than George in terms of conversational effort, but a great deal more in terms of supervision.

The Curious Incident of the Dog in the Night-Time, by Mark Haddon, is a novel about a fifteen-year-old called Christopher who has Asperger's syndrome. There's a scene when Christopher's father has to break bad news to him:

Father said, 'I'm afraid you won't be seeing your mother for a while.'

He didn't look at me when he said this. He kept on looking through the window . . . this was nice, having Father speak to me but not look at me.

This is the classic autistic reaction. What's important to Christopher is not the mood or the content of his father's doom-laden pronouncement, but the fact that, for once, he's not being looked at. Christopher doesn't immediately, intuitively ask himself why his father's looking out of the window, but no neurotypical person would be able to suppress such a question. The scene struck a chord with me. Both boys, but most particularly George, are far more comfortable with oblique contact. They're like wild deer in the way they cautiously approach, make contact, dart away again. And this can be more restful than the constant invasive chatter of normal children.

Many of the most aggravating habits of normal children are refreshingly absent. The boys have plenty of aggravating habits of their own, of course, but they don't whinge, compete, squabble or blame other people for their own shortcomings. They don't exaggerate minor injuries or try to get someone else into trouble. From George and Sam I never hear those tiresome phrases like 'It's not fair' or 'He started it' or 'It wasn't me' or 'Are we nearly there?' (which Jake's asking before we've pulled out of the drive). They may get cross with me when I thwart their desires, but they never criticize me, or anyone else. They never clamour for expensive treats or insist upon their rights; they are unmoved by crazes and playground fashions. They haven't the least notion of 'cool'. They are immune to peer pressure. They are always completely themselves.

And besides, they're very beautiful. There's an autistic 'look', which Asperger noted in his original papers. 'Elfin', 'ethereal' and 'dreamy' are the adjectives that come up most often. There are many exceptions to the rule, and some autistic children can be very plain indeed, but often they are outstandingly good-looking – much better-looking than one would expect from observing their parents. They have symmetrical faces, with dainty, regular features and large, bright eyes. They often look younger than they are; perhaps their faces, never distorted by the base emotions such as selfishness, malice and guile, retain that unclouded purity that is so attractive in babies. I've yet to come across a scientific explanation for the look, but it seems to me to be just as likely a part of the syndrome as an excellent rote memory or advanced spatial abilities.

Sam is a handsome, well-knit boy, with glossy dark hair, an elegant neck, and a rather haughty expression, almost like an Indian brave. His ceaseless motion keeps his muscles toned; his lack of self-awareness gives his movements an unconscious grace. George is a high-cheekboned beauty, with luminous eyes, like a supermodel on drugs. The boys have no opinions about their looks, which only enhances the effect. I have never seen Sam look in a mirror. George sometimes does, but only to pull faces. When they show preferences for certain clothes, they're guided by comfort or colour, or by some weird criteria of their own. I don't think they ever dress to improve their appearance, or to impress anybody else. The only awareness either of them has ever expressed to me is when George asks me to cut his hair 'like a mushroom', in other words with a straight pudding-bowl fringe. Similarly, I've never noticed the boys judging anyone else according to how they look, with the exception of George's taste for little girls with long blonde hair, and his dislike of men with big black beards.

Whether we admit it or not, we are hugely affected by physical appearances. Despite plenty of evidence to the contrary, we associate good looks with intelligence. At one end of the scale, people with cerebral palsy, whose condition has affected their control of their facial muscles, have a hard job convincing the able-bodied that they are of normal intelligence. At the other extreme, beautiful, serene, autistic faces, with 'speaking eyes', give an unshakeable impression of hidden ability, of a normal child locked up. Autistic beauty augments the fairy-tale feeling that the child is in suspended animation, enclosed just out of reach in glass or ice, or that the child is a changeling, a being from another world somehow left in our charge.

The beauty of autistic children does them a service and a disservice. It's good, because people are attracted to them; they want to work with such a lovely child – they want to help. But it's bad, because people find it hard to believe that their handicap is as profound as it really is. Many parents find it stressful to go about in public with their good-looking, anarchic child. One glance at a Down's child and people know they may have to make certain allowances. One glance at an autistic child will not explain nearly so much. I carry a printed card in my wallet which reads, 'This young person has autism,' followed by a brief explanation. The idea is that you present this card to soothe an irate shopkeeper or café owner, but I must admit I've never yet had the presence of mind to do so.

It's hard to observe a handsome, physically fit child behaving strangely without feeling that they're 'putting it on', that the child could control himself if he really wanted to. No one looks at a child in a wheelchair and thinks, 'Oh, for goodness'

sake, of course you can walk! Why don't you just pull yourself together?' No one looks at a child in a wheelchair and
blames his parents for his immobility: 'Why on earth haven't
you taught him to walk yet?' But people do look at autistic
children charging through crowds or throwing food about or
(George's speciality) taking things out of litter bins, and they
think – or sometimes say – 'Why don't you keep your children under control?' George and I had to queue in the building society, not so long ago, and George was in a panic. 'Don't
touch me! Don't speak to me! Don't look at me!' he shrieked.
A whiskery old lady in a headscarf bravely approached him –
she was considerably shorter than he was – and admonished
him. 'Young man! Don't be so darned rude to your mother.'
George opened his mouth as wide as it would go and screamed
in her face. I did my best to explain, but she wasn't having any
truck with this autism malarkey. Nothing would dissuade her
from the belief that what was needed was a jolly good hiding.
Most people find it hard to grasp that it's just as impossible for
an autist to 'behave' in public as it is for a child with paralysed
legs to get up and walk. Autistic good looks distract from the
severity of the condition. I know a mother who took her little
boy to hospital for his diagnosis and was told, 'He's beautiful.
What are you worrying about?'

I suppose some people find it sad that a child with a perfect
face is not 'normal'. I don't; for me, their angelic faces perfectly
express their innocence and strange integrity. I find the boys'
looks a huge compensation and solace. I never tire of gazing at
them. Though, of course, as their mother I would find them
exquisite even if they looked like gargoyles, I'm always pleased
when other people comment favourably on their appearance, as
they very often do. It's something positive that can always be said
because it's always true. Their behaviour often leaves much to be
desired, their appearance never does. And I can be as vain as I
like on their behalf because there's no danger of swelling their
heads. Vanity and autism are mutually exclusive.

The boys are disconcerting, messy, destructive, asocial and

unpredictable, unless you know them well. They are also non-malevolent, unworldly, handsome and intriguing. Autism is a fascinating subject. Books or programmes about savants with extraordinary 'islands of ability' always attract public attention. My sons are very far from being savants, but still, it's interesting – if frustrating – to try and work out the reasons behind their oddities. Why does Sam take the stairs in a series of jumps, both feet together? Why, when George fell in a river, did he lie on his back, supported by his billowing anorak, and say, 'That's our stew and dumplings gone west'? Jessy Park used to fill her glass with juice to a level determined by that day's weather and phase of the moon. Ben Jackson had to carry a Lilliput Lane ceramic house, a carriage clock, a soup ladle and a 'circle yellow dummy'. Donna Williams could hear a snake slither past the house when she was indoors. If you have to have a child with a disability, at least autism's an interesting one. On good days – on *very* good days – autism is its own compensation.

Postscript
What's Wrong with Being Autistic?

Seven years have passed since *George and Sam* was first published. Life with autistic people can feel static. They resist change. The introduction of anything new, whether it's a 'life skill', a foodstuff or a pair of shoes, usually meets with single-minded resistance. So I'm encouraged and surprised, re-reading the book, to find that much has changed, most of it (not all) for the better. Day to day, progress moves at a glacial pace, but looking back over a number of years, I can see we've come a long way.

George is now twenty-one, Sam nineteen. In theory, the dreaded process of adolescence is over, and we're all still standing. Jake, thirteen, has reached the point where George was when I left off writing the book – in physical terms, that is.

I've just filled in the census form; it still gives me a little jolt to record that this place, our home, is no longer George's primary address. George is in the second year of a three-year residential programme at the Mount Camphill Community, a Rudolf Steiner college about fifteen miles away. Jake calls the Mount 'George's university'. When he comes home for the holidays, like any other student George reverts to his old ways, lounging in front of the TV, taking all morning to dress, and being waited on hand and foot by his indulgent mother.

He comes home from college looking clean and fit. His skin is clear; his eyes are bright. The Steiner regime emphasizes physical and spiritual health. Fruit and vegetables are grown organically in the lovely kitchen garden; bread is baked on the premises. Garden and bakery are partly staffed by students. George spends a lot of time out of doors. The timetable is a balance of arts and crafts, practical skills, music and drama, and exercise. There's no television, no junk food; mobile phones don't work in the deep Wealden valley where the community occupies an old monastery. Festivals such as Harvest and St John's Day (midsummer) are enthusiastically celebrated. The Mount is the only special-needs environment I've ever been in which is not overheated.

I've always thought that I would only consider a residential placement for either of the boys if I believed it was right for them, not because it would make life easier for me. I miss George very much, but I now feel that he needs the degree of independence that the gentle support of the Steiner system can give him. George is a young adult; it is appropriate – even vital – that his activities, and the relationships he makes with others, have little to do with me.

Seven years ago, when I finished writing the book, I could not have imagined that George could have survived, let alone functioned so well, away from home. He is still vulnerable, naive, with little initiative or practical sense, sometimes over-compliant, passive. He still needs a sheltered environment and a lot of guidance and supervision, and I imagine he always will. But his social confidence, his ability to tolerate, even enjoy, the company of others, has increased enormously. At social events – for instance, a recent large family party for his grandfather's eightieth birthday – little or no special provision has to be made for him. He almost has a 'range of interests' – in the summer holidays he attends a special-needs art workshop and produces huge meditative abstracts, somewhere between Mark Rothko and Franz Kline. He enjoys golf with Vikki, his helper; he goes to her house and barrows her fallen leaves, does the crossword, has a cup of tea. His encyclopaedic knowledge of rock and pop enables him to have meaningful, if repetitive, conversations with those who share his enthusiasm. The days of semi-starvation are long gone; eating out is now a great pleasure, and his manners are good enough even for a smart restaurant. The striking progress he has made demonstrates the importance, for any autist, of being in the right environment. George has been lucky – luckier than most.

From eleven to sixteen, he attended the ASD unit attached to our state-run special-needs secondary school in Hastings. This was a wholly autistic environment: small, predictable, with a familiar cast of characters. At this stage, George's acute anxieties – mainly centred on change and growing up – would have prevented him from coping with a wider timetable, larger numbers and frequent changes of classroom. By the age of sixteen, he was calmer, and ready to be stretched a little further. By great good fortune he got a funded place at St Mary's College in Bexhill. St Mary's pupils have various forms of learning difficulty, moderate to high-functioning autism included. It does not cater for very severe impairments; it would not have been the right place for Sam. Indeed, George was in their 'nurture group': the lowest level of functioning.

St Mary's was exactly the right environment for George. His three years there transformed him. Staff outnumber students; every conceivable therapy is offered, and there is a twenty-four hour curriculum, so that a particular problem can be worked on throughout the student's waking hours. George began as a day boy. He stayed late one evening a week, going to a club, shopping for a simple supper, listening to music with his housemates. Eventually he was ready for weekly boarding. Everything was done at his own pace.

George loved St Mary's. He formed close attachments to students and staff. The presence of chatty, cheery, non-autistic peers was good for him (though a few years earlier he would have been unable to cope). He was well-liked; his self-esteem grew. The secure sense of belonging emboldened him; his eating became less faddy, and he abandoned the one set of clothes ('jade and turquoise') that was all he would wear when he arrived. The leavers' prom, held at a local hotel, was a triumph. George, handsome in his suit and tie, sat and ate with his friends, danced with his kind, self-appointed girlfriend and, with support from a staff member, sang 'Stand by Me' to the assembled throng.

Leaving was hard. Special-needs students get an extra year at school, but for many they need even more. Whatever their IQ level, many autists seem to be developmentally delayed; I feel that a good school would benefit both my sons well into their twenties. But we were, as I say, lucky. The confidence and independence

George gained boarding weekly at St Mary's enabled him to move on to his fully residential place at the Mount, where he has his own bedroom, his own possessions and his own small responsibilities. As I write, he's halfway through his time there. Those two heart-sinking words loom again: What Next?

I'm not going to attempt to answer that right now. Instead, I'll think about Sam. I see that in my Prologue I comment on the closeness of the two boys. At that stage, I would have said that keeping George and Sam together as much as possible was a priority.

That changed, dramatically, with adolescence. George somehow managed to be both passive and controlling; Sam, despite his belligerent and independent nature, didn't know how to prevent George from controlling him. George's daily greeting to Sam would be to pull the waistband of his trousers to check whether Sam was wearing the 'right' underpants. If not, he would try to strip him. George would interfere with Sam's food – he'd tip away a little of his juice, nibble the corners of his biscuits, remove one of three sausages. This would be irritating for anybody, but particularly for Sam, who a) dislikes being touched and b) has a 'thing' about the wholeness of what he eats. When they watched TV, George would tell Sam where to sit. When Sam played with noisy toys, sound-sensitive George would confiscate them. Their cheery closeness evaporated. Sam would glower, bite his fingers and growl in warning when George hoved into sight. When George started boarding, the breathing space it created for Sam was a great benefit.

Early adolescence, for George, created intense anxiety, manifested in shrieking, stubbornness and extreme eccentricity, but never in aggression. Sam was very different. He became violent and destructive. I think hormones had a lot to do with it; I also feel that, autistic or not, Sam would always have been something of a coiled spring. If they'd been 'normal' teenagers, Sam would have been out trashing cars and getting drunk, while George would have flopped about in his bedroom writing soulful poems and watching his hair grow.

For Sam, physical discomfort influences much of his behaviour. During his adolescent years, when he was changing fast, he was still experiencing eating difficulties. He would chew up quite a wide range of things, but then spit them out; there wasn't much that he would swallow. For several years he must have been under-nourished; his hunger could only be assuaged with crispy salty snacks of little nutritional value. The swallowing problem disappeared quite suddenly when he was about seventeen. I have no idea why. Now he swallows most of what he embarks on, and the range of acceptable foodstuffs, though still small, is much wider than it was. His temper has improved accordingly, though the problem hasn't quite gone away. I still pussyfoot round him, avoiding the confrontations likely to trigger an outburst. Sam hates the word 'no'.

Sam's discomforts go beyond eating. He seems to feel great tension, which he relieves by rocking, by playing loud and hard on his keyboard, or by drawing so hard that the pen goes through the paper. He sometimes hits himself on the head, deliberately, bites his hands, or stamps. These are warning signs. He feels being crowded as a physical threat; the worst thing you can do, if he's in a rage, is to try physical restraint.

His aggression is usually directed against inanimate objects. He went through a phase, years ago, of dropping milk bottles out of his bedroom window because he enjoyed the crash. I nailed up the window and, oddly, it didn't occur to him to throw bottles out of a different window. Problem solved, I thought, but I was wrong. He began dropping mugs or glasses on to the hard brick floor of our scullery, apparently just for the sound effect. This was a nuisance, but it happened so seldom that I took no action. Then, as his teenage anger mounted, he took to hurling down more and more breakables, no longer for fun, but as an expression of rage. We locked up all the china and glass: we eat off melamine and tin when Sam's around.

Without Sam's ABA training, it would hardly have been possible to keep him at home during his most destructive period, when he was about fourteen and fifteen. The compliance ABA had taught him meant that some disasters could be averted. When he was about to embark on a smashing spree, I would say, 'Go and sit in the car'; he would obey, and off we would go to the bottle bank for some legitimate smashing. However, such commands were unheeded once his rage had passed the point of no return. If this happened – usually if someone had physically intervened – his fury would bring about a state change so marked that his teachers wondered if he was having seizures. It is quite common for autists to develop epilepsy during adolescence, so I took him to the doctor, but epilepsy was ruled out.

During these outbursts, people, as well as objects, were in danger. The worst incident at school led to the flooring of several members of staff, after which Sam was put on a reduced timetable. For a year, he was at home with me for about half the time he should have been at school. At home, aggression was usually directed against me or my partner, Simon – in other words, against the people who were trying to control him. I don't remember him ever attacking a stranger and, thank goodness, he never hurt Jake. George sometimes received a (well-deserved) bite or pinch, but never a sustained attack.

Simon is bigger and stronger than Sam. When it seemed that removing Sam from the scene was the only option, Simon would do the manhandling, steering him out to the car to take him for a calming drive, listening to music. But the manhandling process often left Simon with puncture marks. As Simon is usually with us only at weekends, I sometimes had to offer myself up as a human punchbag. The worst incident I remember was once when Sam was raging in the kitchen I decided to operate the 'time out' principle. I bundled him out into the garden, told him he could come back in when he was sensible, and bolted the door. Sam didn't wait until he was sensible. He punched through the window, Tom-and-Jerry-style. There was a fist-shaped hole in the glass, but not a scratch on Sam. He reached his hand in, drew the bolt, came roaring back into the kitchen and knocked me down. There was little I could do other than allow myself to be kicked and bitten until the storm had passed.

I didn't enjoy this sort of incident, but I was never afraid. I knew Sam was stronger than me, but I also sensed that he didn't know how to use his full strength, and I relied on being able to outwit him. I also knew that the rage would end as inexplicably as it had begun, leaving Sam calm and apparently rather shocked.

It has been some time since we've had such an incident. Maybe we're better at spotting the warning signs; maybe Sam is through the worst of adolescent turbulence. But I still sense suppressed aggression in him, and this makes me reject the idea of a residential place. All too easily I can imagine how such behaviour could lead him to be classed as unmanageable: I see options closing for him. I do not want him to be 'controlled' by drugs. For now, I will continue to work at creating a living environment that keeps him calm and content.

I realize that what I've just written makes life with Sam sound pretty terrible. Funnily enough, it doesn't feel that way. Sam's adolescent years have actually been easier than the later part of his childhood; the period from about six to nine or ten. Sam's 'crash', as I call it in Chapter 8, has been, I think, the worst aspect of bringing up my boys – though George's quasi-anorexia ran it close. The time when Sam lost his skills, lost his smile, screamed in daily pain, never ceased his restless quest for sugar, found solace in nothing and nobody – that was bad. The adolescent aggression was only ever occasional, though it could be extreme. Days, even weeks, could go by without any real problems at all. His ability to enjoy things, to use his time purposefully, has steadily increased throughout the teenage years. There are still times when Sam is bored, frustrated or cross, but there are many more times when he seems happy: playing his keyboard, drawing and colouring, watching TV, 'cooking', 'reading', dancing, running outside, splashing in the bath. Sam has never regained the social instincts he had as a small child; he remains aloof from most people, most of the time. He dislikes crowds and, if the house is full of people, he makes himself scarce. I'd like this to change, but more for my sake than for his.

It has been much harder to find the right educational environment for Sam than for George. Sometimes I think Sam's needs and desires are almost incompatible with a school of any sort. However, my sanity, and my breadwinning, depended on having him out of the house for a considerable stretch each day. The law obliges the state to educate all special-needs children until the age of nineteen, so Sam has had to put up with it.

Like George, he attended the local secondary ASD facility, where the staff did their best, but the fact that his ability level was much lower than that of the other children, combined with the physically rather cramped setting meant that tensions tended to mount. At sixteen, the only place I could find for him was Grove Park, a state-run unit catering for extreme physical and mental disabilities. Most of the pupils were not on the autistic spectrum. Sam would be one of the few who were fit and strong. Was this the right setting for someone of his great energy? And was it fair to unleash him on his frail classmates?

I have been pleasantly surprised. The staff, able, committed and numerous, manage the contrasting needs of all their pupils with skill and humour. The building is more spacious, light and airy than his old school, and this has had a calming effect. Sam is now coming to the end of his three years at Grove Park. Academically, his progress has been unspectacular, but the change in his behaviour has been marked. No one could call him unmanageable now. He understands his routine, but accepts deviations from it. He derives pleasure from some of the activities, co-operates with speech therapy and music therapy, tolerates trips into the 'community' – shopping, cafés, train rides, theatres. His 'life skills' are not marvellous – he's not a well-groomed young man – but neither are they non-existent. He has not made friends, nor shown any desire to do so, but he coexists peacefully with most of his peers. Those he dislikes are the ones who make loud peculiar noises; a case of the pot calling the kettle black if ever there was one.

And now, because he's nineteen, it's time to destroy this settled and largely peaceful routine and start all over again. What does the future hold for Sam? Well, there isn't a suitable local college, so because I don't believe he's ready for a residential place, unlike

George, he's going to have a home-based programme, with visits to a day centre and a respite house. Until this is up and running, I can't comment on its efficacy. We'll see.

When people ask about autistic adolescence, what they really want to know about is sex. Well, I can't speak for everyone, but in our case the whole business has been less dreadful than I had imagined. To date, neither George nor Sam has made a sexual advance to another human being. Both, certainly, are fully physically mature and functioning, but as far as I can tell (which may not be very far) neither has even theoretically connected sexual sensations with bodily contact with others.

At St Mary's George had a girlfriend, the lovely, high-functioning, non-autistic Emma. She was good for his confidence; he enjoyed dancing with her and being singled out by her, but I believe that was as far as it went. At the Mount, he expressed a faint romantic interest in an autistic girl, but this didn't amount to more than enjoying being in her general proximity. As for Sam, he's never proved that he can distinguish between male and female. 'What's Grandfather, Sam?' 'A lady.' George might, very occasionally, linger over a picture of a pretty girl in a magazine; Sam would much rather look at a tractor.

It's been surprisingly easy to teach the boys that there is only one place for their solitary sexual activity – the bedroom. In early adolescence we had a few awkward incidents involving the removal of trousers in public, but only a few. Overall, their sexual behaviour is infinitely easier to manage than their toilet habits – George still leaves it in a mess, Sam still flushes away yoghurt pots, candles, rubber ducks, whatever, with expensive and inconvenient consequences. Their sexual aloofness is a measure of the profundity of their 'otherness', but I must say it simplifies matters.

That 'otherness', however well managed, never goes away. I'm so used to it that I forget how odd our home life must look to other people, with locks on many doors, piles of magazines in boxes for Sam to rip up, and the television permanently tuned to the CBeebies channel. George complains his foot hurts – I remove his shoe to find not a sock, but a skiing mitten. Sam strips for his bath – I catch my breath – is that a rare and terrible skin disease? No; he's drawn all over his legs and torso with felt-tips. Making George's bed, I find his treasures beneath his pillow: a broken CD cover, a label peeled off a jar of Nutella, a postcard from my god-mother, the printed-out lyrics to Fleetwood Mac's 'Man of the World'. Have I lost the turkey-baster, the nutcrackers, the rabbit-shaped jelly mould, any number of Tupperware lids? They'll be wherever Sam was last seen. A saucepan, left to scorch on the Aga, contains the remains of Sam's 'cooking' – chocolate mousse, curry and sultanas. The TV remote balanced on top of a door jamb; six spoons lined up to tackle one bowl of cereal; pieces of evidence of George's alternative world view are all over the house.

An autistic child becomes an autistic adult. Since I wrote the book, no new breakthroughs or theories have convinced me that a 'cure' is either possible or desirable. Some aspects of autism can cause great discomfort or distress. When one encounters an individual locked in a world of screaming and self-harming, it would be strange not to wish for some safe treatment that could alleviate the suffering. But a desire to control some symptoms is not the same as wishing autism undone. Gentle George, embarked on one of his huge, semi-abstract paintings, absorbed in his blues and pinks and greys; how should he be different? Sam, rollicking away at his keyboard in what feels like a one-man attempt to recreate Pink Floyd's recording stu-dio at their most experimental phase, 'singing' in an eldritch screech that gives him, at least, great satisfaction – this is what Sam is.

Watching the boys come through adolescence has confirmed my view that acceptance, tolerance and – where possible – celebration of autism is the best coping strategy. A couple of years ago there was speculation in the media about the possibility of a prenatal test to detect autism.* Jake picked up on the story, so I explained the implications to him – if autism was observable in an unborn baby, the mother might choose to end the pregnancy.

* At the time of writing (2011), no such test has been developed.

Such an idea was new to Jake, and unwelcome. 'Why would any-one do that?' he demanded. 'What's wrong with being autistic?'

Jake has never lived in a household not ruled by autism, and his acceptance is unquestioning. Yes, he has wished for non-autistic siblings, especially when he was younger, but he has found excel-lent substitutes amongst his friends, step-siblings, half-siblings, neighbours and cousins. It's second nature to hide his desirable possessions from Sam, but if he does find his chocolate advent calendar ransacked, his rugby gumshield munched out of shape or his can of Lynx emptied, he doesn't apportion blame, any more than he blames his beloved cat Yano for catching mice. At school, Jake was 'doing' *Paradise Lost*. We discussed how, before they ate the forbidden fruit, Adam and Eve had no knowledge of good and evil. 'Just like Sam,' said Jake. George, as typified by his eating hab-its, must have had a little nibble of the fruit, because he does have a rudimentary moral awareness. Sam has none.

Jake is in year eight at our local comprehensive, where he thrives. Always a sociable child, very much a team player, he often brings friends home, with no shred of worry or embarrassment about his brothers' behaviour. It helps that we have a large house and garden; it's easy to give everyone their own space. The only bad legacy of growing up with George and Sam that I can detect in Jake is a mild claustrophobia – he hates lifts and locked doors, presumably a legacy of his toddler days when I locked him in his bedroom to protect him from Sam's rampages.

Jake is lucky to live at a time when social stigmas are relatively weak. In previous generations, eyebrows might have been raised at his working mother and her permanent-but-not-married partner, his 'handicapped' brothers very much in evidence, his father, remarried and with a new family, making regular appearances, the floating population of friends, relatives and helpers – Jake never quite knows whom he'll find sitting at the kitchen table. But the twenty-first-century definition of family seems blessedly flexible, and if Jake does ever yearn for a conventional, Janet-and-John existence, he's never let on. It shocks and worries me to hear of abuse of and prejudice towards the disabled, but in Jake's experience, and in mine, people are sympathetic and well-meaning. For Jake, the greatest benefit of having autistic brothers has been the benevolent tolerance of human variety. He finds bigotry of any kind baffling.

Writing the book brought me into contact with many readers. Their responses have been overwhelmingly supportive, helpful and generous. I can only think of one letter that wasn't – it came from someone who thought my children would have been perfectly normal if only I'd disciplined them properly – whacked them, in other words. This huge imbalance in favour of goodwill is just as well, as goodwill is what George and Sam will always rely on. They will never fend for themselves, never contribute, in economic terms, to society. My attitude so far is best expressed as 'We'll cross that bridge when we come to it,' but I do realize that the thirty-year age gap between my sons and me means that one day I won't be there to help them cross that bridge. It is unrealistic to expect families alone to support those who cannot support themselves, but there is a worrying shortfall in the facilities available to adults with special needs. In a civilized society, my sons will not only be fed and housed, but stimulated, educated and allowed to express themselves, for the whole of their lives. Any political party that recognizes this, and which acknowledges and remunerates carers appropriately for the supremely important job they do, will get my vote.

What do my sons want for their own future? It's not possible to say. Social workers, health professionals and other concerned parties are, rightly, trained to ask the 'service user' about their wishes, to involve them in the consultative process, but with George and Sam this is a struggle. Sam lives wholly in the present. I don't believe he has the capacity to envisage a past or a future. I don't think he can imagine himself in a context he hasn't already experienced. Any question put to him on this subject, as on most, will be ignored, or met with a flat 'No', or even 'Go away'.

George can think about the future, a little, but he doesn't much like it. He's very interested in his own past, repeating endlessly the dates when he attended his various educational establishments. He used to dislike photographic evidence showing that he had physically changed; now, he's fascinated by it. The past falls into a fairly satisfactory pattern; the future is still worryingly amorphous. If asked what job he wants to do, he'll reply 'a zookeeper'. I hope, for the safety of the animals and the general public, that his ambition is never realized. I don't think he truly does want to be a zookeeper; I think he's just plucked the idea from the range of options he's encountered in the children's picture books he still enjoys.

'Are there any questions you'd like to ask me, George?' says the social worker at the end of a review meeting. George thinks for a moment. 'What colour is Tom Jones?' he asks. He has a huge mental repertoire of rock and pop music, and he always wants to know two facts about a singer: are they black or white, and are they alive or dead – 'in the ground'? (He came across a picture of Michael Jackson in an early incarnation. 'He's brown!' George exclaimed, 'but he dyed himself white!') For the foreseeable future, all decisions about the boys' needs will have to be made by me.

It's a big responsibility, and one I only feel qualified to take because I make it my business to understand my sons as well as I can. Years and years ago, I saw Donna Williams on the television. Asked for advice to parents, she said, 'Be your child's anthropologist.' With people who do not instinctively communicate verbally – even if they can talk – one has to pick up other clues to assess their needs, their well-being, their desires. All you can do is observe, as closely and as empathetically as possible. Autistic people can't, usually, put themselves in someone else's shoes. I, in theory, can, so that's what I try to do, but it's not easy, with someone who experiences the world so very differently. I'll sum up the extent of this difference with one small example. Sam really, truly, wants to eat deodorant. I really, truly, do not.

George's concern about which of his favourite rock stars are dead (it's a depressingly long list) is a manifestation of his long-standing preoccupation with death. He does not, exactly, mourn the demise of John Lennon, Marvin Gaye, Freddy Mercury, Les Gray of Mud; it's more that he wants, somehow, to pinpoint facts about them, to anchor them. He talks about his own death; he says he wants to be 'buried in the ground at Whatlington [our village]'. I interpret this not so much as a death wish as a request for reassurance that the place with which he has been familiar all his life will always provide him with a haven. I think it's a variation on the desire – shared by many neurotypicals – that, when they come home, their bedroom should be just how they left it.

I'm sympathetic to George's wish. I, too, want to be buried in the ground at Whatlington. And if I die in the knowledge that society will care for and respect my sons, I'll lie quietly in my grave.

Appendix
Mind the Gap

The *Mind the Gap* columns, which were the genesis of this book, ran in the *Guardian* from 2001 until 2003. Here are the columns in their entirety, together with two extra pieces (16 May 2001 and 15 January 2003) which appeared outside the series.

'It forces you to rethink everything you thought you knew about being human'

16 May 2001

When George, the elder of my two autistic sons, was diagnosed, we were told that the incidence of autism was one in a thousand. That was seven years ago. Now, parents of newly diagnosed children are often told that it is one in a hundred. Such figures are only informed guesses, but my experience bears them out. In our early days, I knew no other families in our predicament. Today, I hardly need look further than the end of the road.

Yet many health professionals deny that autism is on the increase. They attribute the figures to greater awareness of the condition and more frequent and accurate diagnosis. Yes, this is part of the story, especially with children at the more able end of the spectrum. The eccentric loner with a high IQ and a record-breaking collection of bus tickets would have been more likely, in the past, to struggle undetected through mainstream education, employment, even marriage. It's quite fun spotting Great Autists of the Past: the case has been made for Kafka, Wittgenstein and Bartók, and I have a pet theory about Cézanne: indifferent to public opinion, disliked touching flesh, had only one friend (Zola), worked alone in a hut, painted subjects obsessively. 'What shall I paint today? I know! How about Mont Sainte-Victoire.' But it is not credible that hundreds of thousands of more severely affected children could have existed, or been ignored or misdiagnosed, until the last few years.

I remember my own baby-boom childhood years clearly. I spent the sixties in a state primary school with a wide social and geographical catchment. Where were the autistic children? There were none there, nor were there any twirling in corners when I went to my friends' houses to play. I never saw any on buses or in shops or on the beach. Children like my sons George and Sam can't be hidden. You notice children who climb on roofs or up chimneys, refuse to wear clothes, leave trails of torn-up rose petals in their wake, sniff strangers by way of greeting, yell out 'Tumble-drier!' every fifteen seconds, bite their own hands until they bleed. Is autism on the increase? Yes, of course it bloody well is.

The question 'Why?' focuses at present on the debate about the measles, mumps and rubella triple vaccine. I don't think George and Sam were affected by MMR. My sons were born autistic, though I only recognized this with hindsight. But I have met many parents who do blame the vaccine, and I can't bring myself to give it to Jake, my youngest and only non-autistic child.★ If the government wants to restore public confidence in MMR immunization, it should commission research more comprehensive than any that has yet been carried out.

Autism was only identified in 1943; the study of it is still in its infancy. The genetic component has only recently been confirmed; many believe that there must be environmental triggers as well. Paul Shattock, of the University of Sunderland, insists that nothing should be ruled out. Pollutants, changes in diet, plastic bottles, heavy metals, prenatal infection ... the investigative net should be cast wide. Why are boys at least four times more likely to develop autism than girls? Why do one in three autists develop epilepsy? Why do many suffer from gut disorders? Why do some benefit from the removal of wheat and dairy products from their diet? In families containing autists, there seems to be a higher than average incidence of other conditions, including dyslexia and Down's syndrome — why? It is generally accepted that environmental factors are linked to the increase in asthma; why is it so hard to accept that the same could be true for autism?

Society would be best served for the future if money was put into research right now. Caring for an autistic person for a lifetime costs £3 million. If the incidence really is one in a hundred, the financial implications are staggering. Many autists need one-to-

★ 2012: Jake did eventually have the MMR at the age of four, with no ill effects.

one supervision for their entire lives. Even those who are highly intelligent – and the spectrum covers every IQ level – lack common sense and an awareness of danger. George is eleven; he can speak clearly and has some rudimentary academic skills, but that didn't stop him from sitting by the fire with both feet propped on a smouldering log, watching entranced as smoke curled up from his shoes.

George and Sam attend a special unit with trained staff, but the large majority of autistic children are not catered for by the education system. The government's policy on special needs is inclusion in mainstream wherever possible. The idea of inclusion (apart from being cheaper) is that the special-needs child will learn from the example of his mainstream peers, that contact with them will 'normalize' the child. While this may be appropriate for other kinds of disability, in the case of autism it is misguided, even harmful. If an autistic child could learn like that, then he wouldn't be autistic.

Autism forces you to re-evaluate everything you thought you knew about being human, including education. What would you look for in a good primary school? A cheerful busyness; bright, frequently changing wall displays; energetic music and drama; team and group activities. Variety, creativity, a sense of adventure, a feeling of belonging. All this is anathema to autistic children, most of whom would function better with blank walls, muted colours, low lighting, no background noise, as few changes as possible, and a slow, painstaking introduction to even the simplest group activity. Many suffer 'overload' from too much stimulus. When they overload, they shut down; and when they have shut down, they learn nothing. Many absorb information more easily from a non-human source such as a television or a computer. Contact with even the gentlest teacher can be overwhelming; tone of voice, changing facial expressions, jangly earrings, the pressure of incomprehensible expectations, all make it impossible to make sense of what is actually being said. I know one boy who cannot tolerate laughter.

The new parents of any child find assumptions challenged. 'I can't survive without eight hours' sleep,' is one of the first beliefs to go, swiftly followed by, 'If you feed them spinach early on, they'll prefer it to chocolate,' and, 'They much prefer wooden toys to all this ugly plastic.' But when you have an autistic child, the challenges are fundamental. Normal children are wired to understand social rules. They observe human behaviour intently, and they copy. They are tameable; they carry inside them a voice that tells them how to act. They may ignore or disobey that voice, but that's a choice. Autistic children have no such instinct, no such voice. They cannot be tamed. Through a system of positive and negative reinforcement, desirable behaviours can be boosted and undesirable ones reduced, but this is training, not taming.

Their powers of generalization are limited. You can teach them that they mustn't take sweets from the post office; this doesn't mean they'll know not to take sweets from Sainsbury's. You can teach them not to bite their baby brother, but it won't stop them from sinking their teeth into anyone else's baby.

Autists are said to lack a 'theory of mind'. They can't guess what you might be thinking. They see no need to impart information, unless it is information about, say, manhole covers or tree frogs. George and Sam never tell me when they've hurt themselves or when they've had a dream, or if anything unusual happened at school. They don't know that I don't already know. One of the earliest diagnostic signs is a baby's failure to use the 'shared point'. George and Sam rarely drew my attention by pointing; at ten months, Jake was pointing for England.

Just as they can't read my mind, so I don't do a very good job of reading theirs. Their motives remain mysterious. The difference is that I see the need to try, and they don't. Donna Williams, who has written one of the best accounts of the autistic experience in her autobiography, *Nobody Nowhere*, says that you have to be your child's anthropologist. You have to watch, and record, and reach your conclusions slowly. You have to accept that you could be wrong about everything. Nobody can do it for you, and it may take twenty years, but if you want to understand your child, it's the only way.

'For the autist, obsessions are a way of life. Thank God the ones that fill my sons' time are (mostly) harmless'

6 June 2001

I miss launderettes – that stale, humming fug, that soap-operatic feeling that all human life passes through their doors. At one time I spent many a peaceful hour watching my autistic son Sam jump up and down in front of the dryers. Our visits to the launderette were purely recreational; cheap, harmless family excursions. From the age of eighteen months, Sam was obsessed by laundry in all its aspects.

It started with washing machines. Sam tried to say 'washing machine' before he attempted 'mummy'. He created them wherever he was – by rotating a sock inside a shoe, or spitting bits of apple into a bucket and shaking it while making whirring noises. One birthday he was given a Barbie Laundry Center in moulded pink plastic; he wouldn't let go of it for twenty-four hours. The interest widened to embrace tumble-dryers, washing lines, clothes pegs, baskets, irons, ironing boards, soap powder, fabric conditioner ('Want 'dishner!'). He would demand to be lifted up to other people's windows to peep at their white goods. When we visited friends, Sam approached their utility rooms as reverently as if he were entering Tutankhamun's tomb. I searched the library for books with pictures of laundry aids. Sam loved them all, from *Mrs Tiggywinkle* to *Tom and Pippo and the Washing Machine*.

He had other obsessions, too: oast houses, broken chairs, barometers, food processors, grandfather clocks, vacuum cleaners, video credits and bottles of lavatory cleaner glimpsed through frosted glass. Sam's interests were useful from my point of view, being easily gratified and relatively safe. We spent a lot of time in Currys – 'Do you need any help?' 'No thanks, just looking.' A key episode of Mr Bean was watched to extinction. This was less safe. Mr Bean gets stuck inside a tumble-drier; I found Sam stuffing himself into the plate-warming oven of our Aga in emulation of his hero.

Then, overnight, Sam lost all these interests. I hoped this would clear mental space for a wider variety, but instead his range diminished to hand-biting, string-twirling and bouncing – little more than physical sensation. At the same time, his language dwindled to almost nothing. That's why I miss launderettes. At least they were something you could talk about.

Obsessive behaviour is one of the commonest traits of autism, and one of the least understood. It may be an attempt to impose order on an incomprehensible world, it may be symptomatic of the fact that autists can observe minute detail but cannot relate the detail to the wider picture. Their tremendous powers of concentration can lead to real expertise, as in the case of Temple Grandin, an American woman who is a world-leading designer of cattle-handling devices. For most autists, however, their obsession is not 'useful'; it is an end in itself. One man collected all available information about the addresses of juvenile courts. When a well-wisher, in an attempt to broaden his horizons, presented him with the addresses of other kinds of courts, he rejected them, complaining, 'They bore me to tears.'

Trains, bus timetables, weather patterns, electrical circuits, street plans and lamp-posts are all common obsessions. In young autists an absorption in the works of the late, great Rev. W. Awdry is almost universal. George, my older autistic son, went through his Tank Engine phase, but failed to obsess on Thomas, James, Gordon or any of the main players. George favoured Douglas, who doesn't feature in many stories, never appears on T-shirts or in pasta shapes, and speaks in a Scottish dialect that induces lockjaw when read aloud. Douglas has an identical twin, Donald, but Donald was nowhere with George. He bored him to tears, too.

Some obsessions recur less frequently. Among trainspotters and stamp collectors at a recent workshop was a youth who stated his hobby as 'rescuing young women from prostitution'. A young man I know has a fascination with Sir Paddy Ashdown, to whom he attributes super-heroic skills. Obsessions can tip over into phobias, and an autistic phobia can be very controlling. Andrew, ten, can make himself physically sick at the mere thought of fruit (any fruit), or seedlings, or penises. Since all three feature prominently in the average primary school day, life with Andrew can be hazardous.

Obsessions come and go according to mysterious and ungovernable laws. We're all right at the moment – George is on sperm whales (better than lavatory cleaner) and Sam just wants to put everything into the bin, which is tiresome but not fatal. The worst I've heard of is a compulsion to inspect the wheels of moving cars. I'm keeping my fingers crossed – it's as effective as anything else.

'Yes, of course autistic kids can be a challenge – but their innocence and unselfishness are a unique joy'

20 June 2001

My friend Clare is directing a project at the Royal Opera House in Covent Garden. Twelve young autistic people, aged ten to sixteen, attend workshops culminating in a performance. Their theme is maps – real maps, imaginary maps, weather maps, maps of the stars. They use music, dance, speech, mime and drawing. I scared Clare witless by telling her that group co-operation would be impossible, that the children would be overwhelmed by the huge mirror-lined studio, that her material was too complicated. Then I went along to watch.

I was wrong on all counts. Eleven years' experience with my two autistic sons had left me unprepared for the extraordinary collaborative and creative powers of this group. The participants were 'high-functioning': that is, they all had fluent speech and were literate. But being high-functioning does not mean 'nearly normal'. Not one of them could have been mistaken for a normal child. Eccentricities of gait, manner and intonation, and unusual preoccupations (varieties of Ribena, other people's toenails) characterized them all in some measure. Robert (approx. twelve stone) found it hard to resist lying on top of Justin (approx. five stone). Alice wanted to show everyone her new bra. Olivia told a joke: 'Knock, knock.' 'Who's there?' 'Victoria.' 'Victoria who?' 'Victoria Beckham.' Boom, boom. But throughout a two-and-a-half-hour workshop they concentrated, followed instructions and combined forces to produce coherent performances. And – most unexpected – they supported and helped each other.

The difficulties of working with autistic people cannot be underestimated. This group were exceptional in their calmness and lack of aggression. But watching them reminded me that, despite all the problems, there is much to celebrate. By its very nature, autism excludes many less attractive human behaviours. The group displayed no spite, no competitiveness, no cynicism, no materialism. They were not remotely 'streetwise'. They made no criticisms of each other or of the adults working with them. They accepted what was offered at face value, and they did not look for more.

'That's boring,' 'It's not fair,' 'I hate you,' 'Are we nearly there?' I must be one of the few mothers who has never heard these phrases uttered by her children. George and Sam, born twenty-one months apart, have never quarrelled. They rarely hurt each other. Their relationship is largely non-verbal, but they like to be together; when they are out of each other's sight they communicate by strange whale-like noises. At eleven and nine, they share baths and car journeys with perfect equanimity, and are often found curled up in one bed like the princes in the tower. They hold all their belongings in common, having virtually no possessive instinct. Poor Jake, who is three and not at all autistic, has to be selfish all on his own. 'No, Sam, it's mine. You can't have it,' he cries, clutching to his chest some toy in which Sam has shown no flicker of interest.

Offer George or Sam a coin and they hand it back, having ascertained it's not chocolate. They are unmoved by playground crazes; advertising has no impact. They bear no malice, they never gang up, never seek to hurt people's feelings. They cannot lie or cheat; Jake can. They express emotions simply and bodily – they literally jump for joy.

These agreeable characteristics are, of course, symptoms of the deficits that define autism. George doesn't lie, not because he has a sense of honour, but because he is oblivious to the subtleties of human interaction. Sam leaves Jake's toy alone not because he's unselfish, but because he has little interest in Jake, and no curiosity about the uses to which one might put the toy. This gratifying lack of guile and greed is a tremendous barrier to their intellectual and social development.

The 'savant' skills demonstrated by a few autists are, similarly, symptoms of the underlying handicap. Some autists have 'islets of ability', but if the 'islet' cannot be linked to the intellectual 'main-land', it is of limited use. But when is a deficit not a deficit? A talent for drawing, or music, or maths, brings pleasure and interest, whatever its origins. My boys are not savants, but like all autists they are true to themselves. There is an incorruptible innocence that deserves to be honoured. Sam likes to hear Fatboy Slim sing-ing, 'I have to celebrate you baby, I have to praise you like I should.' Sometimes, that seems appropriate.

'It's summer, and the kids' sleeping problems are worse than ever – time for some tips from Margaret Thatcher'

4 July 2001

On the hottest night of the year so far, George, eleven, went to sleep at midnight. At which point three-year-old Jake awoke. Jake stayed up until two. Just as he nodded off, Sam, nine, sprang into life. Sam didn't sleep again until seven, when George came down for his breakfast, fresh as a daisy. Yes, you worked it out correctly: I had no proper sleep at all.

But it's not quite true to say that I had absolutely none because, over the past eleven years, I've learned how to doze quite effectively while chaos rampages around me.

The concept of the 'power nap' is one of the few good things I got from Margaret Thatcher. So if you pieced together all my scraps and wisps of sleep, you would probably total two or three hours. And to be fair, this night was not typical. Jake's usually fine, and Sam's much better than he was. But the last time I could rely on sleeping through the night, the Berlin Wall had only just fallen and Nelson Mandela was still in jail.

Sleeping problems are almost universal among autistic children. Looking back, it's the first symptom that manifested itself in George. We didn't know he was autistic until he was four but, from the day of his birth, we knew he wasn't sleepy.

He was born, very angry, after a long and difficult labour, at ten in the morning, and he kept his eyes open all day. He had a look of the utmost vigilance, as if someone had played a trick on him and he was going to make sure it didn't happen again. His eyes were large and bright, and they drew lots of attention.

'Isn't he alert?' everyone remarked. 'He's going to be very intelligent.'

He kept the rest of the ward awake all night. Desperate, I rang for the duty nurse. 'Change his nappy!' she barked, and vanished.

The pattern, or lack of pattern, was set. George never slept for more than an hour and a half. He was happy awake, as long as he was being held up so that he could look around. After three weeks, the health visitor ordered me to get a dummy.

'Otherwise,' she warned me, 'you will die.'

The dummy helped. Gradually, George's sleeps lengthened, but he still spent most of his time awake. Eleven years on, he often wakes in the early hours, and gets into bed with me. Sam was a more placid baby, though I now realize that he wasn't sleeping as much as I thought. He just lay in his cot, fingering his soft owl. George's autism took the form of over-vigilance; Sam's of detached indifference. Once Sam was beyond the cot stage, the trouble began. He became wildly excited at bedtime – laughing and shouting. We spent all evening returning him to bed, wishing him goodnight, closing the door. But there wasn't any point. We drove him round in the car late at night. I went to the doctor.

'Oh dear,' she said. 'I am sorry. Well, goodbye.'

I went again, and at last wangled some dope out of her.

'I have to warn you,' she said, 'that this makes most children sleep, but in a minority of cases it has the opposite effect.'

Well, guess what? Sam swallowed the medicine, and that night his head hardly touched the pillow. Autists, for mysterious reasons, are often able to 'override' medication.

I decided to do it the continental way, keeping him up with me and pretending I was enjoying his company. The pretence wore thin when, between midnight and seven in the morning, he would wake up as many as eight times. The removal of gluten from his diet, followed by three secretin injections, helped dramatically. He now sleeps solidly for eight hours – with the occasional exception.

Autists, it seems, are out of synch with their bodily needs. They feel discomfort, but cannot easily identify it as hunger, thirst, cold or a need to sleep or to urinate. Non-autistic babies learn in time to respond to the dictates of their body clocks; autistic ones may not. Donna Williams describes this dislocation in her autobiography, *Nobody Nowhere*. She also describes a terror of falling asleep: 'Frightening as my mother had become, I would go into her room ... Unknown to my mother, I lay stiff and silent under her bed, almost too afraid even to breathe ... and waited for the light to come.'

This mother was a drunken, abusive monster. If her daughter was driven to seek shelter from so unsatisfactory a source, how can I deny my sons nocturnal access to me, if that seems to be what they need?

'So you think you've got fussy eaters? George and Sam take the problem to new heights'

1 August 2001

It's never sensible to leave any of my children alone in the kitchen, but one bleary dawn George went down ahead of me. I staggered after him. The cat had been sick on the table. Worse, he had been sick in the place where George sits. Gentle reader, you would be well advised to skip a few lines. George sat down in his place and began to eat the sick.

This is the second most disgusting thing I've seen this year, I reflected as I scrubbed his hands and swilled out his mouth. (The prize-winning incident also involved cat sick; I shall save it for another occasion.) But George, who is eleven and autistic, showed no disgust. He ate the sick because it was in the place where, most days, he'll find a bowl of Coco Pops waiting for him.

Most autists have problems with eating – or rather, the eating habits of most autists are seen as problematic by their carers. Sometimes absolutely anything will be consumed, with no discrimination and no awareness of satiety. But extreme faddiness is much more common. Many insist on sameness. Food has to be presented in unvarying ways – three sausages on an orange plate at five o'clock sharp; dry Frosties, but only from miniature boxes; Walkers prawn cocktail crisps, but not if the packet's emblazoned with a promotional Spice Girl.

Sometimes food of only one colour is acceptable. Take red; does this mean tomatoes, strawberries, red peppers, delicately rare beef? It does not. It means red Smarties (throw the rest away), Hula Hoops in a red bag, Ribena, ketchup if you're lucky. On holiday in France, I had to evade George each day for long enough to slip Penguins out of their blue, green or yellow jackets into the single travel-stained red wrapper I'd had the foresight to preserve.

'Oh, but all children are fussy!' I hear you cry. 'My Archie hardly eats a thing.' In my experience, this turns out to mean that Archie only likes two kinds of green vegetables and isn't terribly good about fish. No, until you've met my Sam, now nine, you don't know what fussy means. For two months Sam ate only the tops of Jaffa Cakes – and when I say he only ate these, I mean it almost literally. I used to throw the bottoms out for the birds. They bounced.

For Sam, food is an adversary. He only reluctantly gives in. He becomes beside himself with hunger, but fails to connect eating with feeling better. He may have trouble with his swallowing muscles; he often gags, and prefers food of a consistent texture, like rice crackers. He used to crumble and scatter food, and preferred eating off the ground, like a shy animal. It's only recently that he'll sit at table, and he won't use cutlery. Sam eating a fried egg with his bare hands is not a pretty sight. He will snatch smoking-hot burgers from the pan with no apparent pain. His appetite has improved immensely since I removed gluten, casein, aspartame and monosodium glutamate from his diet; his self-chosen staples are now an eccentric but reasonably wholesome mixture of eggs, rice, marzipan, dried blueberries, sorbets, burgers and chips.

His attitude to food is calmer now. There was a hideous phase when he became a sugar junkie. He thought about nothing else. Cupboards were raided, pockets picked, a friend's wedding cake swiftly and efficiently stripped. There wasn't enough sugar in the world for Sam. But even during this, his worst phase, he was a sturdy, healthy child, with clear skin, glossy hair, and excellent muscle tone. In fact, the only child who 'failed to thrive' was non-autistic Jake, who eats a balanced diet, enjoys helping me cook, but weighed only sixteen pounds at a year old and is still the smallest child in his school.

The voice of common sense tells me, 'They'll eat when they're hungry.' No, they won't. George once ate only three Twiglets in four days, and he wasn't ill. 'Let them try what's on your plate.' Neither boy shows the slightest curiosity about adult food – unlike three-year-old Jake, whose standard greeting to his grandmother is, 'What's in your sandwich?' 'Provide an interesting range of foods.' Well, I enjoy food, I'm a reasonably adventurous cook, I don't eat junk, and my attitude has made no difference. For years the boys put everything into their mouths – paint, paper, sand, earth, spiders, stones, other people's medicines ... We had some spectacular nappies. But faced with anything of nutritional value, their lips remained firmly sealed.

You have probably heard of the 'holy fools' of old Russia; solitary figures who were eccentric, irrational, often mute, sometimes naked, tolerant of extremes of cold and hunger, indifferent to social status, and revered as 'blessed' by their more conventional countrymen. It seems highly likely that these 'fools' were autistic.

The fools ignored questions, which was seen as proof of wisdom. Those who spoke muttered incoherently, parroted, or used bizarre phrases. Their odd speech habits were thought to indicate prophetic powers. When Grisha, in St Petersburg before the revolution, shouted and ranted, bystanders would crowd around and listen, because they believed that the Holy Spirit was working through him. Significance was read into actions as well as words.

When Nicholas of Novgorod pelted a visitor with cabbages, it was assumed that he was illustrating the petty squabbles of the townsfolk. Pelagija Serebrenikova was admired because she threw stones into a flooded pit, then waded in to pull them out. Fools could address tsars or bishops with impunity. It is unlikely that the fools themselves would have had much interest in their influence, but the respect accorded them opened doors for impostors such as Rasputin.

It is extremely difficult for the non-autist not to impose interpretations on autistic behaviour. We are hardwired to fit all actions and remarks into an emotional and social pattern. The underlying consistency of motive is essential to our sense of what it means to be human. But in observing autists, we need to suspend assumptions. If one of my autistic sons rejects a present – as they often do – this has nothing to do with their feelings about the donor. If they fail to cry at the death of a pet or a person, this does not –

necessarily – mean they are indifferent. Conversely, if they laugh, it may not even mean they are happy.

George has always been prone to gnostic utterances, and I'm never sure how much significance to attach to them. To his bawling baby brother, George said: 'Jake, Tinky Winky created you for good, but you've turned out evil.' This was an adaptation of a line from *Wallace and Gromit*. It wasn't used at random, but one should not infer that George has any real apprehension of, or interest in, the nature of good and evil.

When he was quite tiny, George fell into a stream. He lay on his back, buoyed up by his billowing anorak, contemplating the sky until I fished him out, whereupon he remarked: 'That's our stew and dumplings gone west.' This line belonged to Elvis, a *Fireman Sam* character who had set fire to the kitchen. Its literal meaning was lost on George, but he had picked up the sense that it was the response to a mishap.

Much of George's vocabulary and sentence structure is lifted from stories, poems and videos, which lends an air of profundity that makes interpretation even more tempting. 'We're lost because the spring has gone,' he declared after unseasonable snow had felled the daffodils. And once he pulled the flaccid slice of dill pickle out of his hamburger and handed it to me saying: 'Mum, this is my conscience.' The holy fool goes to McDonald's.

'Why is he doing that?' People often ask this about the boys, and I rarely know the answer. Sam spent a lot of time in rapt contemplation of a broken chair. 'It's as if he can see things we can't see,' said a friend, and she could be right. I don't believe Sam sees ghosts, but his sensory perceptions are certainly different from ours. He systematically flushed all his underwear down the lavatory. I don't know why, but he wasn't – as one might assume – doing it to annoy me, any more than I imagine Nicholas the holy cabbage-hurler was trying to hurt his visitor. It just provided some sort of satisfaction.

Most children attribute human ideas, feelings and intentions to their toys from about eighteen months. Such play is a rehearsal for the complex social game in which they will be involved for the rest of their lives. A key feature of an autistic child is that there is little or no symbolic play. The more able may eventually attach meaning to inanimate objects – the autistic writer Donna Williams describes this – but such symbolism is private, unshared, closed. Though we are baffled by autism we may at least gain, through studying the differences, a greater understanding of ourselves.

'Sam has absolutely nothing in common with the average nine-year-old – apart from an irrepressible lust for life'

29 August 2001

'So what is it that's different about your children?' I am often asked this by people who haven't met them. Curiously enough, I've no pat reply. Described separately, autistic characteristics don't sound so very peculiar. Fussy eating, poor sleeping, fixations on particular objects or activities, dislike of change, destructiveness . . . 'Oh, but aren't lots of children like that?'

The truth is that autists do *everything* differently. I find it hard to answer the question because I don't know where to start. Physical appearance is as good a place as any. Sam is nine. He is a handsome, athletic-looking boy, but he has never looked in a mirror nor taken part in any organized sporting activity. Today he's wearing shorts and a sweatshirt. Both are on back to front; the sweatshirt is punctured all over, like a colander, because Sam has found some scissors. His plimsolls – he won't wear proper shoes – are on the wrong feet.

The shoe size is an approximation because he won't have his feet measured. He's not wearing underpants. The clothes are the fifth set he's had on this morning, because one of his 'stims' (self-stimulatory behaviours) is to wet himself, just a little bit, and then change all his clothes.

Lift Sam's shirt, and you'll find swirls of felt-pen all over his tummy. This is done for physical sensation, not for visual effect. His hands are swollen and calloused from years of being bitten and banged together. I've never been able to cut his fingernails, they just have to take care of themselves. A fine white line runs from his nose to his mouth. This is a duelling scar – the duel was with our late peacock. When the peacock displayed, Sam loved to burrow into the fluffy feathers at its rear end. The peacock, understandably, wheeled round once and lashed out with its spurs. This didn't put Sam off.

The first thing Sam did today was to stuff his pyjamas down the lavatory. He couldn't flush it, because I've put the chain out of reach. I issue lavatory paper in small rations, too – to leave out a whole roll is asking for trouble. Next he took one look at his breakfast and slid it, bowls and all, into the bin. He poured his juice – and my tea – down the sink, then went into the garden to pursue his hobbies of pulling bricks out of the path or climbing on our (slippery, tiled) roof.

It's not all bad. Sam's in a pretty cheerful mood at the moment. He loves the trampoline and climbing frame. He'll listen to the stories that three-year-old Jake likes, although if I leave him alone with the books he'll tear them up. He'll 'dance' to music – Jimmy Cliff at the moment. He loves tickles, and sometimes accepts a cuddle though he's quite likely to follow it with a pinch. On the beach or in a wood he'll run for hours in any weather, happy and indefatigable. At some point he'll have a fit of giggles, and at some other point he'll sob and sob, and refuse comfort. I can rarely trace the reason for either the laughter or the tears.

Sam's usual facial expression is impassive, even haughty – he looks down his nose like a Red Indian chief. His repertoire includes a mischievous grin, a smile of welcome for favoured visitors, and an expression of fury. But he has never shown embarrassment, self-consciousness or shame, and rarely fear. He can talk, but doesn't often see the point. When forced to speak, his voice sounds rusty with disuse.

There's almost no overlap between Sam's day and that of a normal nine-year-old. There is no imaginative play, no competition, no peer-group interaction. Sam would rather play with a burst balloon than a football, or a scrap of string than a PlayStation. He has no intellectual curiosity. He can be cajoled into doing a jigsaw, building a tower, or sorting shapes, and he completes these tasks without complaint, but he never seeks them out. Without adult intervention, he would exist entirely in the realm of physical sensation.

And yet, somehow, he is full of life and character, even fun. He is humorous and lovable and – up to a point – loving. Sam's world has no past, no future, no moral code, no aim beyond immediate gratification, but it is recognizably his own place. I am not invited to join him in it, but I find it fascinating to watch.

19 September 2001

'He can't be autistic,' I said, when worries about George began to surface, 'He's too cuddly.' My understanding of autism didn't extend much beyond *Rain Man.* I shared the common misconception that autists were always aloof, shunning human touch.

Some autistic babies stiffen and cry in their mothers' arms, and only relax when left alone. Others, like George and Sam, delight in being lifted, tickled and bounced. This variety of response makes early diagnosis difficult. George was passionately attached to me. At his six-week check the doctor said, 'There's a baby who is in love with his mother' – a remark that did much to compensate for the ragged nights, hourly feeds, and George's insistence that I hold and gaze at him at all times. Some mothers use breastfeeding to catch up with Proust or the lesser Trollopes, or at least with day-time TV. If I stopped looking at George for even a second, he refused to feed.

Sam, much less demanding, accepted affection from everyone with a placid smile. He didn't seem to single me out, and switched from breast to bottle with supreme indifference. Neither ever had a normal response to touch, but the differences were subtle, and I only fully recognized them after the birth of Jake. Jake was a snug little parcel. He nestled in my arms in a way the others never quite did, and he explored me in a way that suggested interest in me as a person, not just an object. Jake was a good fit.

The peculiarities in George and Sam's responses have become more marked, but neither ever withdrew from physical contact. Rather, it has to be on their terms. As toddlers they wouldn't hold hands or sit on my lap, but they loved to be carried or squeezed or to lean against me. George has always preferred to sleep clinging on to my back like a baby koala. It's not that comfortable now that he's eleven and his feet are as big as mine. Neither likes impulsive gestures. Sam will accept kisses and hugs, but he needs advance warning.

The autist's sense of touch is heightened. The world of the proximal senses is both fascinating and frightening. Temple Grandin, in her autobiography *Emergence: Labeled Autistic*, describes how, as a child, her stiff petticoat felt like barbed wire. She finds firm, even pressure calming, and has invented a 'squeeze box' for herself, based on her own designs for cattle-handling devices. A strong, confident hug is usually more acceptable than a gentle pat. 'Kissing better' doesn't work; autists don't believe in mind magic. A consoling embrace may be the worst thing for a child who is upset. This is hard for parents. Even now, I find it almost impossible to suppress the instinct to hold a crying child, even though eleven years of experience should tell me to leave them alone.

All babies put everything into their mouths. Lips and tongues are more efficient tools for exploration than clumsy infant fingers, but by two most have stopped this. At eleven and nine, George and Sam still do it. Some autists touch, lick and smell people as if they were objects, which can lead to misunderstandings. Autists, who have no 'theory of mind' – that is, no ability to guess how someone else might be thinking or feeling – are no respecters of personal space. George, on holiday in France, flashed a brilliant smile at a pretty woman in a bikini. She beamed back, but her expression changed when George seized her breasts and rotated them in one swift movement. After a faltering '*Je suis désolée* . . .' the limits of my French were reached. Another little boy I know goes up to people in the street and pees on them.

Autistic responses to pain and pleasure can be blurred. When Sam was eighteen months old, he used to sting his face with nettles deliberately. George hates to touch anything with his fingertips – he used to lift food and drink with his elbows – but sore throats and earaches are endured without complaint. Touching people has more to do with physical sensation than emotional expression. It's clear that the boys feel affection for familiar people, and they make some kind of connection between affection and physical contact, but there is little sense of reciprocation. They would never think to cheer or greet another person with an embrace. I've always had a physical relationship with George and Sam, but I had been a mother for ten years before I received a kiss from any child of mine.

'No one knows why autistic children are often so beautiful, but it can be a great comfort to their parents'

10 October 2001

The recent suicide of Helen Rogan received considerable media attention. Her body was found below the Hounds Ghyll viaduct, in Consett, Co. Durham, with that of her 11-year-old son Mark. Mrs Rogan was a single mother: Mark was autistic.

I have no intention of commenting on Helen Rogan's despair. It's not something I've experienced. But one comment from their neighbour struck a chord: 'Mark was a beautiful little boy. To look at him, nobody would have known he was suffering any illness.'

It is surprising fact that many – though by no means all – autistic children are exceptionally good-looking. Of course, every mother believes her children to be the most beautiful on earth, but anyone who knows my sons would agree: George and Sam are extremely physically attractive.

Hans Asperger, who published a pioneering account of autism in 1944, remarked on the ethereal beauty of his patients almost as if it were a diagnostic symptom. No one, so far as I know, has yet advanced a hypothesis to explain this.

Is it the absence of the more disfiguring human emotions – guile, malice, greed – that keeps the autistic face characteristically beatific? The eyes are large and bright, the smile undirected and serene. The autist often gives the impression either of concentrating on an inner world, or of looking through and beyond us to something out of reach.

For us ordinary mortals, does beauty have to contain an element of inaccessibility? One thinks of the beauties of fairy tales, untouchable in rose briars or glass coffins; the handsome prince whose face can be glimpsed only at midnight, and who then vanishes. Then again, John Wyndham's Midwich cuckoos were beautiful, brilliant children planted by aliens among ordinary families in an English village. In *Autism: Explaining the Enigma*, Uta Frith writes: 'Parents of autistic children find this story deeply evocative of . . . their own experiences.'

Certainly, we struggle to associate beauty with impaired intelligence. Asperger writes of the autist's 'strikingly intelligent physiognomy'; such an appearance can be misleading. While IQs of every level can be found on the autistic spectrum, in the majority of cases there is some mental retardation, and the handicap is often profound. Yet it is hard to believe that a truly handsome child is not withholding some hidden intelligence. One mother I know, whose three-year-old is undergoing the diagnostic process, was told by a health professional, 'He's beautiful. What are you worrying about?'

It's ironic that these children are, typically, devoid of vanity. George and Sam do not consider themselves handsome, because they have no objective means of considering themselves at all. They react to other people's looks, but only according to their own criteria – George likes blond hair; he doesn't like beards, especially black ones. They have no notion of fashion, but wear their eccentrically assembled clothes with grace.

Some parents report that their children's good looks cause them to be unfairly judged. The kind of in-supermarket behaviour that would be overlooked in a child with a visible condition, like Down's, provokes disapproving comments.

'It's so sad, she's such a pretty child.' I've often heard this said. But why is it sad? My children's beauty has always been a source of solace to me. When you've had a terrible night with a small baby, you can restore your affection for the child by dressing it up and making it look really sweet. Similarly, I can rise above some of the more 'challenging' behaviours of George and Sam through the simple satisfaction of gazing at their perfect faces.

It means, too, that there is always something positive for other people to say about them. People want to like attractive children, and that is a good start. It can't be sad for the child. It can only be sad for the parent who still clings to the fantasy of what they hoped their child would be, and that is a fantasy that you really do have to get rid of. For me, their appearance comes under the heading of 'Reasons to be Cheerful'. I never tire of being told how beautiful my children are because, unlike most aspects of this baffling condition, it is something certain. Yes, they are gorgeous, aren't they? Thank you very much.

'Sending off an autistic child's stools for analysis is an interesting idea. Until you come to collect the samples'

14 November 2001

'Have you had their stools analysed?' asked another mother during one of the many note-comparing conversations in which the parents of autistic children indulge with a kind of gloomy pride.

No, I hadn't, and I didn't fancy it much. I'd had their urine analysed, removed gluten and casein from Sam's diet, treated them for thrush, injected Sam with secretin, put them through Auditory Integration Training, but so far I'd avoided this one. I knew what would happen. First, I'd reject stool sampling as not practicable, then I'd push the idea to the back of my mind, then I'd allow myself to listen to the arguments, and finally I would – as it were – bite the bullet.

With a heavy heart I took the number of the dietician who reads entrails – or rather, the contents of entrails – and, yes, eventually I rang her. She was reassuring: intelligent, concerned. Stools analysis, she explained, can reveal the presence of harmful parasites. It's not an allergy test, but it shows up deficiencies or intolerances. 'Just collect three samples and pop them into containers.'

That shouldn't be difficult, I thought, since there hasn't been an inch of floor space uncrapped on in my house in the past eleven years. I sent off a hefty cheque, and received a box full of pots and scoops. The samples, said the accompanying literature, should be collected on three consecutive days. George only goes about twice a week. I would have to ignore this instruction.

'The sample must be uncontaminated by urine.' How could this be achieved? Autistic children won't oblige with the little vessels provided. In the matter of defecation, George and Sam have always been free spirits. The days of Turner-Prize-winning displays on walls and windows are (touch wood) over, but performing to order is not within their repertoire. Months of teaching Sam not to poo in the bath had to be undone. Bathwater, I reckoned, must be less contaminating than urine, so Sam's bath was cleared of boats, penguins, clockwork frogs and the like, and I hovered in my plastic gloves, scoop poised. I had to act fast to prevent the precious morsels from disintegrating.

George, a child of nature, prefers to do it in the garden. I had discouraged this, but now I was shooing him out in all weathers. At last, a substantial prize lay steaming on the path. Out I hurried. George was nowhere in sight. As I shovelled, it crossed my mind that this might not be his own production, but that of a fox or badger. I looked forward to the laboratory report: 'We recommend that you no longer feed your son on slugs, earthworms and old crisp packets.'

Three plastic tubes per day, each to be labelled with the date and hour of collection. You mix the stuff with special liquid until it looks like pea soup, then you stopper it and mail it to the appealingly named Great Smokies Diagnostic Laboratory. I was called by a lab worker. 'Could you give me the date of collection?' 'I filled out the labels,' I tersely replied. 'Unfortunately, there has been leakage in transit. The labelling is obscured.' My heart went out to the poor woman. When she was at primary school and the other girls wanted to be air hostesses or ballerinas, did she say, 'When I grow up I'd like to open leaky parcels of other people's shit?'

Great Smokies sent long and fascinating reports. Both boys were rampant with bad bacteria – pseudomonas, citrobacter freundii, giardia lamblia cysts. Their gut flora resembled my flowerbeds after next door's sheep have broken in. The dietician recommended supplements and antidotes; six different potions, totalling nineteen daily doses. All that remained was for me to insert these potions into the boys.

I mixed them into their drinks. They spat, and threw their beakers away. I stirred them into icing sugar. They abandoned it after a couple of licks. 'Mix them with ketchup,' suggested the dietician. 'That disguises most tastes.'

Tastes, maybe, but not colours. The ketchup turned pale orange.

The boys smelt a rat – or something worse. These supplements are disgusting. After a few more tries – spoonfuls of honey, freezing it into ice lollies, baking it into gingerbread like marijuana – I gave up. I have a vivid apprehension of the menagerie of undesirables rampaging through my sons' bowels, and a box of expensive supplements sitting in silent reproach. Oh, and my bank balance developed a leaky gut. Any cures for that?

12 December 2001

Jake (aged three, not autistic, stirring the Christmas pudding): 'I wish I will see a reindeer. What do you wish for, Mum?'

Me (weedily): 'I wish that everyone has a happy Christmas.'

Jake (exasperated): 'Oh, Mum, you could have wished to see a bat in the day. George, what do you wish for?'

George (staring at the pudding): 'I wish for a pudding.'

Jake: 'What about you, Sam?'

But Sam has no wish. Sam does not have the means of expressing a wish, but nor – I think – can he grasp the concept. Autistic people tend not to project forward or backwards. They live in the moment. Their capacity for abstract thought is limited; they don't ask themselves, 'What if?' They are absorbed by what they experience directly, through the senses – hence George's 'wish' for a pudding that was already there.

It is at Christmas that the contrast between my boys and other people's children shows up most vividly. The differences are not all bad. George and Sam do not clamour for presents. They are immune to the blandishments of advertising. Avarice and acquisitiveness don't exist for them. The things they most enjoy about Christmas are tinsel to finger and flap, candles to blow, cake icing to nibble, log fires to throw things into. George, at nearly twelve, has just begun to show an interest in Father Christmas. He has written a letter, though it contains only two requests: for firewood and a stick of rock. Sam is as indifferent to Santa as he is to most adults, real or imaginary. Jake opens his advent calendar every morning and counts the remaining days. George and Sam show not a flicker of anticipation. They'll be excited, but only when the tree is up, when things glitter and dangle in front of their eyes.

Years ago, when George was Jake's age, when asked what he wanted for Christmas, he replied, 'Aphids.' A kind godfather approximated with a box of stick insects. It was only a long time afterwards that I understood George's request. In a book called *The Bad-Tempered Ladybird*, the constant refrain of the eponymous hero is, 'I want those aphids.' George had associated the word 'want' with the word 'aphids'. As so often – far more often than we realized in those days – he had misunderstood the point of the question.

The boys have no desires – or only rudimentary desires – because, like all autists, they are 'mind-blind'. They cannot put themselves into the position of another person. When we covet our neighbour's ox, it's because we want the ox, but – more importantly – it's because we want whatever our neighbour's got, just because he's got it. We compare ourselves to our neighbour, we strive to be like him, or try to avoid turning out like him – delete as applicable. It's called society. George and Sam might possibly covet their neighbour's ox – or their neighbour's lollipop – but they don't give a stuff, one way or another, about their neighbour's feelings or opinions. They don't know their neighbour has feelings or opinions. For the autist, there is truly no such thing as society.

Clara Claiborne Park, in *The Siege*, her excellent account of her autistic daughter Jessy, describes 'a tiny golden child ... circling round and round a spot on the floor in mysterious, self-absorbed delight ... She doesn't want any objects. Instead, she circles her spot.' The 'siege' Park laid was to force Jessy out of her charmed circle, to plant and nurture want and need in her, because without them there is no growth.

The sequel to *The Siege*, the story of Jessy's emergence as an adult, is called *Exiting Nirvana*. It is a painful irony that we parents must destroy our children's isolated Nirvana if we want to have them with us in our world. We are snakes in Eden, but our unfallen children are untemptable, so we must force-feed them the fruit of the tree of knowledge of good and evil. Autism is incurable; an autistic child becomes an autistic adult. But we should strive to extend the overlap between their understanding of the world and ours.

The essential characteristics of social behaviour have their obverse: there is no generosity without greed, no kindness without spite, no love without hate. I need to drag my autistic sons into some kind of recognition of social behaviour if they are to be at ease in our world. So my Christmas pudding wish is that, by next year, George and Sam will have learned what wishes mean.

6 February 2002

By the time George was three and a half, I was worried. The sunny, attention-seeking baby with prodigious skills – colours recognized by eighteen months, singing long songs word-perfect at twenty months, spelling short words at two – had become a nervous, antisocial little boy with echolalic speech patterns and little interest in play.

At his routine developmental check, the health visitor set out a puzzle of animal shapes. An elephant arched its trunk over smaller animals. 'What's that, George?' 'It's an elephant.' 'Well done. And that?' 'It's a cherry cake.' It was a hippo. 'This one?' 'It's a chocolate cake.' No. it's a lion. 'What about this?' 'It's an almond cake.' Well, close, but actually it was a rhino. 'He's got a sense of humour, hasn't he?' said the health visitor.

But he hadn't. George was naming the animals as cakes because in a book called *The Elephant and the Bad Baby* the elephant's trunk reached over a row of cakes in the same way as it did on this puzzle. George was using one clue only – position – to identify objects. The important characteristics were ignored.

The health visitor wasn't worried, but she agreed to let a speech therapist see him. She – I suspect – knew instantly what was wrong. He was given a physical check-up – no problems. An expert from Guy's Hospital came to see him, and diagnosed Asperger's syndrome – the more 'sociable' form of autism. He has since been demoted, and is now simply autistic, though, compared with Sam, his condition is mild.

At this point we had no concerns about cheerful two-year-old Sam. It was another year before his hearing tests were unsatisfactory; perhaps his indistinct speech was due to glue ear? No, it was more than that. An educational psychologist dismissed the theory that any peculiarities came from copying George: 'You can't copy something as fundamental as eye contact.' She presented Sam with the usual tests – building blocks, shape-sorting. He wouldn't co-operate. 'Oh, he can do all these things,' I said. 'He just doesn't want to.' 'The point is,' she said, 'that at three and a half, he should want to.'

She got him into an excellent special-needs nursery, where he prospered. 'We can just call it language delay,' she said. 'We don't need to label him.' I disagreed. Labels help. A label gets you a statement of special educational need, Disability Living Allowance, sympathy and tolerance for misbehaviour. You get to occupy the moral high ground: a comfortable, if sometimes lonely, spot.

So there we were, with two very different eccentric sons, both exhibiting the 'triad of impairments' necessary for a diagnosis of autism. These are: impaired communication, impaired social interaction and impaired imagination. Every person with autism has all three, if only to a minor extent.

I've heard horrendous stories of misdiagnosis, delayed diagnosis and endless referrals. We were relatively lucky; George was just four when he got his 'label'; Sam was four and a half. But, paradoxically, it would have helped if, as babies, their symptoms had been more severe, so that intervention could have started earlier.

I am convinced that one must lay siege to an autistic child. There is no cure for autism. There is no 'normal' child screaming to get out. It is in everyone's best interests to modify their less acceptable behaviours. The sooner the siege begins, the greater the results will be.

*'By helping his older, autistic brothers with their therapy,
four-year-old Jake discovers that learning is fun'*

On Sam's tenth birthday, his brother Jake, then three, was excited,
though not for the obvious reasons. 'Can we wake up Sam?' he
begged, 'Now he's ten, he'll be able to talk, won't he?'

We woke Sam, and found his ten-year-old self not markedly
more communicative than before, though later he gratified Jake by
asking for 'Play-Doh, please' with unusual clarity. But it made me
realize how much Jake must think about his brother's condition. I
had already heard him explain to a playmate that 'My brother's
rather rough, because he's French', and months ago he had
instructed me that 'We must teach Sam how to be kind.' But Jake's
great excitement on his brother's birthday morning was particularly poignant, echoing the dream of every parent that one day
their autistic child will wake and the autism will have been ma-
gicked away.

It is important to abandon this dream. It is even more important
to replace it with the hope that, through hard and patient labour,
one can bring autism into line with normal behaviour to the point
of happy coexistence. Progress is possible. Last Friday I took Sam
to Guy's Hospital for six hours of tests – medical, behavioural, 'academic'. This involved coping with rush-hour trains and the horrors
of London Bridge McDonald's at lunchtime, as well as the extraction from Sam of blood, urine and co-operative behaviour.

It would have been a difficult day for any child, let alone someone as bewildered as Sam. He didn't complete every assessment,
but he did pretty well. We got through with the minimum of upset
and achieved a degree of compliance that would have been impossible even a year ago. That's progress.

I explained Sam's outing to Jake. 'Will the doctors mind if he flaps their toys?' he asked. Then his small brow furrowed: 'I hope it never happens to me.' These two comments encapsulate what it means to be non-autistic. They show an understanding of social norms, concern about the possible outcome of transgressing these norms, an ability to put oneself in another's position, and to project the future, both immediate and theoretical. Jake can draw a nearly accurate mental map of his position in relation to what he knows of the wider world. So can most children. George and Sam can't.

Jake's circumstances are unusual. His older brothers do not behave as if they are older in any respect except for sheer physical strength. They have absolutely no sense of responsibility – towards him, or anything else. They can only play with him to a limited extent, and then only under heavy adult supervision. They cannot be left alone with him for a second, because they will hurt him. They ride roughshod over his feelings, and his Brio layout. In creating a proper family life for him, I am working with unpromising material. But it has to be done.

The ABA (Lovaas) therapy programme that I run for George and Sam is hugely helpful. The therapy, which breaks learning down into tiny steps and gives instant rewards – usually sweets – for success, is the reason why Sam is now compliant enough to be tested at Guy's, and why his bottom will now make contact with a train seat for more than half a second.

The therapists come to our house and often involve Jake in their activities. He holds up his fingers for George to do his sums on; he is the stooge for teaching turn-taking games to Sam. ABA can include treasure hunts, I-spy, musical bumps; Jake has an unshakeable belief that learning is fun. He's just four now, and he can read, tell the time, play board games, because he's soaked it all up along the way. Much more importantly, he is intimately involved with George and Sam's progress. He points out toys or material we could use with them. ABA has penetrated their autistic aloofness for him.

The connections that exist naturally between most siblings are constructed artificially in Jake's case. If the bridges have to be built out of Dolly Mixtures, never mind. The great thing is that he should see his brothers as a blessing, not a burden – or at least, as a burden worth the carrying. George and Sam can't teach him much by example, but by living and working with them he may learn to be tolerant, to celebrate differences, to overcome difficulties through ingenuity, and that love is unconditional. If he does, he'll be a lucky boy.

'My autistic son George will soon be a teenager – loud music,
spots and all. But he still loves the Teletubbies'

13 March 2002

George has changed. For years, he was 'the easy one' – all things being relative – but this is no longer so. He has turned twelve, and adolescence has begun.

Much has been written about autistic children, less about autistic adolescents. I'd done little more than vaguely imagine my sons as taller, stronger versions of their present selves. But now I think of my teaching days, and how the mothers would weep at parents' evenings – 'What's happened to my little boy?' It's all beginning for George, and it's rather fascinating.

George displays the symptoms in a simplified, almost abbreviated form. He rejects authority. He is automatically negative, even about things he likes, and is enraged when he realizes he has accidentally talked himself out of vanilla fudge or lemonade. The smell of his trainers enters a room before he does. He won't get out of bed. After years of 5 a.m. starts, I thought I'd welcome this, but it brings its own stresses – with the school taxi waiting while George pulls on his underpants with agonizing slowness. Once up, he won't stir from his favourite spot on top of the Aga. To get him through the door and off to trampolining club or the library, a treasure hunt has to be laid from Aga to car seat. He'll do almost nothing now without bribes or coercion; the bribes are getting weaker, the threats more transparent.

His grandmother and I took to referring to him as 'Kevin' after Harry Enfield's great creation, but when he introduced himself to a visitor as 'George Kevin Smith', we realized we needed a new code. The phrases George uses are essence of teen spirit. 'Don't look at me!' 'Don't ask me that!' 'I don't want to be clean!' 'I want holes in my teeth!'

Though ignorant of fashion, he likes to customize his clothes. His pants have to stick out of the top of his trousers. His socks have to flap three inches from the end of his toes. He won't wear school uniform. He prefers to wear pink. He tears holes in his trousers, wears T-shirts on top of jumpers. Somebody told him that, with the white collar of his rugby shirt back to front, he 'looked like a vicar'. George took this as a compliment, and won't wear anything the right way round: 'I will look like a vicar! I will!'

Despite my best intentions, food has become a battleground. George supports his fast-growing frame on three Galaxy Ripples and half a portion of chicken curry per day. Hunger must be playing a part in his inertia. George, once hyperactive, is now in hibernation. His only exercise is dancing to rock music, played – of course – too loud.

He has become more socially aware, for the first time wanting to be part of a crowd. He invited all his old class to his birthday party. I had misgivings, but the guests were delightful; the occasion bore only a passing resemblance to an out-take from *One Flew Over the Cuckoo's Nest*. He likes Dido, and the Pop Idol he matily refers to as 'William', but last night his choice of video was *Teletubbies Bedtime*.

And that's where the differences begin. No normal twelve-year-old could watch *Teletubbies* except in a spirit of irony. Irony doesn't exist for George Kevin Smith. Satire, black humour, a mocking reappraisal of the adult world, its flaws newly revealed to the average teenager ... all this is irrelevant to George. So, too, is the youthful idealism that believes the world can be reinvented.

For George, the world doesn't exist beyond the limits of his own experience. What other people think or know does not matter. Like a little emperor, he demands that his 'friends' be brought into his presence, but he cannot imagine that they have lives that go on when he's not there. His increased sociability is encouraging, but he still has no empathy.

The painful, comic struggle of adolescence, turning children into adults with a coherent social function, exists only in part for George. The emergence of his identity is actually more like that of a three-year-old. His sense of self may never be whole enough to bear the pressure of social responsibility. George becomes distressed at talk of growing up. 'I won't be a man; I will be a boy!' And why upset him? Perhaps he never will be a man in any sense other than the physical. Perhaps never-never land isn't a bad place to be.

'The annual Easter egg hunt raises a difficult problem – how do I explain to my sons the meaning of death?'

27 March 2002

'When Jesus came alive again on Easter Day, was it in time for his egg hunt?' asked Jake. The question made me realize that I had never attempted to tell the Easter story to his older brothers. For George and Sam, Easter is simply a chocolate-fest – and, since Sam started his gluten- and casein-free diet, a muted one at that. After Eight eggs are all right, apparently, and so are little eggs called Whizzers. The colours are reminiscent of the drab palette of the Camden Town painters – dingy mustard, weak cocoa, sticking-plaster pink – and, like all gf/cf products, they are ridiculously expensive, but they pass muster for egg hunts and for those nests made out of squashed-together Rice Krispies.

George has invited his friends to an egg hunt, so, if the weather's good, I'll have ten autistic boys, plus Jake, charging round the garden. Sam, and Oliver, who is on the same diet, will have to be directed away from the more attractive treasures on to the trail of the dreary Whizzers. Autists aren't good at looking for things – they don't understand secrecy, because it involves taking on someone else's point of view – so the eggs will have to be prom-inently displayed. And if it rains . . . we'll cross that bridge when we come to it.

But eggs it is, and hot cross buns – consumed furtively, out of Sam's way – but resurrection won't come into it. Talking about death has always been a problem. I've spent ten years persuading George and Sam to accept the finality of death. To tell them a story about someone who rose again seems an unnecessary com-plication.

The first death in George's experience was that of Oscar, my neighbour's pony. George was three at the time. He still talks about

Oscar. Autists have excellent memories — indeed, I sometimes think that part of the trouble is that they don't know how to forget. Oscar was followed by Conan the cat, Darius the peacock, various hens, and a brisk succession of hamsters. The peacock was the one that hit Sam hardest. For years he beseeched me to bring him back. One afternoon, astonishingly, a white peacock stalked up our drive. Darius was blue. Sam bellowed, 'White Darius!' and called me to come and see — an extremely rare event. A characteristic of autism is the failure to draw other people's attention to things, manifested in autistic babies as the absence of the 'shared point'. Sam almost never wants to share experiences, but this was important. The white peacock was a neighbour's escapee. His name turned out to be Terence. 'White Terence' is still one of the phrases Sam repeats to himself during his almost constant, incoherent private vocalizing.

Five years ago my aunt died. She had been a kind and constant presence in the boys' lives. George was furious with me. 'Get her out of the fox's tummy!' he ordered — he knew of no other method of dying. I explained, but he got muddled and, to this day, blames me for her disappearance — 'Mummy, spit Great-Aunt Hilary out!' I told the boys that though we couldn't see her any more, we could think about her and remember the nice things we did with her. 'Remember orange jelly,' intoned Sam. I think my aunt would have been pleased with that epitaph.

Now George is twelve, and has decided that he wants to die. 'I'll be inside a fox,' he declares. 'Don't find me, Mum.' It is not pleasant to hear one's child wish for death, but I'm less troubled by it than I would be if the comment came from a normal child. I think — hope — that George simply sees death as a convenient way of avoiding the demands that are constantly put upon him — similar to pulling the duvet over one's head, but more effective.

Jake, weeping, will ask, 'When you are dead, who will be my mummy?' Stories and videos have to be censored. I haven't dared read him the first Babar book yet, with its uncompromising early bereavement. But George and Sam never ask questions that go beyond the here and now. The action of the imagination that asks, 'What will happen to me, to you, to everyone I know?' and which leads eventually to 'What is life for?' will probably always be beyond them. Jake, at four, already finds huge interest and consolation in the Easter story. For George and Sam, it would be just another bewilderment in a bewildering world.

'How do you keep two autistic boys out of mischief during the school holidays? With considerable difficulty'

George and Sam went back to school today. For the last fortnight every spoonful of coffee, pinch of salt and squidge of toothpaste has involved unlocking a door. There are locks on the larder, the bathroom, my bedroom, Jake's bedroom, and the room where Sam does his Lovaas therapy. It does slow life down rather, and I'm always losing the keys.

If there weren't locks, Sam would empty bags of sugar down his throat. He would stuff the teapot full of teabags, and add water. He would plunge his fist into golden syrup and pour himself a bowl of Frosties – but he wouldn't stop pouring until the packet was empty.

The other day, I switched on the kettle and the house filled with the aroma of cooking marmalade. Sam had poured orange juice into the kettle – I'd forgotten to lock it up.

Both boys squeeze out toothpaste tubes. Sam can't resist tipping shampoo and bubble bath down the sink. He eats lipstick, and licks deodorant. (You should try it sometime ...) He uses a pack of eighty babywipes to clean up a tiny spillage. George turns everything into a 'flapper' – he is never without a bendy straw, strip of cardboard, or a daffodil stalk. Flower arrangements are in peril (he drinks the water out of the vases, too), and so are the constructions Jake brings home from nursery school – a 'bottle pumping machine' made of loo rolls and yoghurt pots, a shoebox lair for a salt-dough cheetah 'who doesn't roar'. Jake does roar when his treasures are tampered with: hence his locked bedroom door.

If I leave out a bowl of fruit, one bite is taken out of everything, including lemons. I can't have an open fire unless there are plenty of other adults to stand guard, because anything from cushions to vital telephone numbers will be thrown in. Even felt-pens are hidden, because Sam bites off the tips. He snaps the round bits off jigsaw pieces. The boys have almost no possessive instinct, which is useful when it comes to other children playing with their toys, but it also means they have no respect for other people's property.

And George will flap anything flappable, like the headless rabbit abandoned by the cat. I know, now, not to take him to municipal gardens during the daffodil season.

There are locks on the garden doors, too. They're not as vital as they were, because – I'm tempting fate here – Sam's running away phase seems to have passed. A couple of years ago, he was off whenever my back was turned – police helicopters came out three times. Sam has an excellent sense of direction and a strong instinct for self-preservation – accounts of the eighteenth-century feral child, the Wild Boy of Aveyron, convince me that he was autistic, like Sam. And 'running away' isn't quite right; Sam just likes exploring. So I worried less about his disappearance than one might imagine. The worst escape was in Hereford, because he didn't know his way. One minute, he and I were inspecting a memorial in the cloisters, and the next I was touring the city in a police car. He turned up a couple of miles away, on the banks of the swollen Wye. 'I thought it was a little unusual,' said the passer-by who called the police, 'because he went up to a dog, took the ball from its mouth, and put it in his own.'

Sam was cross when the new locks went on. Tom Kitten-like, he scrambled up the chimney. I heard a scurry of soot, and saw two sandalled feet dangling above the (unlit) fire. I decided that intervention might make matters worse – Sam's always been very contra-suggestive – and left him to make his own way down.

The good thing about autistic habits – for my boys, at least – is that they don't last for ever. 'Challenging' behaviour will disappear as mysteriously as it came. Unscrewing light bulbs and smashing them – that was a bad one, but the days when I had to walk round a dark house with one bulb in my pocket and a candle in my hand seem to be over. And, to the relief of my guests, I'm now able to leave paper out in the lavatories, instead of issuing it only on request. But I admit that, once we'd waved the boys off this morning, Jake and I set our breakfast honey on the table with an audible sigh of relief.

'Sockless wellingtons are the boys' footwear of choice now – at least they're not wearing trainers in bed'

8 May 2002

Sunday lunch with friends. George wore his wellingtons, not because it was a rainy day, but because at the moment wellingtons are all he will wear on his feet. Footwear has always been an issue for both George and Sam. When they were tiny, they always wanted to be barefoot. Actually, they always wanted to be naked and barefoot, even in the depth of winter. Then, when George was six, he wore his shoes, but on the wrong feet. He kept this up for a whole term. No use insisting; the minute I wasn't looking, he'd swap them back. The autistic child will almost always win these battles because the non-autistic adult is weakened by having several thousand things on his or her mind. The child has only one thing on his mind – shoes, in this case – and brings all his very considerable mental energy to bear until he has established his point. The autist never loses interest.

Both boys went through a phase of wearing my shoes. George had some minimal element of pretend play – he'd clack round the house in high heels saying, 'George is a mummy.' But Sam wasn't playing – he just wanted my shoes. He would teeter up the steps to school, where they would be whisked away by a waiting member of staff. I think he was then barefoot until home-time.

I never got Sam back into his own leather shoes, but he learned to tolerate trainers. More than tolerate – he wore them in bed. He used to wear his school clothes in bed, too, which did save time in the morning. If I could stay awake – and as Sam was often still up at midnight, I couldn't always – I used to sneak in and remove them once he was asleep. Now he stows them neatly under his bed, and accepts pyjamas, too. The only eccentricity is that he pushes the tongues into the toe, and wears them that way.

I can't get Sam into a shoe shop, so I just have to guess at the size. I realize I still feel tense when Jake has his feet measured, because I'm expecting trouble, even though for a normal four-year-old there's no reason why there should be any. I'm still not quite used to normality.

George also converted to trainers but, because he wouldn't wear socks, the stench was more than flesh-and-blood could stand. For a while, he tolerated those leather clodhoppers with a Velcro strap, but only when he'd ripped out the inner sole and left them overnight in the garden to get nice and stiff.

Now these, too, have been rejected, and it is sockless wellingtons or nothing. Does this matter? Medically, probably not. Both pairs of feet look healthy to me, albeit slightly blackened. They never seem to get cuts or splinters. George recently walked barefoot to the bluebell woods, through thistles and nettles, a round trip of about a mile; he sustained no injuries.

Like the soles of their feet, my skin has thickened over the years. I don't mind escorting a barefoot twelve-year-old into hospital or accompanying a pair of giant leopard-shaped slippers on the train. There's an argument that one should help them to look as normal as possible, and I tend to agree. But these variations on the footwear theme have their equivalent in every aspect of life. Clothes, crockery, cutlery, toys, baths, sleeping arrangements – the boys customize everything. They dedicate their lives to reinventing the wheel, but reinventing it square. Or triangular. Or star-shaped. And it's hard to find the energy to tackle it all.

Anyway, I took them to my friends' house on my own, armed only with gluten-free sausages and a bit of ribbon for Sam to play with. And they sat at the table, at least for a while, played (a bit) with the other children, didn't break anything much, and didn't run away. After twelve years, we approximated a normal family Sunday. Never mind the wellingtons. I was pretty pleased with that.

'"To be far off and very little" was the wish of one autistic child, but we must pester them away from this notion'

22 May 2002

There's a story called 'Wooden Tony', which offers a rather beautiful description of autism. It was published in 1882, sixty-two years before the condition was identified, but I suspect that Lucy Lane Clifford, the author, wrote from first-hand experience. She was 'the wife of the philosopher and mathematician W. K. Clifford': that phrase rings a warning bell.

'Wooden Tony' is an inversion of the Pinocchio story. Pinocchio wants to be a real boy; to do so he must develop a conscience. He becomes fully human once he is altruistic enough to save his 'father's' life. Tony, by contrast, longs to become wooden, to achieve separation from other humans, including his parents. He wants to be 'little and far off'; with autistic literal-mindedness, he sees objects in the distance as physically tiny. His mother explains perspective, but Tony, with an autist's unteachability, 'would not understand'.

Tony is the son of a Swiss woodcarver. Other boys chop wood, gather edelweiss, tend goats, but Tony does nothing. 'When his mother tried to make him useful, he looked so frightened that at last she left him alone.' Any parent who has struggled to involve their autistic child in daily activities will recognize this, as they will recognize her anxiety for his future – 'Who besides me will care for thee if thou art stupid?'

Tony 'had few words with which to talk'. His mother defends him: 'Perhaps he thinks of more than he cares to say.' He has the typical autistic physiognomy – 'a pale face and wide open eyes'. Like my own son Sam, he regresses into his own world: 'That was before he had grown so silent, before the time when the great cobweb seemed to have wrapped him round, before he had wandered into a dream and shut the door on the waking world.' He is entranced by sensory stimuli: 'He would sit by the doorway listening to the falling avalanche, and letting the warm sun fall on his head.' My older son George used to sit for hours watching rippling water, or dust motes. Tony has fixations. His eyes keep wandering towards 'a dark knotty piece of wood', which becomes an object of fear. I remember Sam dancing round a broken chair-back, which seemed to attract and horrify him in equal measure.

And Tony has a special talent. It's these 'savant' skills that people find most interesting, as if they somehow validated autism. Like my George, Tony has a beautiful singing voice. He sings 'a song learnt in some strange fashion, unknown to any near him'. His mother says, 'There is not room for an evil thought anywhere within sound of [his song].' Autists have little moral sense, but neither do they bear malice. Their innocence is peculiarly attractive.

Tony believes that when his father carves toys, 'chip by chip [he takes] away the walls that held the little ... men and women in prison.' Tony wants to be such a toy. He gets his wish when a dealer offers to 'take the song from his lips and send it over the world'. They walk to Geneva. Unlike the distractable Pinocchio, oblivious Tony 'kept his eyes on the long, straight road'. The dealer commands 'sing', and he does so 'mechanically, as though he were a puppet'. The dealer twangs a wire, and the song 'goes out' of Tony. By the time they reach Geneva, his desired separation from humans is complete. 'They seemed to be made of a different texture, of different flesh and blood from himself.' Tony was 'not tired, or warm, or cold, or glad, or sorry, but only in a dream'. This perfectly describes autistic detachment.

Tony has turned into wood. The dealer installs him in a clock tower. His song plays automatically as he is jerked out on the striking of each hour. Tony has 'kinship with the things that belonged to Nature's firstness'. His parents come to Geneva in search of him; his mother recognizes him inside the clock. 'Tony is there. He is wooden.' His father reminds her that Tony's song was the only useful part of him, but she is not comforted. 'It is Tony that I want, my son Tony who sat by the door and sang, or by the fire watching the wood smoulder.' Tony is indifferent to her grief. He has fulfilled what is perhaps the essential autistic wish – 'to be far off and very little'.

This wish needs thwarting. I nibble away at the challenge-free cocoon of physical sensation the boys spin for themselves. I pester them to join my world, but try to respect their autism too – it's a difficult balance. But I don't want the fate of Tony's mother, who had to leave him behind a closed door, in darkness, forever out of reach.

5 June 2002

On 6 May 1935, the silver jubilee of George V was celebrated by my family and other inhabitants of our village in the field next to our house. My grandfather recorded the event in his diary, which he kept every day of his adult life. A pavilion was rigged up, 'made of poles covered with rick cloths'. A 'fine large union flag' was attached. The committee 'cut up meat and made sandwiches'. An oak was planted, near those that commemorated the two previous coronations. My grandmother shovelled in the first spadeful and then 'everyone put in some earth'.

There were sports after lunch. My father and his siblings took part in the races. My uncle lit the bonfire. My grandfather 'brought out the lantern I carried in the Eton procession of 1897 before Queen Victoria'.

In 2002, our golden jubilee celebration will be rather different. The venue will be the same, because I live in the house where my father grew up. But the celebrants will be pupils from the ASD (autistic spectrum disorder) units attended by my sons George and Sam.

George is very keen to see his 'friends', and often asks, 'When are the boys coming to my house?' So the jubilee seemed like a good excuse. This new sociability is probably the biggest advance George has made this year, but I've put 'friends' in inverted commas because not all the boys know that George regards them as such. Some are mute. Some, like Sam, are socially indifferent. But some are highly vocal and, like George, show enthusiasm for each other's company.

Instead of the rick cloths, we'll have a bouncy castle. Tea urns will be replaced by large bottles of juice. The food would be unrecognizable to a time traveller from 1935, but at least all those horrid, crispy, nuggety things beloved by twenty-first-century children are appropriately golden in hue. The postprandial sports will be non-competitive; autists don't compete, because they don't compare themselves with other people. There will be trampolining, swinging, scrambling over the climbing frame and, I expect, the usual amount of autistic spinning and flapping. Some kindly adults will, I'm sure, play football with non-autistic Jake (aka Michael Owen), but the other children are unlikely to take part, because co-operating in a team runs counter to what it means to be autistic.

Jake is interested in the jubilee. He shed tears for the Queen Mum, thinks that her late husband slew a dragon, and is intrigued to hear about the third prize that his grandfather won in the four-year-olds' race on that warm May afternoon sixty-seven years ago. Jake is four, too; he understands that his grandfather was once a child, and that he himself will one day be an old man. He is familiar with the jubilee oak in our field. He measures himself against the copper beech that we planted in honour of his birth. He knows that he has a place in the family, the village, the country. He is firmly anchored in time and place.

George and Sam have no such understanding. Trees were planted for their births, too; George's only response has been to snap off twigs to use as flappers. They don't know what a jubilee is; they only know the word 'queen' because it comes up a lot in ABC books, like yacht and xylophone. George actively resists attempts to interest him in his own history – he rejects early photographs of himself, denies that he was ever a baby, or will ever grow older. Sam is interested in photographs that show familiar objects – his old dummy, his cuddly owl. He ignores pictures of people, himself included.

I have heard talk of the 'autistic community'; this, to me, is a contradiction in terms. But our non-autistic community – family, helpers, friends – will enjoy the pleasure the boys derive from the jubilee party, whether, as in Sam's case, that pleasure is primarily sensual – physical exertion, fizzy drinks, flapping flags – or whether, as for George, approximately social. Part of the meaning of the jubilee is to celebrate the lives of whoever is around, whatever they may be like. I think we will plant an oak tree. Sam will enjoy the hole; he likes seeing worms wriggling in mud. George will enjoy watching people take turns to shovel in earth; he likes roll-calls of people he knows.

And Jake? He'll describe the scene to his teacher, his school friends, anyone who will listen . . . and, one day, he'll show the tree to his grandchildren.

*'Taking my autistic sons to the doctor or dentist is a
nightmare — everything involves an unholy struggle'*

26 June 2002

George has cradle cap. At least, that is what it looks like. His scalp
is covered with yellowish-brown patches the texture of rough
sticking plaster. It is not a pretty sight and, as George is twelve
years old, I can't cover it with a lacy bonnet.

At first, I thought it was biscuit crumbs. Both George and Sam
have been through phases of storing bits of food in their hair, possibly with a view to later snacking, so I wasn't particularly surprised.
I went to brush them off, but was pushed away by George who,
like most autistic people, dislikes uninvited touch. There is no red-
ness or irritation, so getting rid of the stuff is purely a cosmetic
exercise — and as George has no self-consciousness about his
appearance, its removal is more for my benefit than for his.

I don't know what causes such a condition, but the deficiencies
of George's diet — sausages, ketchup, Refreshers, full stop — could
have something to do with it. I bought from the health-food shop,
at vast expense, a preparation extracted from the fruit of the Ki-
gelia africana, also known, appropriately enough, as the sausage
tree. The sausage seeds are spread by hippos; it is the same type of
tree under which David Livingstone spent the night before 'discovering' the Victoria Falls ... but I digress. The tincture seems to
be working and, in exchange for Refreshers, George allowed me
to comb out some of the patches.

Why haven't I taken him to the doctor? Well, my GP operates
a first-come, first-served system, which can mean a wait of more
than two hours. Two hours in the waiting room with George, Sam
and a throng of nervous geriatrics is something I tend to avoid,
especially since the health authority forbade toys in the surgery
because they harbour germs. This, plus the near impossibility of

getting either boy to swallow any medicine they might be prescribed, means that they have seen the doctor a great deal less than most children. Sam, who is ten years old, has only ever had one course of antibiotics – and that was when he was a baby.

No antibiotics is probably good, but the boys' unapproachability does cause problems. Teeth, for instance. They have an excellent special-needs dentist, but even he sometimes can't prise open a pair of sealed lips. Both boys have had decay – inevitably, since yes, they do eat sweets, and no, of course they don't brush their teeth properly.

It's not possible to carry out treatment in the chair, so they have had fillings and extractions under general anaesthetic. Last time, I had to drive George round and round Bexhill for an hour and a half before he was calm enough to enter the hospital. He wouldn't be weighed, so I had to stand on the scales with him in my arms, and have my own weight subtracted. I won't be able to do that for much longer. It took six adults, including me, to hold him down for the anaesthetic mask. It sounds terrible, but it is the only way – coaxing and cajoling only make him more frantic.

The recovery, by contrast, was fine. Other children were moaning and having to be rewarded with Bob the Builders and Barbies, but George is like an animal when he's ill – he just lies, still and silent, until he's better. The tooth was a huge, craggy, adult molar, blackened and hollowed like a bombed citadel. It was presented to him in a dainty bag adorned with a blue elf and a pink fairy perched on a crescent moon, but he showed no interest. As neither money nor make-believe mean anything to George or Sam, I haven't bothered with the Tooth Fairy yet, but I can see that Jake, my non-autistic four-year-old, isn't going to settle for less than the standard rate.

Nail-cutting, nit-combing, the application of suncream … any of the routine physical interventions of motherhood involve an unholy struggle. But paradoxically, I have a closer acquaintance with my sons' bodies than most of my friends do with their normal children. George and Sam have absolutely no idea about modesty. Their social indifference means that they do not understand taboos.

I'm loath to destroy this prelapsarian innocence, but I do need to make them as socially acceptable as possible, which means removing ugly cradle cap and – much harder – instilling inhibitions about the public removal of one's trousers. I expect to have an unimpeded view of their fast-approaching adolescence. The spectacle will be interesting and alarming in equal measure.

*'With no sense of competition and no concept of camaraderie,
can my autistic sons ever enjoy sport?'*

17 July 2002

The sports day season is upon us. I'm lucky, I suppose – I only have
to marshal the grandparents, the white shorts and the camcorder
for one of my three sons. George and Sam attend autistic units;
their teachers have wisely decided that to involve them in such an
event would, at best, be pointless.

Jake's nursery sports day – or sports half-hour – happened last
week. Jake started talking about it on the first day of the summer
term. When I asked if they had done any practising at school he
replied, 'Yeah, lots. Archie usually beats me in training.' His every
move was recorded for posterity; there is a particularly good photograph of him clutching a yellow bean bag and looking proud. The
four-year-old girls' race was a close run thing; Jake asked if he
could see the picture of 'Ruby and Ellie's photo-finish'.

Is Jake taking it all a little too seriously? Quite possibly; but the
sporting instinct is in his blood. (Not my share – I spent five boarding school years faking periods and verrucas.) Jake has picked the
Grand National winner two years running. He watched the World
Cup: England versus Argentina or a goalless draw between Micro-
nesia and Uzbekistan would afford equal satisfaction. His favourite
video is of England's 1966 triumph; Nobby Stiles, Jackie Charlton
et al. have entered his fantasy play. During Wimbledon he became
a Henmaniac.

Jake loves the rules, the scoring, the loyalty, the taking of sides,
but he also loves the people. He loves the way team games involve
a group reaction. His favourite 1966 moment is when Bobby
Moore is hoisted on to his team-mates' shoulders and everybody
cheers. For Jake, sport is human society writ small; it all makes perfect sense to him.

It doesn't make any sense at all to his autistic brothers. I well remember their nursery sports days. George was towed from bean bag to hula-hoop by one of those kind-but-bossy little girls; Sam ran backwards. Sam is the most physically fit ten-year-old I have ever seen. His muscle tone is fantastic; he can run for hours and never tire. But neither he nor George have a shred of competitive instinct, because they don't compare themselves to other children. The camaraderie, the intricate social structure of most sports, are beyond them.

Luke Jackson, who is thirteen, and has Asperger's syndrome, explains the problem in his excellent book *Freaks, Geeks and Asperger Syndrome*. Luke attends a mainstream school. He struggles with all group activities, but organized games are the worst. Like many with AS, Luke has poor coordination, but that is not his only difficulty. It isn't pleasant to be the one nobody wants in their team; the teacher allocates him to a random team 'like a spare piece of luggage that no one can be bothered to carry'. But Luke is not longing to be chosen, far from it; team sports seem pointless and disjointed to him. He has the over-heightened senses characteristic of the condition; 'I cannot work out where the noise is coming from or who it is directed at and it all becomes very confusing and ... frightening.' A friend of mine with an 'able autistic' son reports a similar problem: 'Shouts of encouragement in sports puzzle Joshua and make him stop what he's doing.'

Jackson pleads eloquently for release: 'I know this must feel like a ... defeatist attitude but, believe me, in this area we are defeated! This is a recognized disability and these problems are part of it.' Instead, he advocates running, working out, or tae kwon do, where there are set routines and patterns. Tae kwon do has improved Luke's coordination and his ability to judge speed and distance. It is also 'about training your inner self to be more aware and more accepting of those around you'.

For George, the equivalent is his trampolining class. He is the only ASD child in the group. When he joined he wouldn't even get on the trampoline; now, he follows instructions just like the others. He enjoys the limited social contact with other children and the physical sensations of the activity. The sensation has to be its own reward; praise, competition or the mastery of new skills per se are not motivators for George. I'm hoping that soon Sam will be biddable enough to join him. Meanwhile, I face a long summer with Jake of endless garden re-enactments of Michael Owen's finest moments.

'The Tweenies *and* The Magic Roundabout *have taught my autistic sons valuable social skills — as well as strange phrases*'

31 July 2002

School holidays mean that our VCR is rarely out of commission. Autistic children with obsessive interests occupy themselves for hours on end, but at present George and Sam have no obsessions.

If left to their own devices they merely 'stim' — which for George means flapping bits of twig or cardboard, and for Sam means banging his hands together or bashing balloons to bits. Getting them to do anything more constructive needs a lot of direction from adults. That's not always possible, so, as six weeks is a lot of 'stimming' time, videos are useful substitute child-minders.

They can be educators, too. George has learned what little he knows about the art of conversation from the likes of *Rosie and Jim* and *The Tweenies*. George is twelve, but still watches the videos he liked when he was three. Recently, *Kipper the Dog* and the strangely mesmeric *Jellikins* have been added to old favourites such as *Tots TV* and *Fireman Sam*. But the format doesn't vary: a catchy theme tune, stories lasting five to ten minutes, and consistent, easily identifiable characters. Autists tend to enjoy repetitive patterns, and videos for the very young are satisfying variations on a theme.

George is an excellent mimic; at one time he spoke fluent Pinguese. At first he echoed video dialogue with little understanding of its meaning, but it provided him with usable speech patterns, and over time he became able to connect real-life encounters with the goings-on inside the Teletubby house or on the good boat *Ragdoll*. These videos have been like foreign-language conversation classes, teaching George how to speak 'human'.

Some lines have unintentionally comic effect. Dougal, from *The*

Magic Roundabout, was a rich source. 'I've been let down by the government,' George announced to general mirth at his trampolining club. And there was the splendidly unfathomable comment: 'This would make Ken Russell spit.' Alas, our one *Magic Roundabout* tape has ground to a halt after years of faithful service.

The videos teach the rudiments of social or moral behaviour as well. The three Tots have small squabbles which are resolved through negotiation and compromise. The Jellikin bears each have a dominant characteristic which somehow chimes with their colours; blue Denny is 'always helpful, always good', red Pepper is more combative. The wistful nuances of Bob the Builder's undeclared passion for Wendy are lost on George, but he understands that Lofty is nervous, and that Spud plays naughty tricks.

Autists often love Disney; exaggerated smiles and tears are useful aids to recognizing the emotions that normal children perceive automatically. I'm with our Archbishop-designate Rowan Williams – I dislike the way the Disney formula degrades and betrays the imagination of childhood – but the boys' Disney phase brought benefits. *Dumbo* was a favourite for years. At first, Sam only liked the credits; then he moved on to the bit when the train goes up the mountain. They both loved the pink elephant sequence, because they are more motivated by visual stimulation than with the story. The first time non-autistic Jake watched *Dumbo*, his eyes grew round with horror. 'They've taken his mummy away!' he sobbed. 'This can't be for children.' And I tend to agree.

Sam is uninterested in plot or character. He likes spotting familiar objects on television; he was taken with *Nigella Bites* because of her food processor. In his laundry phase he loved an episode of *Old Bear* where part of a washing machine could be glimpsed. Mr Bean at the launderette had Sam in thrall. It has been suggested that Mr Bean is himself autistic. When I see him packing a single espadrille because the pair won't fit in his suitcase I'm inclined to agree, but Mr Bean gets a distinctly non-autistic pleasure out of doing other people down.

I ought to move the boys on to something more age-appropriate.

I've been lazy about this, partly because Kipper, Pingu et al. never draw blood or zap aliens and are not style-conscious; it is nice to avoid the noisier and more brutal elements of youth culture.

For the time being, the singsong of the boys' videos mingles with other summer holiday sounds – bees, lawnmowers, coast-bound traffic – and the never-ending autistic hum emitted by George and Sam to form the aural backdrop of our family life.

'Going on holiday with autistic kids is hard enough as it is without missing the exit to the Little Chef'

21 August 2002

Jake and I are off to Spain next week. George and Sam will stay at home with their grandparents. They won't mind – well, they will mind my absence, but at least they won't feel as if they're missing a treat. Being autistic, they don't regard a change of scene as a treat. And they don't moan about English weather – they like wind and rain.

Jake, four, asks lots of questions about Spain. How will we understand what people say? Do any 'swallowing' animals live there? Has Spain ever won the World Cup? But his older brothers have no such curiosity. They don't understand the concept of a foreign country. I don't think they know that they live in England. They live in our house, and that's it.

George and Sam don't expect to understand much of the conversation going on around them; other languages are only marginally less 'foreign' than English. I sing them French songs, and they enjoy them, and try to repeat them, but they have never asked what the words mean. George does French at school; with his mimic's ear, he picks up vocabulary quickly, but he has no concept of an entire nation speaking nothing else. George likes echoing, but making himself understood has never been his priority.

I have taken them abroad in the past. The first time was before their autism was diagnosed; George was three and Sam eighteen months. George disliked the aeroplane intensely. I couldn't have fastened his safety belt without breaking bones, so he lay on the floor and screamed, and I held him in place with my feet during take-off. The complimentary crayons and colouring book offered by the helpful air hostess were as effective as a box of Band-Aids at a motorway pile-up.

Once we had arrived, things improved. The boys liked sand, stones, water, mud and lollipops. They disliked crowds and unfamiliar food. A plastic bowl of tinned spaghetti bolognese was a feature of all our expeditions. George wore the same pyjama top, night and day, for the week. Cultural experiences were kept to a minimum, though I do remember Sam charging the length of a Romanesque church, with a thunderous cry of 'Cake!', before blowing out all the votive candles.

George still hates planes, so for the past two years we have stuck to England. Both boys are good in the car – it's only Jake who asks 'Are we nearly there?' before we have reached the end of the drive. Sam had a phase of throwing things out of the window – I shudder at the memory of a trail of cassette boxes, lolly wrappers and plastic beakers the length of the M4, which I, as sole adult, was powerless to prevent. I resolved never to travel alone with them again, and was vindicated last year when, in the ultimate holiday nightmare, the car broke down – terminally – en route to Devon. You are supposed to get the children out in these circumstances, but loitering by the dual carriageway isn't an option with George and Sam. My travelling companion took Jake on a wild-flower hunt while I sat in the sweltering car with the other two, awaiting death or the RAC, whichever came first.

Eating out is a challenge. My aunt and godmother were reduced to helpless school-speech-day giggles during a very wet trip to a children's farm in Dorset. We sat in the cafe taking turns to dash out and glimpse barn owls through the sodden gloom. George smothered a pile of chips with ketchup, sucked them, then spat them, torpedo-style, the length of the refectory table.

Returning from that holiday, we missed the turning for the Little Chef (onion rings, lots of napkins, other children behaving badly) and found ourselves in a rather grander establishment (tinkly Vivaldi, twentysomethings in conference suits, sun-dried everything). The waitress gave us each a menu the size of a Monopoly board. Sam threw his back at her. She persevered; she had been trained to present a menu to each diner, and that was exactly what she was going to do. I scanned mine in search of anything amid the seared, pan-fried, oil-drizzled goodies that the boys might eat, but in vain.

'Well,' said my godmother afterwards, 'I enjoyed my salad.'

'Yes,' said Jake, 'and I enjoyed my sugar.'

They all did. We left a pile of sucked sugar sachets and a very large tip, and headed for home.

'If you ask George if he likes school, he'll answer "No" – but then that's his answer to almost any question'

2 September 2002

Once again it's the season of mists, mellow fruitfulness, and new pencil cases. Children are excited, or anxious, or even terrified at the prospect of a new school year; few will be indifferent. For mothers, there's a flurry of last-minute shopping for school clothes, sports equipment, books and stationery.

It's not like that in this household. Compared to most mothers, I've little preparation to do. This is just as well as, with two autistic sons and one normal four-year-old, even the simplest shopping expedition involves complicated babysitting arrangements. Granny is out looking for tracksuit trousers – Sam dislikes zips and seams. Both boys have been barefoot all summer, but now, somehow, I really have to get their feet measured. I can't go on guessing any longer. The question is, how to achieve this without endangering other shoppers.

But there's nothing for George or Sam in the supermarket racks of 'back-to-school essentials'. Neither of them have ever needed a calculator, a musical instrument, football boots, not even a ruler. They understand – I think – that they are going back to school soon, but they do not know which year they are in, or even the name of their class.

Both boys attend ASD (autistic spectrum disorder) units attached to special-needs schools; Sam's primary, George's secondary. Each unit has a maximum capacity of eight, and a high staff-to-pupil ratio. Not high enough, though; ideally, autists should have one-to-one attention, or even more, because it's almost impossible for them to learn in a group. In Sam's unit the ages range from seven to eleven. They are all boys, which is often the way it goes with autism. Some have no speech, and almost no academic skills – but then there's one boy who, intellectually, outstrips his mainstream peers, but has the social nous of a toddler. Why is he grouped with the likes of my Sam, who can count to ten on a good day? Because there's nowhere else for him to go.

The schools have a 'uniform' sweatshirt, but wearing it is optional. George chooses to wear Sam's – part of a desire to hide behind his younger brother which has been going on for years. Sam, who would prefer to wear nothing at all, puts on whatever comes to hand, usually back to front. In place of the cricket bat, trombone, laptop or whatever it is the modern schoolboy requires, George and Sam take bags of spare trousers, in case of what are inaccurately called accidents. Both boys enjoy wetting themselves; it helps to pass the time.

Sam has a lunchbox, contents wheat- and dairy-free, which returns almost untouched. George, whose diet is improving, still likes to pretend that he eats no food at all. A lunchbox is too blatant a reminder that this cannot be true, so I smuggle supplies, well wrapped, into the boot of his taxi. On arrival these are conveyed to his teacher by some similar sleight of hand.

The boys have no homework. Notebooks convey messages between the school and me, usually things like, 'Sorry about Sam's face, he got hold of my marker pen.' I've had a restful time so far, with no SATS results, no complicated timetables, no prize-givings, no after-school activities, no friends home to play.

Jake is about to start at the village primary school. He will wear a tie – already a source of some anxiety for both of us. He has been asked to complete a booklet entitled 'All About Me' (his favourite subject). He has taken it very seriously. For the first time in twelve years of motherhood I'll have a child who will worry if he isn't wearing the right kind of socks. It'll be a steep learning curve for me.

Do George and Sam like school? It's hard to say. If you asked George, he'd say 'No' – but then that's his answer to almost any question. Sam isn't yet able to express an answer to any question about personal preferences. Certainly, the teachers and assistants couldn't try harder. But autism is a condition that is antithetical to any kind of communal activity, however sensitively organized.

Me, I love September. After six weeks of uninterrupted quality time with my sons, the ring of the doorbell heralding the arrival of the taxis is music to my ears. But then, you don't have to have autistic children to appreciate that.

'Sam loves to touch stinging nettles and electric fences. Autism means he lives in a different sensory universe'

25 September 2002

When Sam was eighteen months old, he blundered into a clump of stinging nettles. I braced myself for the screams. None came. Indeed, no sooner had I dragged him out than he sought a fresh bunch and stung himself across the face, quite deliberately.

The same thing happened when he first encountered an electric fence. Even at two, Sam was a fast runner. Before I could reach him, he'd charged straight into the fence. Oh no, I thought, he'll never want to go for a walk again. Not a bit of it. He spent the next few weeks plotting to repeat the experience – and succeeded. On neither occasion did he cry.

This was long before Sam's autism was diagnosed. His indifference to pain surprised me, but I wasn't worried. I just thought I had a brave, tough son, who was perhaps somewhat bloody-minded. And when he was diagnosed at four, his condition was described in terms of a social and intellectual deficit. No mention was made of his abnormal sensory responses.

Autism is identified by the presence, to a greater or lesser degree, of a 'triad of impairments' – of social interaction, communication and imagination. Yet almost everyone on the spectrum also has sensory abnormalities. Temple Grandin, a very able autistic woman, devotes much time to perfecting a 'squeeze box' to provide the pressure that gives her the tactile balance she requires. The autistic author Donna Williams can't function under strip lighting; it makes her see figures as jerky and disjointed. Sam, like many others, has problems with spatial orientation; sometimes he rocks back and forth on his feet, unable to move forward, as if the ground in front of him might swallow him up.

Such abnormalities are not always problems. Many autists

experience pleasure in sights, sounds and textures more intensely than we could without recourse to drugs. Donna Williams could hear a snake passing the house while she was indoors.

I heard about a boy who saw the *Spiderman* film. Adults were talking about the removal of the twin towers from all the scenes. No, said the boy, the twin towers are in it. No, they're not, said the adults, they can't be. They watched the film again. The twin towers are visible, once, fleetingly, as a reflection in one of Spiderman's eyes. George, my other autistic son, used to gaze, literally entranced, at sparkling water or dust motes dancing in a sunbeam. He has always been absorbed by colour – he fixated on a red plastic teddy when only a few days old. For years, he has produced abstract paintings and drawings which have the vibrance of a Mark Rothko or a Howard Hodgkin.

Clare Sainsbury, in her autobiographical book *Martian in the Playground*, attributes these anomalies to the cerebellum, which acts as a 'volume knob' on the senses. The volume may be turned too high, in which case a light touch may be felt as a blow, or too low, as in the case of Sam and the nettles. Many autists are highly sound-sensitive, but it's not simply a case of noise level. Some loud noises may be acceptable, even gratifying – George turns the TV up as high as it will go – while others (vacuum cleaners, hand-driers and the like) will be unendurable.

And there may be little overlap with what we neurotypicals find repulsive or acceptable. George sniffs every plate before choosing one, but he lies on top of our old dog, while the rest of us are felled by her near-lethal halitosis.

I believe that sensory abnormalities should form part of the diagnostic criteria. What difference would this make? Well, it would encourage us to see autism as a physical condition, not just a mental one. It's not just that my sons can't or won't communicate or play with other children; George and Sam are autistic in every fibre of their beings. If the physicality of autism was accepted, schools and work places could remove or adapt things that cause sensory distress – bells, strong-smelling cleaning fluids, strip light-ing, whatever. And, looking to the future, more research could be done on the kind of messages the autistic nerves or brain are transmitting.

We've rejected the once universally held belief that autism is an emotional disturbance caused by a hard, over-intellectual 'refrigerator mother'. But we still assess an autistic child in terms of educational handicap, and fail to recognize him as the differently wired being he really is.

'It's hard to take photographs of autistic children. How they might appear never seems to cross their minds'

16 October 2002

Jake's in the newspaper this week. The local paper publishes pictures of the Reception classes of the village schools: Jake is cross-legged in the front row, smiling the rather squinty smile he reserves for momentous occasions. He pores over the photograph: 'That's David – he's silly at lunch. That's Paul – he's my friend. Danny – he's funny! Lucy – she's got orange hair. Annie – she's the same as Lucy, except her hair's different.'

My oldest son, George, also started off at a village primary. I remember a similar photograph from those days. The children stood in the playground forming a perfect grinning triangle – except for a grey blur in the top corner. That was George, escaping. Unintentionally, the photographer had neatly encapsulated autism.

Sam, my second son, is also autistic. His class photo is marvellously expressive of the autistic child's indifference to the whole business. He attends an autistic unit – eight boys, no girls; but there are only seven in the photo because one was having a screaming fit at the time. Tim is barefoot, Alex wears only socks, Martin's trainers are flapping open. Sam and Craig are being held in place by members of staff. No one is looking at the camera.

George and Sam are handsome boys, but it's hard to take a good picture of them. Their eyes are closed or averted, or they're simply on the move. George dislikes photos of himself – if I display framed pictures round the house, he turns them face down. He rejected all images of himself as a baby or toddler – 'That's not me! It's Sam.' He can't bear talk of the past, or the future – 'I'm not going to be a big boy one day.' It is as if his sense of self is too fragile to countenance the possibility of change.

Jake, by contrast, is consoled by photographs. When he wept

because, as he said, 'I want to make time go backwards. I wish I could see our trampoline when it was new,' I got out the album, and he was cheered by the sight of his father struggling with the new trampoline while four-month-old Jake looked on from his bouncy chair. Sam had a look too, and was pleased to spot familiar objects – his soft owl, his dummy – but showed little interest in the people. George just said, 'Put the pictures away.'

Last week, I went to an exhibition of photographs taken at the TreeHouse school. TreeHouse was set up by parents in 1998; it's the first UK school to teach autistic children according to the ABA method (Applied Behaviour Analysis). The photographer, Stefanie Hafner, spent a lot of time getting to know children and staff – the ratio is one-to-one. These are not simply portrait studies of often very attractive children. Like the ABA approach, which breaks learning down into tiny chunks, Hafner has photographed details in close-up – a hand, an ear, the back of a head. The images get close to the way an autistic child experiences the world: lacking 'central coherence', the autist characteristically sees the minutiae, not the bigger picture.

Hafner's approach also reflects the patient observation that we 'neurotypical' parents need to use if we hope to understand our children's behaviour. Autists very rarely explain or describe the way they see the world, which is why autobiographical accounts are particularly valuable. A symptom of the condition is an absence of 'theory of mind'; an inability to see things from another's point of view. When George was little, he used to say 'Want it', without realizing that I didn't know what 'it' was. 'Want it!' he would shout, with increasing emphasis and frustration, when I asked for clarification.

So we have to study our children like anthropologists. Concrete fact often means more to autists than words, and the TreeHouse photographs have a strong physicality. A little boy stretches out on a ledge, looking as if he'd like to be a wooden slat himself as he presses his body into the space, which is, satisfyingly, just the right width, and loses himself in the feel and smell of the wood.

We can only guess what this child is experiencing. But we can be sure that he's not giving a moment's thought to how he might appear to the photographer. That's autism.

'We thought George and Sam would be useful in an experiment on autism. George and Sam had other ideas'

13 November 2002

George and Sam have been to Addenbrooke's Hospital, in Cambridge, to have their brains scanned. Their brains didn't get scanned, as it turned out, but nobody could say we didn't try.

I have no worries about the physical health of my sons' brains. The scanning was not diagnostic, or even for their benefit. The Cambridge Department of Experimental Psychology is investigating emotion in autistic people. A magnetic resonance imaging (MRI) scanner is used to record brain activity in people with and without autism. The project requires boys with autism or Asperger's syndrome, aged between ten and fourteen, right-handed, with no history of seizures. George and Sam fit the criteria, so, in the interests of science, off we went.

The Addenbrooke's unit is state of the art. The huge scanner is protected by *Star Trek*-style doors, there's a special viewing area, and everything is immaculately clean, or was until we arrived. Chris Ashwin, who is in charge of the project, had taken great trouble; he'd provided favourite videos and a sack of jelly beans to coax the boys into compliance. We all had to sign forms declaring that we had no false hips, penile extensions and the like, we removed keys and coins from our pockets because of the powerful magnets, and then we were ready to begin.

The boys practised pressing a switch every time they saw a picture. Some of the images were human faces expressing exaggerated emotions, others were patterns with no emotive content. Brain cells use more oxygen when active; as the brain responds to the pictures, the scanner measures changes in oxygen levels. The hypothesis is that activity in the autistic brain will differ from that in the 'neurotypical' brain in response to emotional and social stimuli.

George and Sam just about mastered pressing the button. Then they were introduced to earplugs. The scanner makes a noise not unlike a road drill, so ears have to be protected. Sam was intrigued by the earplugs; they were squidgy, pale peach in colour, and they looked distinctly edible. Most things look edible to Sam, except, of course, food. He made several attempts to ingest the earplugs, but decided he preferred the jelly beans.

Once the earplugs are in, headphones have to be worn on top. I'd brought some of the boys' CDs with me; the plan was that, once inside the scanner, they could listen to familiar music to relax them before beginning the button-pushing tasks. This looked as if it might work. To the strains of The Kinks, they began to enter the long tunnel of the scanner.

Not for long. They popped up again like meerkats once they realized they were meant to lie flat on their backs with their heads down. Sam, in particular, hates this position – he'll never lie down and rinse his hair in the bath. Shampooing him involves throwing jugfuls of water at a moving target, like washing a dog. A large stuffed snake was introduced into the tunnel as an enticement. George, who is not motivated by stuffed snakes, wandered off in search of some Fanta, but Sam quite enjoyed chasing the snake into the tunnel. Only on his tummy, though; he was still not going to lie on his back.

Time was ticking by. Bags of chips were fetched from Burger King; these, plus crumbs from Sam's friable gluten-free biscuits, gave the waiting-room carpet something of a forest-floor effect. Four-year-old Jake had finished his activity book, and was becoming restless. He was keen to have a 'photograph' of his (non-autistic) brain; he followed instructions to the letter, was inserted into the scanner, and was given the illusion that he was taking part in the project.

I reckon if we'd tried every day for a week, we could have trained the boys to co-operate, but the procedure involved too many different steps for them to master in one session, so we gave up. Our failure illustrates a real problem: how do you investigate a condition of which erratic and non-compliant behaviour are major symptoms? Thirty volunteers are needed; it's likely they'll all be from the high-functioning end of the spectrum. Getting an image of an unsedated deeply autistic brain is extremely difficult.

I hope the project succeeds. New scanning techniques offer exciting possibilities for understanding not just autism, but conditions like dementia and schizophrenia as well. Going home, Sam said 'Want tunnel' several times. Too late.

'Inclusion in the mainstream is the new mantra. But autism is more than a learning difficulty, it's a way of being'

11 December 2002

I have just been to Sam's annual review. If you have a child with a statement of special educational need, you have a yearly meeting with the head, the class teacher, someone from the local authority, and other interested parties (speech therapist, social worker, educational psychologist ...). Together, you decide whether the wording of the statement still applies, and whether your child is being educated in the right place. This year's review was particularly important because Sam is in year six. Next September, he must start at secondary school.

Sam is in an ASD (autistic spectrum disorder) facility attached to a special-needs primary school. There are eight boys in the unit, no girls, two job-sharing teachers, and four general assistants. There is a speech therapist, and extra helpers for activities like swimming and music. It sounds like a lot of staff, but, believe me, they are all needed. Autistic children only learn one-to-one. Class teaching doesn't work. And if – as often happens – one child throws a wobbly and mops up the attention of three or four members of staff, the remaining seven children are pretty much all at sea.

Sam has a 'severe autistic impairment'. He also has 'severe learning difficulties'. To me, the autism is by far the greater problem. There is an excellent local school for children with severe learning difficulties, but I don't want Sam to go there because I believe his school environment should be wholly attuned to the needs of autism, and that he should be managed by staff who really understand the condition. I want him to go to the ASD facility attended by his older brother, George; it is a very similar set-up to his present school, but for children of eleven and up.

Why am I so set on an autistic environment for Sam? Doesn't being with other autists intensify his 'challenging' behaviour? Would he benefit from being in a class with non-autistic children? Should he be in a school which specifically caters for his apparently low IQ?

No, no and no. A central characteristic of autism is the lack of imitative behaviour. One autistic child will only pick up 'bad habits' from another in the most transient, superficial way. Sam just might imitate, say, Joe's peculiar high-pitched hoot for a few days, but he doesn't think 'Ah, Joe uses that noise to get out of swimming so if I hoot I'll get out of swimming too.' Sam cannot think that way because he cannot put himself into someone else's shoes. He has no 'theory of mind'.

By the same token, Sam would not learn 'normal' habits through contact with non-autistic children. Most children, even those with intellectual impairments, are profoundly social beings. They sort out their group dynamics through observation and imitation. Sam is not a social being. He prefers some adults to others, but has no concept of friendship. He is indifferent to what other children do. He has a reduced sense of his own identity. I showed him a photograph of Ian, our nanny, holding him. In the picture, Sam was wearing a red jumper. 'What is Ian doing?' I asked. 'Ian holding red jumper,' Sam replied. Never mind that there was a Sam inside it.

What about Sam's 'severe' intellectual impairment? Why do I regard addressing his autism as the priority? Well, for a start, the autism makes an accurate assessment of his abilities very difficult. I have no doubt that Sam has learning difficulties. I also have no doubt that, like most autistic children, he is cleverer than he can or will show us. Another autistic trait, particularly marked in Sam's case, is lack of motivation. Sam wants to be left alone; he is not concerned with showing us what he can do. He has no intellectual curiosity, no goals beyond unlocking the cupboard and taking out the sweet tin. The core of any educational programme for Sam has to be to find a way of galvanizing him. Indifference, not IQ, is the main issue.

The present government favours a policy of 'inclusion in

mainstream wherever possible'. Special schools and units are being closed up and down the country. In the case of autism, this policy is idiotic and harmful. Both George and Sam have special needs – the needs of an autistic child. The overlap between their requirements and those of a normal eleven- or twelve-year-old scarcely exists.

'I've invented a new game show for Channel 4,' announced Jake, my four-year-old. 'It's called *Rewind Your Life*. You start, Mummy. Rewind your life to the moment when you burst out of Granny Ann's tummy.'

Channel 4 haven't taken up the option yet, but tonight Jake will be on television. He is appearing not in a game show, but in a documentary called *The Autism Puzzle,* made for BBC4 by Saskia Baron. Forty-two years ago, Saskia's brother Timothy was one of the first children in Britain to be diagnosed with autism. Michael Baron, their father, was a founder member of the National Autistic Society, which last year celebrated its fortieth birthday. Saskia's film combines footage from the sixties and seventies, interviews with parents, researchers, psychologists, teachers and autistic adults, and fly-on-the-wall observation of two autistic families, one of which is mine.

We have already seen the pilot video. Non-autistic Jake, shown playing football, is hopeful that he will be spotted by Gérard Houllier's talent scouts. Sam, eleven, who hadn't seemed to notice that he was being filmed, watched the end product with interest. He enjoyed spotting familiar objects – our fridge, our trampoline, and, in a brief archive sequence, his toy owl (now a shadow of its former self), in all its original glory of white fluff and smart leather claws. He didn't pay much attention to people, though he did emit throaty chuckles at the antics of some of the other autists in the film, and I'm tempted to believe this indicated some kind of empathetic recognition.

Sam is quite similar to Timothy Baron, who is shown watching an old film of his arrival at Somerset Court, the residential home where he lived for many years. 'Coach!' exclaims Timothy with apparent pleasure. 'Suitcase! Yellow shirt!' 'Who's that?' asks Saskia, interested to see whether her brother can recognize Sybil Elgar, the pioneering teacher who worked with him for twenty years. No response. One could not even be sure that Tim recognized himself. As contestants on *Rewind Your Life,* neither Sam nor Tim would get past first base.

How do autists see the world? *The Autism Puzzle* shows eye-tracking experiments which indicate that autists watching scenes of social interaction look only at the lower half of the face, mainly the mouth. They cannot pick up clues from the wider social picture. They fail to notice Richard Burton glowering drunkenly in a corner as Elizabeth Taylor holds forth in *Who's Afraid of Virginia Woolf?*. Brain-imaging shows that the autistic brain reacts in the same way to inanimate objects as to faces expressing extreme emotions. Socially, therefore, autists are missing the point. It is hoped that this research will lead to earlier diagnosis; it might be possible to train an autistic baby to make 'appropriate' social responses before the neural pathways harden.

The autistic spectrum is wide; no two autists are the same. The programme makes this point: it shows a sensitive, caring grandfather with Asperger's syndrome (a mild form of autism), and David Braunsberg, a talented, articulate autistic artist, as well as the likes of my Sam flapping and humming in a world of his own, oblivious to the camera. The difference between my own two autistic sons is enormous. While Sam watched the video with calm enjoyment, George, twelve, objected so strongly that we had to switch it off and take it away. George has a thin-skinned reaction to all photographs, films, or even mentions of himself. He destroyed his school report. 'Don't look at me! Don't talk about me!' he tells us every few minutes. He cannot bear strongly delineated faces; if Cherie Blair is on the front of the newspaper, she will have books, toys and placemats piled on top of her.

George wouldn't get far on *Rewind Your Life* either, not because he does not notice things, but because he notices them too acutely.

His problem is a painfully accurate memory, and no way of editing it. The past and the future are both frightening – 'I wasn't a baby once! I didn't wear nappies! I won't grow up! I don't want to be a horrible man with a black beard!'

Saskia uses a clip of Leo Kanner, the psychologist who first defined autism in 1943. Kanner describes one of the two key symptoms as 'extreme aloneness from the beginning of life'. But George has never been 'alone' in Kanner's sense. He has strong social reactions, sometimes negative, often inappropriate. He has always been selectively affectionate, but he is also profoundly odd.

The Autism Puzzle points out that diagnostic criteria have expanded to include many people whom Kanner would probably not have recognized as autistic. Together with the numbers receiving the diagnosis, public awareness and media interest have increased astonishingly since George was first diagnosed nine years ago. Then, I was told, the incidence was one in a thousand; now it's one in a hundred. It is a condition that mainstream society has to learn to assimilate. Saskia's affectionate, level-headed film admirably sums up the state of play forty years after the founding of the first autism-specific school. She shows us autistic difficulty, autistic talent, anxiety, humour, energy, sorrow and delight. Autism is neither a disease, nor a product of emotional disturbance. It is more accurate to see it as a social handicap than an intellectual one. There is no cure, but nor should a cure be needed. In a responsible society, it can be accommodated, and even – sometimes – celebrated.

'Two of my sons, Jake and George, share a birthday – but only one shows any interest in celebrating it'

29 January 2003

Yesterday, we celebrated the birthdays of two of my three sons. Jake was born on his brother George's eighth birthday. Now, they are thirteen and five – momentous ages, both.

Five marks the end of infancy. I remember my own fifth birthday. I received a money box in the shape of a clock, and five imperial pennies to put in it. I was awed by my new maturity. I was to be responsible for my own pocket money, and I was to learn to tell the time. I had a powerful sense of transition, exciting, daunting and largely welcome.

Jake has a similar feeling. He is a proper schoolboy now, with an interior life that is separate from mine. For the first time, he did not announce his wish to the world when he cut his cake. 'It's a secret,' he said, 'I'll tell you this time next year.' He asked to have a party in the village hall, rather than at home, because 'my little people might be scared of George and Sam – they might not understand about being autistic.'

One thing the 'little people' would certainly not understand is George's aversion to having a birthday at all. Last year, he chose to invite his school friends, and enjoyed it. This year, he didn't want any of it – cards, presents, party food. Especially not party food. George knows food is linked to growing, and he doesn't want to grow. He fights for control over his hunger. 'Be quiet, my tummy,' he says, when he thinks he's alone. 'You're not hungry, my tummy. Stop rumbling.'

George starves himself for days. I've tried cajoling, rewarding and threatening, and they're all counter-productive. Now, if he won't eat, I stop offering food. This is hard; the maternal impulse to nour-ish one's children is not easily overruled. Making no comment,

I leave food where I know he can reach it. Eventually, like a wild deer, George creeps up and begins to nibble. After a few days, he'll get himself back on track, and I will serve his meals at the table.

This sounds like classic anorexia, except that George has no interest in what he looks like. We don't possess bathroom scales, but if we did, George would not be interested in weighing himself. I know this because he has no sense of modesty, and shows no teenage desire for an inviolate private space. He has a strong idea of himself as a child – 'I will stay little' – but no idea of how others react to his physical appearance. Neither the onset of puberty nor his appalling eating habits have damaged his outstanding beauty, but he is as unaware of this as he has always been. As for peer pressure, it's simply not an issue. One thing autistic classmates never do is put pressure on each other. No trends are set, no fads catch on, because autists neither lead nor follow.

George's dread of growing older expresses a profound autistic anxiety about change. Some autists can't bear to have furniture moved. George is calm about that, but his desire for 'the preservation of sameness' comes out in his attempts to keep himself frozen in time. Why, then, did we persist in celebrating his birthday? Wouldn't it be kinder to allow this breatharian refusenik the control he wants?

As usual, I'm aiming for a compromise, a meeting ground, between his world view and ours. We neurotypicals have a strong need to give presents, to make cakes, to sing Happy Birthday to our children, to show that we love them; for us, love means giving attention. George will encounter this universally accepted impulse throughout his life. I have to teach him to accept it, and hope that acceptance may lead to pleasure. The fact that George and Jake share a birthday is helpful. Presents, cards, cakes and people could all be brought into the house because they were 'for Jake'. Once George had accepted that, he inched his way towards enjoying his birthday. He blew out his candles. He risked eating a piece of chocolate. He even opened a present, because it was clearly a video. Something familiar and safe. 'I want this,' said George, in a rare burst of affirmation. 'Let's put it on.'

'Why do my autistic sons tip shampoo down the drain and flush pants down the loo? I suppose they find it fun'

19 February 2003

It is Monday morning, and I am going to write this column before I start to get the house back to its weekday self. That's a big task. I am not a particularly orderly person. The house is old, and resists newness; it has a rambling, inconsequential layout, more like a geriatric's anecdote than a Corbusian aesthetic discourse. That's fine – I have no taste for minimalism. It is just that by the end of a wet February weekend things are looking – well, pretty autistic.

To start with, there is George's litter collection. Not just any old litter: on his bedroom windowsill, the kitchen table, and the play-room floor are grouped mint wrappers, yellow plastic lollipop sticks arranged in fan shapes, the papers you peel off the back of sticking plasters, and the dark, sweet-scented envelopes that After Eights come in, which retain their plumpness and look – triumph of hope over experience – as if they just might still have a choc-olate inside them. I don't know why George likes these things, but, as Shakespeare's Troilus says, 'What's aught, but as 'tis valued?' If George's papers get thrown away, he will rummage in dustbins and retrieve them. I daren't dispose of all of them, but I think I will risk a cull.

Then there are the videos. We own a great many. George has taken nearly all of them out of their boxes. He has flattened out some of the boxes and dotted them round the house. He has removed the printed covers, so the boxes are anonymous. Others have been put on the shelves back to front, so you can't see what they are. This means that when George comes home and asks for *Learn, Sing and Play the Montessori Way,* or *Bananas in Pyjamas in Springtime,* it will take me about forty minutes to find them.

Nestling among George's sweet wrappers are the remains of

Sam's biscuits. Sam gets through a lot of biscuits, but I don't think he has ever eaten a whole one. He chips away at them, leaving a circle of broken fragments behind him like a goblin ring. The kitchen floor resembles an archaeological dig, covered as it is by these brittle tesserae. Sam's wheat- and dairy-free diet means that the biscuits come at vast expense from the so-called well-being section of the supermarket. That's several pounds' worth I'm crunching underfoot. Looking closer, I see that a scrubbing brush is called for: yesterday, I failed to deal adequately with Sam's Jackson Pollock moment with the poster paints.

Sam has lost interest in flushing underwear down the lavatory, I am pleased to say, but he still likes tipping shampoo down the drain. George is, at present, focusing on soap. For his recent birthday he received ten bars, and they have nearly all gone. In the bath he rubs his feet with them, which seems to induce a trance-like state – a kind of DIY reflexology. Downstairs, he has taken to rubbing soap on to the rims of tumblers. Do you remember, in the early seventies, when it seemed the height of sophistication to drink Coke out of a glass that had been rimmed with frosted sugar? Well, in our house it's like that with soap, only less tasty.

I keep a lot of things under lock and key – most foodstuffs, cleaning materials, the hamster. I would love to leave a bowl of fruit out on the table – a humble ambition, you might think, but Sam takes one bite from each of the fruit and then throws it away. It is only recently that I have been able to reintroduce vases of flowers. There was a time when George would strip the flowers off and use the stalks as flappers, and Sam would drink the water.

I can't properly explain why autistic children behave like this. Their sensory experiences are so different from mine that I have to assume they derive a satisfaction from smearing toothpaste or shredding cardboard boxes that I cannot hope to share.

They are also largely undeterred by disapproval. When Sam wants to tip shampoo away, he is powerfully motivated. My admonitions don't penetrate – indeed, he may hardly hear them. He can be trained away from some of his less acceptable habits, but the training, which involves redirection and reinforcement for doing the right thing (i.e., a sweet) has to be consistent and oft-repeated. I have any number of other thoughts in my head when I am dealing with Sam; my concentration wavers. Sam's doesn't. He has only one thought — get that shampoo down the plug-hole, and do it now. As a winning strategy, it's hard to beat.

'I have no idea how Sam and George will cope as adults but one thing I know – they'll never earn a living'

12 March 2003

I was at a party, talking to a woman about my autistic sons, when she surprised me by saying, 'But of course, they'll grow out of it, won't they?' I looked at her, startled. 'Oh,' she said, 'I thought autism was one of those things you grew out of.' Well, no. If they were going to grow out of it, why would I be making such a fuss?

Autism is a lifelong, incurable condition. It is misleading to look at it any other way. But it is also a highly unpredictable condition, with room for enormous change and development. I am encouraged to hear that learning can continue well into adulthood. Clara Park, author of two books about her autistic daughter Jessy, says that Jessy continues to make progress in her mid-forties. Jessy, a mute, unreachable child, underwent rapid intellectual and social development in her teens, once the right motivators had been found. Now, she is a talented, commercially successful artist. She has a regular nine-to-five job in a mail-sorting office. She cooks, shops and cleans. But, her mother emphasizes, she is still autistic, and always will be. Jessy's life is now highly satisfactory, but it is worlds away from the social and emotional intricacies of a neuro-typical woman of her age, or indeed of any age.

Not that anyone is aiming for a 'normal' social life for her, least of all Jessy herself. Clara is pleased about her continued development because each small step leads her towards the final goal – a fulfilled, secure, independent life after her parents' death. But fulfilment for an autist is very different from the usual definition.

Jessy's success exceeds the wildest dreams of most parents of autistic children. But it is not a miracle; it's an achievement based on an accumulation of small, attainable goals. I have truly no idea what Sam and George will be like as adults. I do not try to look far ahead. Right now, I want Sam to learn to eat with cutlery (have you ever seen someone eat a fried egg with bare hands?). And I want George to wipe his own bottom, preferably with lavatory paper rather than any spare garment that comes to hand. Lately, George has reached certificate-level in trampolining. He doesn't care for certificates – he has less competitive spirit than an earthworm. But I am pleased, because it shows he has been able to do the same thing as normal children, to the same level. He will never be normal, but the more his world can overlap with ours, the easier it will be for all concerned.

So progress happens, but there can be tremendous regression, too. You think everything is going swimmingly and then you hit a powerful undertow. And the frustrating thing is, you rarely know why. All you can be sure of, when you have an autistic child, is that you are the proud possessor of something very, very odd. Looking after Sam, in particular, reminds me of one of the strange creatures in Dr Seuss's *One Fish, Two Fish, Red Fish, Blue Fish* (a seminal text in our family). The Seuss children are carrying a large, tusked, whiskery creature they name Clark in a glass jar. They found him in the park, and decide to keep him and name him Clark: 'He will live at our house. He will grow and grow,/Will our mother like this? We don't know.' Clark's expression is ambiguous, neither fierce nor wholly benign, just 'other'. As he grows, will he burst out of his jar, or will the jar grow with him? All I know is, I've got Sam for keeps. The best I can do is watch him, and try to understand his needs.

Statistics about autistic adults make gloomy reading, if looked at with 'normal' hopes and ambitions in mind. Only a tiny minority marry, and only a slightly less tiny minority hold down 'real' jobs. But, except at the most able end of the spectrum, such normality is unlikely to appeal to an autist. Worrying about whether George or Sam will ever have a 'relationship' is about as pointless as trying to find a bride for the be-tusked Clark. Nor do I expect them ever to earn their keep. In the context, their lack of awareness of their condition is probably a blessing. Life is much more painful for the very able autist who wants to get out of his glass jar and join the normal world.

'Parents of autistic children would love a little help from their friends – but the last thing they will do is ask for it'

2 April 2003

I have read or listened to many parents' accounts of life with an autistic child. One comment that recurs far too often is that parents have lost friends. They feel socially isolated; they hardly ever go out. They are almost imprisoned by their child's autism.

This is sad and unnecessary. Autism is now thought to affect about one in a hundred children. When my elder son George was diagnosed in 1994, the figure quoted was one in a thousand. Whatever the reasons for the increase, the chances of having contact with a child diagnosed with autism are obviously much greater than they were. So, the question of how best to respond is one that many, many people will be seeking to answer.

What kind of help can you provide if the child of one of your friends or relations turns out to be autistic? Your friend probably won't ask for help; she will have all the usual inhibitions about that. You need to use your non-autistic powers of empathy, and think yourself into her position. Take the summer holidays. Can your friend take her child shopping, or do the bright lights and buzzing over-stimulus of the supermarket drive him beserk? Is he inclined to wander, but too big to fit in the trolley? Six weeks is a long time not to go to Sainsbury's. Offer to babysit while your friend shops, if you feel confident about keeping him safe. If you don't, then suggest you do the shopping for her.

Would the child benefit from swimming, riding, or just going to the beach or playground? Can your friend manage such a trip on her own? Her child might be the running-away kind, like my Sam, or he might have no road sense. Offer to accompany her, as an extra pair of hands (and legs). Or look after her other children while she takes the autistic one.

We 'autistic' parents suffer from a shortage of babysitters. Our children can't simply be left with an inexperienced local teenager. We need someone who knows our child well, or someone who has masses of experience of the condition. The former are easier to come by – and you, as a friend or relative, can make it your business to get to know that child.

The best babysitting arrangement is to have more than one adult. That is expensive, so if you volunteer to be the back-up babysitter for nothing, then you are really doing your friend a favour. I go out a lot. A quiet evening in watching the telly is not something I can take for granted – my sons require constant supervision until they finally fall asleep, at some hideously late hour. So, if I want child-free time, I have to leave the house.

And child-free time is vital. I am absolutely certain that I look after my sons with more energy and enthusiasm if I can refresh myself with regular escapes.

It is easy to be nervous of autistic children. They are unpredictable; one day you feel that you have made real contact, the next day they ignore you. They make eerie noises, they bite their hands or bang their heads, they defecate in ingenious places. Your own children may be scared of them. You may feel you simply can't have such a child in your house. But if you can overcome your qualms, then making your house available is a great act of friendship. Find out what the child can't tolerate, and temporarily banish it. If the child's on a special diet, respect it. Lock up forbidden fruits, and ask the mother in advance which edible treats are allowed. Expect less than nothing in the way of good manners or gratitude. Instruct your children not to bombard their autistic visitor with offers of toys; explain that the kindest thing is to leave him alone, to allow him to orientate himself in his own way, at his own pace.

Take nothing personally. It is almost impossible for an autist to be deliberately rude or hurtful; he can't truly take your feelings into consideration. The rejection of your present isn't a rejection of you. You are probably less interesting to him than, say, your vacuum cleaner.

Appreciate the child. Autism isn't a tragedy, it is a different way of being. I much prefer a show of affectionate interest in my sons to the 'Poor you, how do you cope?' approach. Even the wildest child must have some plus points. If you are a friend, you can find them, and celebrate them.

'When a child is diagnosed as autistic, there is no point wishing for a cure. Acceptance is the only way to cope'

23 April 2003

I've been talking to a woman whose son has been diagnosed as autistic. He is her only child. Like my George, as a baby he was so attractive – almost magnetic. He seemed exceptionally bright; gifted, even. Now he's three and a half, and she's watching in dismay as he undergoes a classic autistic regression, losing the skills of which she had been so proud.

Should she go ahead and have the second child she'd always planned? She knows there's a real chance she might have another autist. After our first two sons were both found to be autistic, we had genetic counselling at the Maudsley Hospital. They estimated the chances of it happening a third time as one in twenty. But this is only an estimate; the genetic component of the condition isn't fully understood. We took the risk, and I'm very glad we did, because in addition to George and Sam I now have my almost pathologically un-autistic Jake.

My caller was wondering whether she could cope with another child with such complex and exhausting needs. But I suspect that what she was most frightened of was 'losing' another child to autism, of being forced to relinquish her hopes for the child she thought she had in the face of mounting evidence of abnormality.

Few parents know they have an autistic baby. I didn't; nothing was spotted by any of the health professionals who dealt with George and Sam. It is only with the benefit of hindsight and the experience of Jake that I can recognize that my first two babies were, indeed, born autistic. The condition takes a while to show its true colours. Unlike a physically obvious condition, such as Down's syndrome, autism can only be diagnosed by behavioural observation. With a young baby, you'd have to be extremely clued up to know what to observe.

This means that most parents have months, even years, of false belief about their child. The extreme physical attractiveness of many autistic infants can add to the impression that a marvellous, normal child had been somehow 'lost'. For some parents, the process of grieving for the child you thought you had takes years to complete. There's a nagging residual feeling that the child could snap out of it; you almost wonder, sometimes, whether they're just putting it on. Documentary-maker Saskia Baron's autistic brother Timothy is now in his forties. Her recurring childhood fantasy was that he was some kind of spy, just acting his autism, and that one day he would unmask himself.

This fantasy was fed by moments – or hours, or even days – when Tim would suddenly seem a lot more normal. He'd always return to his autistic ways, but these flashes gave the misleading impression that there was a 'real' Tim inside, that you only had to find the right key to let him out. All of us who deal with autists have experienced this. Out of the blue you get some great eye contact, some clear and meaningful speech, even some action which feels empathetic. Sam is not very verbal and is usually emotionally aloof or indifferent, but once, when George was upset he went over to his brother and patted him on the head. 'Don't cry, Georgie sweetheart,' he said.

Autists who've written autobiographical accounts describe occasions when the mists lift, when the neurotypical world suddenly seems to make more sense. But, like most autistic experiences, such moments are only fragments. Autists can learn some coping strategies, but their condition will never be 'cured'. And the rest of us must learn to stop wishing for a cure. Acceptance is all.

That natural early assumption that your baby is normal affects a lot of things. Many parents choose mainstream school for their rising-fives because they haven't shaken off the impression that a mainstream child is what they have. Inclusion in the mainstream rarely works, but it takes some of us years to understand that 'special needs' means exactly what it says.

I wasted a great deal of time with my two, thinking they were only 'mildly' affected. They're not. They're both profoundly handicapped, both George, the 'gifted' baby, and Sam, the cheery toddler. If I had my time again, I'd intervene straight away with a gluten-free, casein-free, additive-free diet, and as much interventionist behavioural therapy as I could manage. I'd keep them out of mainstream school until I was certain they were ready for it – and I'd try to accept that that day might never come. And yes, I'd go for that next pregnancy. No question.

'I am fascinated by autism and love my sons, but it is relentless.
I cope by making sure I still have a life outside'

14 May 2003

As autism is a spectrum disorder, autists exhibit wildly differing traits. Their idiosyncrasies, deficits and abilities can make one autist almost as unlike another as he is from a non-autistic person. But if autists themselves often have little in common, there is one experience that unites all their parents: being asked the question, 'How do you cope?'

I cope with help. I can, and often do, manage my three boys on my own, but our quality of life is much better if there are other adults around. On my own, I cannot let my vigilance slacken. Sam might pull a boiling pan off the stove, or drag Jake across the floor, or take himself off for an unannounced walk, destination unknown. George is less dangerous, but he'll let the hamster out, or raid the dustbin to augment his litter collection. Only yesterday, George peed on his toy box. 'Sorry!' he grinned, using my sweater to mop it up.

Coping alone is possible, but it's more about keeping them alive than about having fun. Help from other adults expands their range of activities, and gives Jake the non-autistic playtime that is his life's blood. I get help from relations, friends, neighbours, our ABA tutors, and from Ian the nanny, the most recent addition to the household. It's important that the boys have good relationships with several adults apart from me. I'm lucky; I haven't had to clamour for respite care. But there is respite help to be had: pester social services and your local Autistic Society.

Don't be too proud to ask. You need to grow a thick skin, both to ask for what you need, and to deal with the extraordinary situations that arise every time you take your child out in public. I have had the odd confrontation in shops or on public transport, along the lines of 'Can't you control your children?' (Answer: No.) But most people are kind and helpful, especially if you explain the situation. And it really is up to you to explain. Autism doesn't announce itself with a wheelchair or a white stick. It isn't immediately obvious why a good-looking thirteen-year-old must dive behind the counter to grab a discarded till roll (George), or why a physically able eleven-year-old cannot stand in a queue (Sam). You need to play your part in educating the public.

Having a child with any disability throws your life off-balance. It's easy to become obsessive, to let outside interests wither away. I'm fascinated by autism, and I observe my sons with keen interest, but I also need breaks from it. An important part of my coping strategy is to maintain an active mental and social life which has nothing to do with autism, and which restores my sense of perspective.

I am constantly searching for an equilibrium between striving to conquer aspects of their condition and accepting them for what they are. I've tried many therapies and interventions, and most have brought benefits, though none have amounted to a cure. I hope I was never looking for a cure; now, I'm sure I'm not. I want Sam to stop scattering his food and biting his hands, but I don't dream of a neurotypical Sam with the usual emotional and intellectual range of a boy of eleven, because no such Sam could possibly exist.

What do I want for my children? I want them to be happy, and to be allowed to be the kind of people that they are. This applies to all three of them, but for George and Sam, happiness won't be made up of the usual ingredients. When you look after autistic children, you have to throw away the childcare recipe book and reach your own conclusions based on patient observation. Loving them is the easy part; what is harder is to square their desires with what those around them can tolerate.

My final coping tip is to enjoy your child as much as you possibly can. You may be saddened to relinquish the ideal of a playful, sociable, imaginative childhood, but there is a refreshing absence of the neurotypical nasties – no competitiveness, possessiveness, envy or spite.

Many, many readers have sent me interesting and supportive letters and emails. It has been my intention to reply to them all; if I have failed to do so, I apologize. This week is Autism Awareness Week, so it seems appropriate to thank the *Guardian* for improving public awareness by running this column for the last two years. For me, it has been a treat. I have been allowed to rabbit on about my children, uninterrupted. Isn't that every mother's dream?

Reading List

There are many excellent books about autism. This is a personal list; it is not meant to be exhaustive.

Tony Attwood, *Asperger's Syndrome: A Guide for Parents and Professionals* (Jessica Kingsley Publishers, 1998).

Simon Baron-Cohen, *The Essential Difference* (Allen Lane, 2003). Fascinating theory of autism as the result of the 'extreme male brain'.

Jill Dawson, *Wild Boy* (Sceptre, 2003). Fictionalized account of the Wild Boy of Aveyron, possibly the earliest fully documented autistic child.

Uta Frith, *Autism: Explaining the Enigma* (Blackwell, 1989; 2nd edn, 2003). My favourite among the 'textbooks'.

Temple Grandin, *Thinking in Pictures* (Vintage, 1996).

Temple Grandin, Margaret M. Scariano, *Emergence: Labeled Autistic* (Warner Books, 1996). Grandin, a high-functioning autistic woman, describes her experiences and mental processes with clarity and insight.

Roy Richard Grinker, *Unstrange Minds: A Father Remaps the World of Autism* (Icon, 2008). A study of how different cultures perceive and handle autism, by the father of an autistic daughter.

Mark Haddon, *The Curious Incident of the Dog in the Night-Time* (Jonathan Cape, 2003). A novel, told from the point of view of an Asperger teenager. It deserves the hype.

Robert Hughes, *Running with Walker* (Jessica Kingsley Publishers, 2003). Life with an autistic son.

Jacqui Jackson, *Multicoloured Mayhem* (Jessica Kingsley Publishers, 2003). Life in a family of seven children, of whom four are on the autistic spectrum. The Jacksons were the subject of a recent TV documentary, *My Family and Autism*.

Luke Jackson, *Freaks, Geeks and Asperger Syndrome: A User Guide to Adolescence* (Jessica Kingsley Publishers, 2002). An insider's account; clear, hard-hitting and informative.

Luke Jackson, *A User Guide to the GF/CF Diet for Autism, Asperger Syndrome and AD/HD* (Jessica Kingsley Publishers, 2002).

Jean Kearns Miller (ed.), *Women from Another Planet?: Our Lives in the Universe of Autism* (Authorhouse, 2003). A collection of personal accounts by women on the spectrum.

Wendy Lawson and Olga Bogdashina, *Sensory Perceptual Issues in Autism and Asperger Syndrome: Different Sensory Experiences, Different Perceptual Worlds* (Jessica Kingsley, 2003). Very readable textbook, containing a lot of first-hand experience.

Marilyn Le Breton, *Diet Intervention and Autism* (Jessica Kingsley Publishers, 2001). Useful recipes, tips and addresses, all based on first-hand experience.

Clara Claiborne Park, *The Siege* (Little, Brown, 1982). A mother's story about bringing up her autistic daughter, Jessy, in 1960s America – the era of 'the refrigerator mother'.

Clara Claiborne Park, *Exiting Nirvana* (Aurum Press, 2001). Takes up where *The Siege* left off. Highly recommended.

Oliver Sacks, *An Anthropologist on Mars* (Picador, 1996). Case histories of neurological disorders of many kinds, including autism. Sacks's writing is intelligent and humane.

Clare Sainsbury, *Martian in the Playground* (Lucky Duck Publishing, 2000). What it's like to be an Asperger child in a mainstream school.

Daniel Tammet, *Born on a Blue Day: A Memoir of Asperger's and an Extraordinary Mind* (Hodder and Stoughton, 2006). The autobiography of an autistic mathematical savant.

Donna Williams, *Nobody Nowhere* (Random House, 1992).

Donna Williams, *Somebody, Somewhere* (Corgi, 1995). Williams's are probably the best-known autobiographical accounts.

Lorna Wing, *The Autistic Spectrum* (Constable, 2003). A handbook for parents and professionals.

Directory of Useful Addresses

NATIONAL AUTISTIC SOCIETY
http://www.autism.org.uk
The National Autistic Society
393 City Road
London EC1V 1NG
Tel: 020 7833 2299
Fax: 020 7833 9666
Email: nas@nas.org.uk

APPLIED BEHAVIOURAL ANALYSIS
http://www.peach.org.uk
PEACH
Parents for the Early intervention of Autism in Children
The Brackens
London Road
Ascot
Berkshire SL5 8BE
Tel: 01344 882248
Fax: 01344 882391
Email: info@peach.org.uk

THE LOVAAS INSTITUTE FOR EARLY INTERVENTION
http://www.lovaas.com
LIFE Administrative Headquarters
Lovaas Institute for Early Intervention
11500 West Olympic Boulevard
Suite 460
Los Angeles, CA 90064
USA

Tel: 001 310 914–5433
Fax: 001 310 914–5463
Email: info@lovaas.com

UK YOUNG AUTISM PROJECT
http://www.ukyap.org
UK Young Autism Project
89 Tilehurst Road
Earlsfield
London SW18 3EX
Tel: 020 3369 9630
Email: enquiries@ukyap.org

AUDITORY INTEGRATION THERAPY
http://www.auditoryintegration.net
690 Boyd Road
Leicester, NC 28748
USA
Tel: 001 828 683 6900
Fax: 001 828 683 0303
Email: health@aithelps.com

AMBITIOUS ABOUT AUTISM
http://www.ambitiousaboutautism.org.uk
Campaigning charity, affiliated to the groundbreaking TreeHouse
School. Specializes in political and educational issues.
Ambitious about Autism
The Pears National Centre for Autism Education
Woodstock Avenue
London N10 3JA
Tel: 020 8815 5444
Email: info@ambitiousaboutautism.org.uk

AUTISTICA
Research charity.
http://www.autistica.org.uk

Autistica
Rotherfield House
7 Fairmile
Henley-on-Thames
Oxfordshire RG9 2JR
Tel: 01491 412311
Fax: 01491 571921
Email: autistica@mail.vresp.com

CHARLOTTE MOORE

GRANDMOTHER'S FOOTSTEPS

Three generations of women, and the secrets of a family home.

When her husband died, it was clear to Verity that she would have to sell Knighton, the beautiful old house where her daughter, Hester, had grown up and where her mother Evelyn before her had come as a young bride.

But this move proves to be a beginning rather than an ending. The discovery of suffragette Evelyn's diary first intrigues Verity but later threatens her peace of mind. And though successful, single and independent Hester is also discovering that the legacies she has inherited from her mother, grandmother and father are forcing her to reassess her past, present and future.

Mother and daughter are about to come to grips with a past that simply will not let go – are they following in grandmother's footsteps?

'Absorbing and civilized . . . beautifully rendered' *Daily Telegraph*

'Offers poignant portraits of women . . . tells their stories with sensitive restraint' *Spectator*

CHARLOTTE MOORE

HANCOX

Hancox is the Tudor hall house in rural Sussex where Charlotte Moore grew up,
and where she lives today. It's been in the family since her ancestor Milicent
Ludlow, young, single and an orphan, took it on in 1891 and began to enlarge the
house and manage the farm. Hancox tells the story of the house and the family
over the following thirty years, in the long run-up to the First World War.
In one sense it's a rural idyll: the arrival of the car disturbs this peaceful agrarian
world, but apart from that the rhythms of the countryside go on as they had for
centuries before. But all was not quite as it seemed: Milicent made a distinguished
marriage but her husband harboured a secret. Milicent herself gradually
succumbed to religious fanaticism. And the death of the youngest boy at Ypres
devastated the family, bringing the idyll to a painful end.

Using extraordinary archive material held at Hancox today, Charlotte Moore
weaves an Edwardian tale of madness and jealousy, love and loss, heroism and
tragedy.

'Hugely enjoyable' Penelope Lively

'As compelling as fiction - except that no novelist would dare invent anything as
rich and strange' *Daily Telegraph*

'Utterly compelling. A marvellous book' *Spectator*

He just wanted a decent book to read ...

Not too much to ask, is it? It was in 1935 when Allen Lane, Managing Director of Bodley Head Publishers, stood on a platform at Exeter railway station looking for something good to read on his journey back to London. His choice was limited to popular magazines and poor-quality paperbacks – the same choice faced every day by the vast majority of readers, few of whom could afford hardbacks. Lane's disappointment and subsequent anger at the range of books generally available led him to found a company – and change the world.

'We believed in the existence in this country of a vast reading public for intelligent books at a low price, and staked everything on it'
Sir Allen Lane, 1902–1970, founder of Penguin Books

The quality paperback had arrived – and not just in bookshops. Lane was adamant that his Penguins should appear in chain stores and tobacconists, and should cost no more than a packet of cigarettes.

Reading habits (and cigarette prices) have changed since 1935, but Penguin still believes in publishing the best books for everybody to enjoy. We still believe that good design costs no more than bad design, and we still believe that quality books published passionately and responsibly make the world a better place.

So wherever you see the little bird – whether it's on a piece of prize-winning literary fiction or a celebrity autobiography, political tour de force or historical masterpiece, a serial-killer thriller, reference book, world classic or a piece of pure escapism – you can bet that it represents the very best that the genre has to offer.

Whatever you like to read – trust Penguin.